Systematic Process Improvement Using ISO 9001:2000 and CMMI®

For a listing of recent titles in the *Artech House Computing Library,* turn to the back of this book.

Systematic Process Improvement Using ISO 9001:2000 and CMMI®

Boris Mutafelija
Harvey Stromberg

Artech House
Boston • London
www.artechhouse.com

Library of Congress Cataloging-in-Publication Data
Mutafelija, Boris.
  Systematic process improvement using ISO 9001:2000 and CMMI® / Boris Mutafelija, Harvey Stromberg.
    p. cm. — (Artech House computing library)
  Includes bibliographical references and index.
  ISBN 1-58053-487-2 (alk. paper)
    1. Quality control—Standards. 2. ISO 9001 Standard. 3. Capability Maturity Model® (Computer software). I. Stromberg, Harvey. II. Title. III. Series.
TS156.M875 2003
658.5'62—dc21   2003041477

British Library Cataloguing in Publication Data
Mutafelija, Boris
  Systematic process improvement using ISO 9001:2000 and CMMI®. — (Artech House computing library)
    1. ISO 9000 Series Standards 2. Capability Maturity Model® (Computer software) I. Title
  II. Stromberg, Harvey
  005.1'0685

ISBN 1-58053-487-2

Cover design by Igor Valdman

The following are service marks of Carnegie Mellon University: CMM® Integration[SM], IDEAL[SM], SCAMPI[SM], and SCE[SM].

The following are registered in the U.S. Patent and Trademark Office by Carnegie Mellon University: Capability Maturity Model®, CMM®, and CMMI®.

© 2003 ARTECH HOUSE, INC.
685 Canton Street
Norwood, MA 02062

All rights reserved. Printed and bound in the United States of America. No part of this book may be reproduced or utilized in any form or by any means, electronic or mechanical, including photocopying, recording, or by any information storage and retrieval system, without permission in writing from the publisher.
  All terms mentioned in this book that are known to be trademarks or service marks have been appropriately capitalized. Artech House cannot attest to the accuracy of this information. Use of a term in this book should not be regarded as affecting the validity of any trademark or service mark.

International Standard Book Number: 1-58053-487-2
Library of Congress Catalog Card Number: 2003041477

10 9 8 7 6 5 4 3 2 1

*To our wives, Mirta and Susan,
and our children, Suzanne, Christopher, Daniel, and Deborah*

Thanks for your support, encouragement, and especially patience.

Disclaimer of Warranty

Special permission to use
1. *Capability Maturity Model® for Software, Version 1.1*, CMU/SEI-93-TR-24, © 1993 by Carnegie Mellon University,
2. *Key Practices of the Capability Maturity Model® for Software, Version 1.1*, CMU/SEI-93-TR-25, © 1993 by Carnegie Mellon University,
3. *Capability Maturity Model Integration® (CMMI®)*, v1.1, Continuous Representation, CMU/SEI-2002-TR-003, © 2001 by Carnegie Mellon University,
4. *Capability Maturity Model Integration® (CMMI®)*, v1.1, Staged Representation, CMU/SEI-2002-TR-004, © 2001 by Carnegie Mellon University,
5. *IDEAL^{SM}: A User's Guide for Software Process Improvement*, CMU/SEI-96-HB-001, © 1996 by Carnegie Mellon University,
6. *Standard CMMI® Appraisal Method for Process Improvement^{SM} (SCAMPI^{SM})*, Version 1.1: Method Definition Document, CMU/SEI-2001-HB-001, © 2001 by Carnegie Mellon University

in *Systematic Process Improvement Using ISO 9001:2000 and CMMI®* is granted by the Software Engineering Institute. The SEI and CMU do not directly or indirectly endorse this work.

NO WARRANTY. THIS CARNEGIE MELLON UNIVERSITY AND SOFTWARE ENGINEERING INSTITUTE MATERIAL IS FURNISHED ON AN "AS IS" BASIS. CARNEGIE MELLON UNIVERSITY MAKES NO WARRANTIES OF ANY KIND, EITHER EXPRESSED OR IMPLIED AS TO ANY MATTER INCLUDING, BUT NOT LIMITED TO, WARRANTY OF FITNESS FOR PURPOSE OR MERCHANTABILITY, EXCLUSIVITY OR RESULTS OBTAINED FROM USE OF THE MATERIAL. CARNEGIE MELLON UNIVERSITY DOES NOT MAKE ANY WARRANTY OF ANY KIND WITH RESPECT TO FREEDOM FROM PATENT, TRADEMARK, OR COPYRIGHT INFRINGEMENT.

Contents

Foreword . . . . *xi*

Preface . . . . *xv*

Acknowledgments . . . . *xix*

1 Introduction 1
1.1 Role of frameworks in developing process improvement strategies   4
1.2 Process improvement approaches   5
1.3 Syngergy   7
References   11

2 Process Improvement 13
2.1 Why worry about process improvement?   13
2.2 Why is process improvement so difficult?   14
2.3 Typical process improvement approaches   15
    2.3.1 Plan–Do–Check–Act   *16*
    2.3.2 ISO 15504, Part 7   *17*
    2.3.3 IDEAL^{SM}   *21*
    2.3.4 Evolutionary spiral process   *24*
    2.3.5 ISO 9004:2000   *26*
    2.3.6 Brute force   *27*
2.4 Summary   27
References   29

3 Framework Introduction 31
3.1 Relationships between frameworks and process improvement approaches   31
3.2 ISO 9001:1994   34
3.3 CMM® for software   35
    3.3.1 CMM® structure   *38*
    3.3.2 Key process areas   *40*
3.4 ISO TR 15504   43
3.5 EIA/IS-731   47
3.6 FAA-iCMM®   53
3.7 Summary   56
References   57

4 Revised Frameworks: ISO 9001:2000 and the CMMI® . 59
4.1 ISO 9001:2000   59
    4.1.1 Quality management principles   *61*
    4.1.2 Process approach and system approach to management   *65*
    4.1.3 ISO 9001:2000 requirements   *66*
4.2 CMMI®   78
    4.2.1 New to CMMI® version 1.1   *80*
    4.2.2 Model representations   *81*
    4.2.3 Maturity versus capability levels   *81*
    4.2.4 Institutionalization   *83*
    4.2.5 Generic Goals and Generic Practices   *86*
    4.2.6 Process Areas   *98*
References   118

5 ISO 9001:2000 and CMMI® Synergy 121
5.1 Commonalities   129
5.2 Differences   131
5.3 Strengths   132
5.4 Weaknesses   133
5.5 Synergy   134
    5.5.1 Institutionalization   *135*
    5.5.2 Process areas and their specific practices   *136*
    5.5.3 Relationship between ISO and the CMMI®   *149*

	5.6	Summary of ISO requirements not covered by the CMMI®	151
	References		152

6 Transitioning from Legacy Standards 153
6.1 Differences between the CMM® and CMMI® — 155
6.1.1 Institutionalization — 155
6.1.2 Maturity level 2 PAs — 161
6.1.3 Maturity level 3 PAs — 166
6.1.4 Maturity level 4 PAs — 171
6.1.5 Maturity level 5 PAs — 172
6.1.6 Continuous CMMI® representation: concept of threads — 173
6.2 Differences between ISO 9001:1994 and ISO 9001:2000 — 175
6.3 Transitioning from the CMM® to the CMMI® — 177
6.3.1 Basic approach—no previous process improvement experience — 180
6.3.2 Transitioning from CMM® maturity level 2 to CMMI® maturity level 2 — 192
6.3.3 Transitioning from CMM® maturity level 3 to CMMI® maturity level 3 — 196
6.3.4 Transitioning from CMM® maturity level 2 to CMMI® maturity level 3 — 198
6.4 Transitioning from ISO 9001:1994 to ISO 9001:2000 — 201
References — 204

7 Approaches Using ISO–CMMI® Synergy 205
7.1 Process improvement — 205
7.2 First phase: Initiating — 206
7.3 Second phase: Diagnosing — 207
7.4 Third phase: Establishing — 209
7.4.1 Process improvement approaches — 209
7.4.2 Potential transition cases — 211
7.4.3 Process improvement planning — 234
7.5 Fourth phase: Acting — 235
7.6 Fifth phase: Learning — 236
References — 237

8 Appraisal/Registration 239
8.1 SCAMPI^{SM}   240
   8.1.1 Some history   *240*
   8.1.2 SCAMPI^{SM} overview   *242*
8.2 ISO 9001:2000 registration process   252
8.3 TickIT   258
8.4 Using SCAMPI^{SM} to prepare for ISO 9001:2000 registration   260
8.5 Summary   261
References   261

9 Document Mapping 263
9.1 Mapping: ISO 9001:2000 to the CMMI®   264
9.2 Inverse mapping: CMMI® to ISO 9001:2000   268
References   281

Acronyms 283

About the Authors 287

Index 289

Foreword

As we began the work in 1998 to bring together three closely related models for process improvement (one for software engineering, one for systems engineering, and one for integrated product development) with the idea of creating the Capability Maturity Model Integrated® (CMMI®), we noted the significant improvements that were being made in the ISO 9000 series that became ISO 9000:2000. We knew that one of the challenges that lay ahead was to ensure that organizations could capitalize on the improvements that both of these efforts made available, resulting in high-quality development.

Many organizations struggle when confronted with multiple standards. Those standards often have different architectures, use different languages, and have different appraisal methods. Usually, organizations address the one standard that is demanded in the next proposal or project or is recognized in the industry as a "must." Sometimes, management reads about the benefits of some new model or standard or hears about it at a conference, and it then becomes important that their next procurement be based on that new standard, model, or framework. What happens next? Standards are revised, the newly developed standards are vastly different, old standards or models will be retired, new appraisal methods are developed—and the cycle starts again.

Boris and Harvey have shown with this work that multiple standards can be addressed simultaneously, by developing a process architecture that is compliant with all of them. This is because there is always a large overlap among the frameworks—most standards and models are based on a set of best practices—so by definition they have to have something in common. Most process improvement professionals have experienced such dilemmas and say that the best approach to process improvement is to have clear goals that support the organization's objectives and strategy. These clear goals need to drive the process improvement goals. Does the company really want to improve its processes or do they want to quickly respond to that new RFP or customer request. As in school, there is no shortcut; no amount of cramming for the finals will result in lasting knowledge. Process improvement takes time and resources, but the rewards have been proven achievable—and sustainable. Organizations whose goal is to "get a level" or "get ISO certified" without regard to the business objectives often struggle to succeed, or to maintain the level or certification. There is no secret; organizations have to set their goals, objectives, and priorities and decide how to conduct process improvement within the business context.

Some organizations will choose to focus on only one of the two frameworks. But because of globalization, many organizations will discover the need to demonstrate compliance with one, or the other, or both documents. Are they compatible? This book points out that ISO 9001:2000 and the CMMI® have a lot in common. In the last several years many organizations started to implement both ISO 9001:1994 and the CMM®, so it seems natural to extend this trend to those newly revised documents. With the revisions of those documents the synergies between them are even more evident. In repeated cases, the model supplements the standard and the standard provides guidance for the model. In the case of software systems and products with large software content, the commonality is very prominent and the book shows how that commonality can be advantageously used for process improvement. In addition, the book shows that the appraisal method used for the CMMI® can be used to prepare organizations for ISO registration.

I have been pleased to see that Boris and Harvey have kept the emphasis on process improvement rather than on the ISO registration or CMMI® maturity level, but they also show what an organization has to do to achieve either one or both. The book provides a systematic process improvement approach, based on the proven IDEAL℠ model, and couples it with the synergy between ISO 9001:2000 and the CMMI® described above. It starts by describing some of the existing frameworks, and then concentrates on ISO and the CMMI®, discusses their newly released revisions, their similarities and differences, and outlines how they provide an effective partnership for improvement.

Next, the book addresses the process of transitioning from the legacy standards to the new revisions, which is then used as a basis for the ultimate, synergistic, unified process improvement approach. Because many organizations already have process improvement experience, the approaches they may take to achieve registration or a maturity level may be quite different. The approach described in the following pages is sensitive to the organization's investment in the previous process improvement achievements and process architectures guiding the adoption of those newly revised documents with added efficiency.

You may wish to read the whole book and find explanations of the major frameworks, including the references to in-depth descriptions of those frameworks, or you may want to jump to the specific case that most closely matches your own improvement environment and find an in-depth transitioning process from the legacy documents to their new revisions, ready for implementation, which will lead to ISO registration, a CMMI® maturity level, or both. I wish you synergistic success on the journey!

Mike Phillips
CMMI® Program Manager
Software Engineering Institute
Pittsburgh, Pennsylvania
March 2003

Preface

After observing and experiencing the difficulties associated with selecting, implementing, and institutionalizing a standard or standards, we have developed a systematic approach to implementing both ISO 9001:2000 and the CMMI® by capitalizing on their synergy. This approach also allows organizations to preserve the process improvement investments made while implementing the legacy standards. The approach encompasses cases in which an organization has no previous process improvement experience as well as those cases in which an organization has already been following one or more standards.

This book does not require process improvement experience or knowledge of a specific standard, but such experience or knowledge is helpful. It is written as a guidebook that practitioners can follow when they implement process improvement based simultaneously on ISO and the CMMI®. It can be used as a textbook for a process improvement course that addresses the details of practical implementation of the two most prominent process improvement standards and contrasts them with other prominent standards and models. The book, for the first time, describes the synergy between ISO 9001 and the CMMI® and the use of that synergy to implement process improvement and get "faster, better, and cheaper" results.

We should stress that the focus of this book is on process improvement, rather than on achieving ISO registration or attaining a CMMI® maturity level. It is our conviction that an organization should first and foremost establish its process improvement goals and only then target ISO registration or a CMMI® maturity level. We have witnessed many organizations that have achieved registration or a maturity level, only to revert to their old "business as usual" with cost overruns, low product quality, and missed deadlines.

Audience for this book

It is important that an organization understand the basic premises of the standards it intends to adopt. The material in this book is presented in a manner that allows all levels of an organization to benefit from it. In particular, the following people will benefit from reading this book:

- *Senior managers*—making decisions on standards selection and implementation. Senior management provides leadership, resources, and funding for process improvement and implementation of standards. They need to understand the underlying principles of each standard and how their synergy can be exploited to make process improvement more efficient and effective.

- *Process improvement practitioners*—developing strategies for process improvement implementation and the transition from legacy to revised standards. Process improvement practitioners develop the processes and practices that will be implemented and institutionalized. They need to identify the processes that can be improved regardless of which standards required them.

- *Evaluators*—making compliance decisions and recommendations. Evaluators compare the actual implemented processes and practices to the standards and judge the degree of compliance. They need to understand the interactions among standards when developing findings and making recommendations.

- *Students of process improvement*—learning the features of each standard and implementation techniques. Students explore each standard and gain the knowledge that will help them understand why and how those standards can be implemented so that they complement each other.

What to expect in this book

To implement process improvement based on a standard, a model, or a combination of models and standards, each standard or model has to be understood in depth. Only then will a full picture of the potential process architecture emerge. Sometimes, both frameworks require exactly the same activities to be performed. In other cases, although the resulting activities are the same, the requirements in each standard may be worded differently, masking potential similarities. Quite often, requirements are at different levels of detail, making it possible to use one standard as a guideline for the other.

In this book we point the reader to the similarities and differences between ISO 9001:2000 and the CMMI®. We reconcile the terminology differences used by those frameworks and then interpret one standard in terms of another, thus guiding the readers to an understanding of their synergy and the use of that synergy for successful process improvement. We introduce a set of process improvement steps that provide efficiency in process improvement implementation.

We understand that many organizations have already invested time and resources using legacy standards. We outline several ways for transitioning from those legacy standards to their new revisions and then show how the synergy between those new revisions can be systematically used in process improvement.

The book is written to gradually guide the reader to an understanding of the needs of an organization that has set process improvement goals for itself. It develops the notion of a systematic process improvement approach based on ISO–CMMI® synergy and is organized in nine chapters.

Chapter 1 introduces the multitude of models and standards and their use in developing process improvement strategies. In Chapter 2 we briefly show how to link organizational business goals to process improvement objectives and describe a process improvement approach. We start the discussion by describing several possible approaches and several standards or frameworks that can be used to guide process improvement. We selected an approach that enables exploitation of the synergy between ISO and the CMMI® and is implemented by adopting the SEI IDEAL^{SM} model.

Chapter 3 discusses some of the best-known frameworks and their relationship to process improvement. Those frameworks provide the basis for understanding the two selected frameworks. Chapter 3 shows that, over the years, standards and models have been successfully used and that it is still possible to use some of them when implementing process improvements. In Chapter 4, ISO 9000:2000 and the CMMI® are explained in detail to enable the reader to understand their synergy. Those two standards were revised and released at the end of 2000 and many organizations are contemplating their use as process improvement frameworks.

Chapter 5 discusses the synergy between ISO 9000:2000 and the CMMI®. Differences between them are discussed. The strengths and weaknesses of each standard are described to provide an understanding of where they will support one another and where some special activities are needed.

In Chapter 6, we describe several approaches for transitioning from the CMM® to the CMMI® and an approach for transitioning from ISO 9001:1994 to ISO 9001:2000 as a basis for showing how to use the ISO–CMMI® synergy in process improvement. We are specifically sensitive to the efforts that organizations have put into developing their process improvement approaches using legacy standards and models. Although many approaches can be devised for transitioning from legacy standards to new standards, the examples presented outline the basic steps from which all other approaches can be derived, depending on the process improvement maturity of an organization.

In Chapter 7, we describe a process improvement approach based on the ISO–CMMI® synergy for an organization with no prior process improvement experience. Then we address several specific cases that can be useful for organizations that have previously implemented process improvements based on one or both of the standards. Chapter 8 covers major appraisal methods and discusses steps for preparing for ISO registration and CMMI® appraisals. Those appraisal methods are not only used for obtaining a formal rating, but also as a tool for determining process improvement opportunities in the diagnosing phase of the IDEAL℠ process improvement cycle.

Finally, in Chapter 9 we provide mappings between ISO 9001:2000 and the CMMI® as a useful tool for judging organizational compliance with ISO, the CMMI®, or both. Mappings are subjective interpretations of each standard's clauses in terms of another standard. They are useful for extrapolating knowledge from the more familiar to the less familiar, but they do not replace a true understanding of the standards.

The outlined approach is based on our experience with organizations that use both ISO and the CMM(I)®. The various cases and the process improvement steps described in the book have been developed to help the reader avoid process improvement traps and dead ends. However, every organization will have to analyze its specific situation, using the approaches described as a guideline. We believe that the steps described in this book will be helpful and will provide sufficient guidance for implementing systematic process improvement using ISO 9001:2000 and the CMMI®.

Acknowledgments

We both work in the process improvement field and have built careers in that field for more than 15 years. However, the roots of our knowledge and process understanding go back to the early days of our professional life when we learned firsthand what works and (painfully) what does not work.

As young engineers, we started working in separate companies, and then worked together for many years, went in different ways, and then again worked together. There are too many people to mention whom, in many ways, contributed to our successes as project managers, process improvement engineers, and software developers. However, we must mention a few that provided leadership and encouraged us to implement a successful and efficient approach to process improvement. Sometimes they gave us an opportunity, sometimes they gave us encouragement, but they always drove us to be the best that we could be. Our thanks to Gene Edelstein, Stu Steele, Ken Nidiffer, Leitha Purcell, Richard Abbott, and Ken Kochbeck. Many thanks to our colleagues in our own organizations and in our clients' organizations, where we worked together to improve processes. Our special thanks go to Tiina Ruonamaa of Artech House, who coaxed and encouraged the writing, reviewing, and production of the manuscript.

Today, we practice process improvement at BearingPoint and Hughes Network Systems, respectively. We wish to express our gratitude to management and our colleagues there who enabled us to reinforce our process improvement approach and provided fertile ground for implementing this "unified" process improvement approach.

Our thanks to the many associates who contributed to our approach with their advice. The errors, however, are all ours.

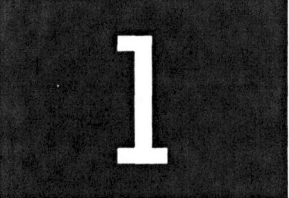

CHAPTER 1

Contents

1.1 Role of frameworks in developing process improvement strategies

1.2 Process improvement approaches

1.3 Synergy

References

Introduction

Evidence is overwhelming that successful organizations continuously improve their processes. Although process improvement is time-consuming and expensive, the evidence shows that the return on investment is high. Improvements can be implemented on an ad hoc basis, but systematic process improvement guided by models or standards is the most effective and efficient approach.

The purpose of most standards is to help its users achieve excellence by following the processes and activities adopted by the most successful enterprises. Unfortunately, standards are often developed independently by standards bodies based on industry-specific needs. Once approved and published, they are periodically updated and revised to reflect the most current experience in that particular field. In many instances, a liaison between the standards bodies is established to make the standards more compatible, but even with such a liaison, each standard usually grows in its own direction with only minimal consideration for the others.

Because standards must limit their scope, they generally cover very specific fields. Over time, activities in other emerging fields may need to be considered, so as a result, additional standards are written or existing standards are modified. Thus, what was at one time a compact well-thought-out set of rules becomes diffused and those rules gradually diverge in unforeseen directions.

In addition, a large body of work, such as more detailed subordinate standards, guidebooks, tutorials, and evaluation methods, usually accompanies each standard. Consultants

1

develop specific guides and tools and registration or certification organizations are formed to provide assessment services. All of these tools and services are supposed to help the users implement the standard and start collecting the promised benefits, but when standards change, the aids that were developed to support them must be reexamined and potentially rewritten.

When standards change, we need a systematic way in which to transition to those new standards without making drastic changes to the existing process assets. In addition, when organizations merge or their programs change, their process improvement approaches may require reexamination and alignment with those changed standards.

Specifically, software is a field in which many standards have been written, rewritten, abandoned, or canceled—only to resurface is some modified form under a new name. When the U.S. Department of Defense declared in the mid-1980s that we were experiencing a "software crisis," many organizations naturally attempted to find solutions to this crisis by over-regulating their software development. Although excessive constraints worked poorly, that period nevertheless resulted in the creation of methods, tools, models, and computer languages intended to help develop software with fewer bugs, enable better prediction of schedules, and reduce the cost of development, operations, and maintenance. This body of work resulted in a much better understanding of the software development process and has brought advances in how software development is approached.

Figure 1.1 shows the "frameworks[1] quagmire" [1], illustrating the relationships among the most prominent standards. As one can see from this figure, it is not easy to select suitable standards from so many choices when developing an organization's process architecture. In many cases, contracting authorities or the marketplace "solves" this problem by prescribing the standards to be used. Although this removes the need to evaluate and select the most appropriate standards, it is not the best way to commit resources and funding to process improvement. What is also evident from the figure is that because of the relationships between the frameworks, a large overlap exists between their features and requirements. In many cases one standard supersedes another or incorporates many of its predecessor's features, thus making development of a standards-based process architecture even more complicated.

Most organizations, if allowed, will select and follow an appropriate standard to guide their improvement activities. Often, however, their customers

---

1. Here, the word *framework* includes process models, international standards, and national quality awards. This definition is somewhat different from the one used in this book.

Introduction 3

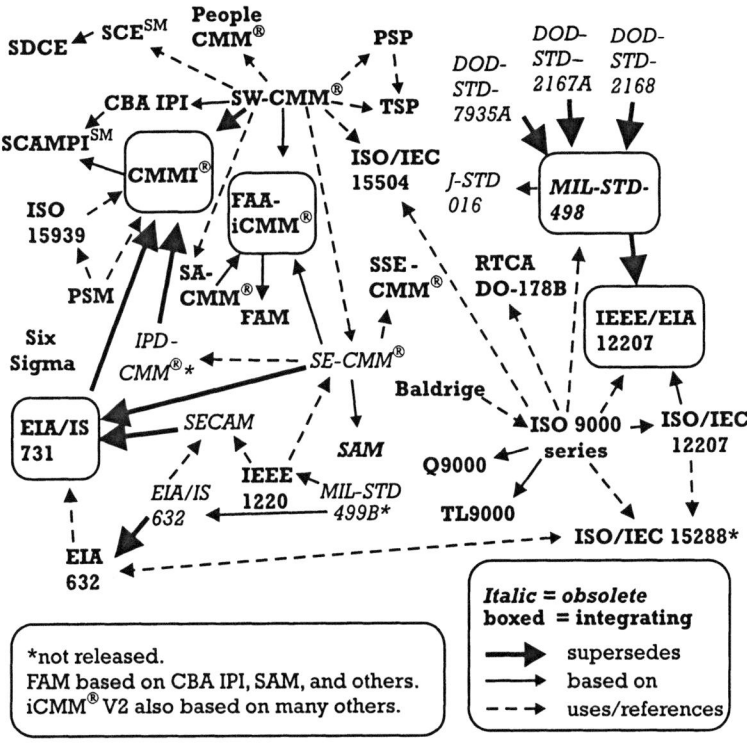

Figure 1.1 Frameworks quagmire. (Copyright © 2001, Software Productivity Consortium NFP, Inc. Used by permission. All rights reserved.)

each require different standards to be used for the same set of activities. In those cases, the organization's processes can be evaluated against each of the standards levied on it by those separate customers. In many instances, a contract or statement of work may require more than one standard or framework. In those cases, an approach to satisfy all required standards or frameworks must be developed.

Some standards, such ISO 9001:1994, imply process improvement but only provide high-level guidelines for its implementation. On the other hand, the Capability Maturity Model® (CMM®) for Software (CMM®-SW), ISO TR 15504, and EIA/IS-731 provide road maps for software process improvement. The goals of these standards are the same: Improve the processes for developing systems and software. The approaches taken to achieve these goals, however, are different.

Although ISO 9001 was revised to emphasize customer satisfaction and the use of a process approach, the Capability Maturity Model Integrated®

(CMMI®) was created to harmonize several capability maturity models: systems engineering, software engineering, acquisition, and integrated product development. The CMMI® consolidates overlapping activities and provides a systematic approach for process institutionalization over all of these domains. In addition, the CMMI® was written with ISO TR 15504 in mind and, as we will see later, has quite a close relationship to it. In the following chapters we will examine the salient features of each standard[2] and explain how to capitalize on their similarities and differences.

What happens when standards or frameworks that have been successfully used are updated or revised? If the revisions are insignificant, or if the organizations using them have mature processes, transition to the new standards may be simple. However, if the standards or frameworks undergo major change, organizations may need to upgrade their governing documents (such as policies, procedures, and processes), and retrain their staff.

The best processes are those that an organization has captured, documented, and then compared to a standard in contrast to those whose creation and implementation is driven by a standard. Process improvements that are identified in an organization's own processes are much easier to implement and institutionalize because buy-in to a familiar process already exists. Process definition driven by a standard or model often produces a "hard-wired" process architecture that mimics the standard's structure and requirements. Such processes are often the easiest to document but, as standards change, will require modifications and updates relative to the standard on which it is based, unrelated to the effectiveness and efficiency of the process itself.

When standards and frameworks are revised, the standardization bodies typically claim to have minimized the impact of changes on users of the predecessor standards. This is often closer to wishful thinking than to reality. In fact, organizations that used the predecessor standards and frameworks as *guidelines* for their processes and documentation will find the transition to the new standard easier than those organizations that created processes echoing the structure of the standard. Thus, a process-focused approach makes change easier to deal with than a standard-focused approach does.

1.1 Role of frameworks in developing process improvement strategies

An important attribute of successful process improvement efforts is the close relationship to the organization's business goals and objectives. Once the business goals are defined, the organization has to accomplish these tasks:

---

2. Although the term *standard* is sometimes used freely, some of the frameworks we discuss (such as the CMM® or CMMI®) have become de facto standards because of their broad use.

- Select a framework that will enable the realization of the goals and objectives.

- Select a process improvement approach.

- Develop and document a process improvement plan.

- Execute the plan with all of the management attributes that accompany any project.

Many of our process improvement colleagues believe that the most effective and efficient way to satisfy more than one standard is to implement them simultaneously rather than sequentially. Such an approach enables process developers to capitalize on the commonalties between those standards and use the strengths of one standard to offset the weaknesses in the other. Our own experiences supported that point of view and prompted us to start investigating a "universal process improvement approach" based on the synergy between ISO 9001:2000 and the CMMI®.

We deliberately avoid specifying goals focused solely on achieving a CMMI® maturity or capability level or attaining ISO registration. We are aware that many organizations will consider those targets to be their process improvement goals, but we firmly believe that such achievements are by-products of consistent and effective process improvement.

We are often asked what advantage one standard has over another. The answer is that it all depends on the process improvement goals and requirements. As we will show in this book, one standard complements the other—where ISO is generic, the CMMI® provides detail, and where the CMMI® is too broad, ISO provides focus. They are both based on the same principles of process engineering, continuous process improvement, and customer satisfaction.

1.2 Process improvement approaches

Process improvement is a major undertaking for any organization. It requires these tasks:

- Analysis of existing processes;

- Changing existing processes;

- Developing new processes;

- Deploying new and modified processes through the organization;

- Training staff to use new or modified processes;
- Sometimes abandoning comfortable old processes.

Most organizations select an approach that will enable them to implement the selected standard(s) and then measure the effectiveness of the new processes. The most fundamental approach is based on Shewhart's *Plan–Do–Check–Act* (PDCA) cycle. In the PDCA cycle, the existing process is compared to the selected (or required) standard or model. Based on the detected "gaps," the organization develops a plan for process improvement, updates or changes processes, measures the improvement, standardizes the new processes, and finally implements them across the organization. The cycle repeats until all goals are achieved.

A more sophisticated approach uses the SEI IDEAL^{SM} model, described in Chapter 2, which distinguishes five phases: Initiating, Diagnosing, Establishing, Acting, and Learning. Its cyclical design implies continuous improvement, in which the learning phase of one cycle is followed by the diagnosing phase of the next cycle. By following those five phases, a systematic process improvement approach to implement one or more frameworks can be devised, as shown in Figure 1.2.

We view the standards or models as frameworks. A *framework* is defined as a set of assumptions, concepts, values, and practices that constitutes a way of viewing reality [2].

With this definition, we move away from the rigid implementation of each clause found in a standard. We take standards as guidelines that have been developed using engineering and management fundamentals and the experiences of the standards writers and successful organizations. The standards thus help users understand the concepts, practices, and values associated with effectively managing, developing, and delivering products and services. Using the preceding definition, all standards and models considered in this book will be considered frameworks.

By selecting a framework, or a set of frameworks, one can develop an approach that will be appropriate for the organization and will result in effective and efficient process improvement. If the selected frameworks are compatible, it will be much easier to develop a satisfactory approach to process improvement than if they address different fields or take different views of the world. For example, before the SEI developed the CMMI®, the *Federal Aviation Administration* (FAA) needed a model that would cover all processes involved in developing and procuring the nation's airspace control systems and developed the FAA-iCMM®,[3] an integrated CMM® based on

---

3. FAA-iCMM® is a registered trademark in the U.S. Patents and Trademark Office.

1.3 Synergy

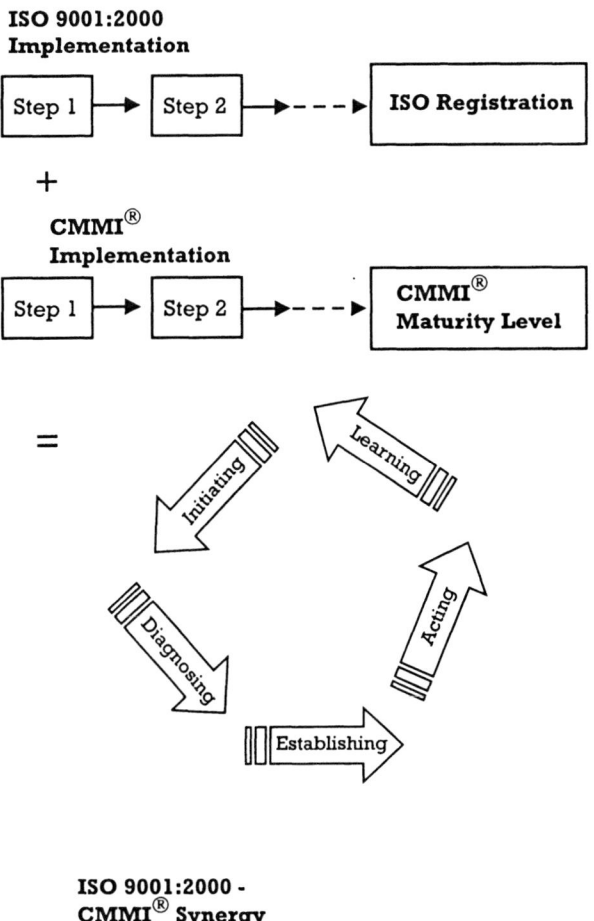

Figure 1.2 Systematic process improvement concept.

several existing CMM®s—software, systems engineering, and acquisition. On the other hand, it would be difficult to develop a coherent framework that would include, for example, the software CMM® and ISO 14001, the environmental management standard.

1.3 Synergy

We have selected two of the most prominent "standards" to show how they can be used synergistically. One is truly an international standard: ISO 9000:2000. The other is a model that has become a de facto standard: the SEI's CMMI®. They were written independently and their purpose and scope are different, but they still have a lot in common. It is this commonality that we are going to explore in this book. Both standards have large followings in the United States and internationally. They are based on predecessor standards created in the late 1980s and early 1990s. Both standards are often required by contracts. Customer representatives (or third-party organizations that are specifically chartered for appraising standard implementation) may examine and evaluate their implementation.

When confronted with requirements for following multiple standards, most organizations will implement one standard, perform an appraisal to confirm that the standard was satisfactorily followed, and then address the next standard.

Some organizations, in their quest for the shortest possible time to achieve ISO registration or a CMM® maturity level, will opt for the cheapest and the least complicated approach. They intend to revisit their processes after achieving registration or process maturity level, but in practice this is seldom done.

By analyzing the requirements of ISO 9001:2000 and the CMMI®, we see that they have many commonalties that can be exploited. If we carry this concept further, by adding more and more details, we realize that we have to account for differences between the maturity of organizations that plan to implement those standards, their commitment to those standards, and their willingness to accept necessary organizational changes. We analyzed several potential approaches and selected one that enables efficient process improvement implementation and capitalizes on the synergy between the standards.

What unifies those two frameworks? When analyzing the principles on which they were built, we noticed that they have more similarities than differences. We were able to use the strengths of one standard to counter the weaknesses of the other, thus further unifying the process improvement approach. For example, both documents are based on the following:

- Process approach;
- Full life cycle;
- Integration of management and production processes;
- Systematic planning;
- Extensive process and product measurements;
- Explicit requirement for the resources needed to implement the processes;

1.3 Synergy

- Educated and well-trained workforce;
- Need for stakeholder involvement and customer satisfaction.

ISO 9001:2000 is a very sparse document, whereas the CMMI® is quite detailed. One will notice that while ISO requires process improvement, it provides only very high-level guidance through ISO 9004:2000. Continual improvement is addressed in new requirements throughout ISO 9001:2000, and some organizations may not be familiar with improvement approaches. Although senior management is required to address its commitment to continual improvement, it is not clear how organizations will indicate that they are continually improving. In contrast, the maturity and capability levels of the CMMI® help organizations chart the way toward reaching their process improvement goals. When the ISO–CMMI® synergy is exploited and combined with the IDEAL℠ process improvement approach, a truly unified process improvement approach emerges.

Figure 1.3 shows an approach using ISO–CMMI® synergy to implement process improvement. To diagnose potential process improvement opportu-

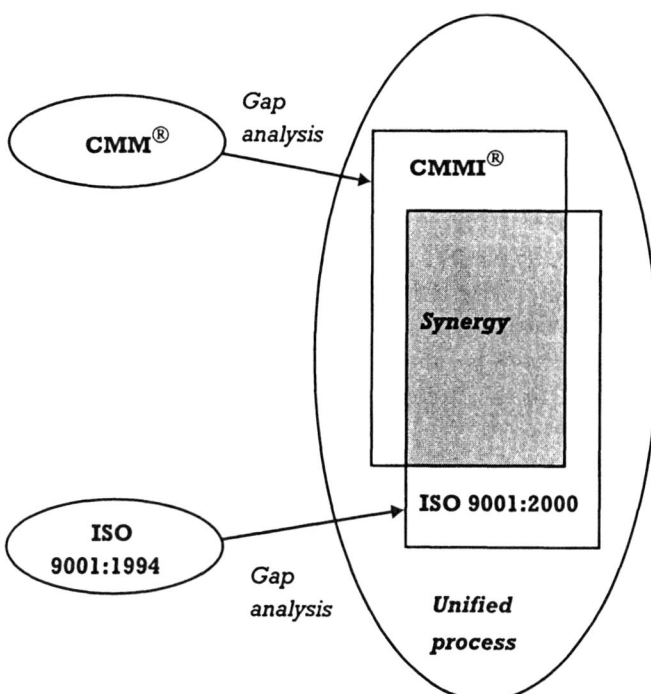

Figure 1.3 Process improvement using ISO and the CMMI®.

nities, gap analyses for each standard have to be performed. Armed with the gap analysis results, process improvement plans can be developed and executed.

We distinguish several cases of process improvement implementation: those in which an organization has some experience in one or both standards and those in which an organization has no experience in process improvement. In each case, the organization will perform a gap analysis to determine the extent of changes required by either standard. Efficiency in process improvement can only be achieved if the synergy between the standards is explored. Invariably, each document will have requirements not covered by the other that will need special attention. Those requirements will become more important for organizations that seek formal assessment of their conformance with the standards than for those organizations that only use the standards for process improvement.

The advantages of this systematic approach are as follows:

- Both standards can be satisfied at the same time.
- Overlaps between the standards are addressed synergistically.
- The strengths of each standard are maximized.
- The weaknesses of each standard are minimized.

For example, customer satisfaction is not explicitly required by the CMMI® but is one of the major themes in ISO 9001:2000. On the other hand, process institutionalization is explicitly required by the CMMI® but is only implied by ISO.

Many of our clients ask us if reaching CMMI® maturity level 2 or maturity level 3 is equivalent to satisfying the ISO requirements. The answer is not simple and we do not encourage such a comparison. However, we would like to provide an indication of the equivalence for those organizations that understand the salient features of each of these documents and have studied their synergy.

There are approximately 130 "shall" statements in ISO 9001:2000. Approximately 40% of these "shall" statements are satisfied by CMMI® maturity level 2 specific practices and generic practices. Approximately 90% of the ISO requirements are satisfied by maturity level 3 practices. Thus, to achieve ISO certification, a CMMI® maturity level 2 organization would have to address the remaining 60% of the ISO 9001 requirements. That gap could be closed by getting to level 3 (to satisfy an additional 50% of the ISO requirements) and then adding those requirements not addressed by the CMMI® or satisfied at higher CMMI® maturity levels.

References

[1] Sheard, S., "Evolution of the Frameworks Quagmire," *IEEE Computer*, July 2001, pp. 96–98.

[2] *American Heritage Dictionary of English Language*, 4th ed., Boston, MA: Houghton Mifflin, 2000.

CHAPTER 2

Contents

2.1 Why worry about process improvement?

2.2 Why is process improvement so difficult?

2.3 Typical process improvement approaches

2.4 Summary

References

Process Improvement

Initiating process improvement after an assessment is challenging. The methods selected may have far-reaching consequences for the success or failure of the process improvement efforts. Most improvement initiatives are based on a problem-solving approach that starts with an analysis of the present situation and continues with planning, execution of the plan, and evaluation of the obtained results. Because many such approaches are available with problem- or domain-specific guidelines, selecting one may be difficult. In this chapter we describe several of the most prominent process improvement approaches, outline their steps, compare them, and finally select one that we think is the most promising for successful process improvement.

2.1 Why worry about process improvement?

It is hard to imagine an organization that cannot be improved. Structured approaches have been developed because they streamline improvement efforts, enable effective planning, logically order the steps to be performed, guide the organization from the initial state to completion, and measure actual performance improvement.

There is more than one approach to process improvement. Some are generic and others are domain specific, but all are based on fundamental problem-solving concepts that require the following:

- Identification of goals;
- Analysis of the present situation;
- Development of an approach;
- Construction of a plan;
- Execution of the plan;
- Measurement of results.

Since the introduction of CMM®-SW, the approaches developed for software process improvement have been extended to cover system and enterprise level issues. The extensions cover the front-end activities of system analysis and design, the back-end system integration and testing activities, and systems engineering process improvement in general. In this book we will use the term *process improvement* to denote both software process improvement and more general systems engineering process improvement.

Effective process improvement programs have measurable goals that are linked to business objectives. Improvement goals are typically stated in terms such as *improving productivity, decreasing the number of defects,* or *increasing the probability of delivering products on time and within the budget.* In a pinch, *achieve ISO registration* or *reach CMM® level 2* can be the initial improvement goal, but it is not very convincing and is not recommended. Linking process improvement goals to business objectives is beyond the scope of this book, but guidelines on the topic can be found in the literature [1].

2.2 Why is process improvement so difficult?

Organizations are systems of complex, concurrent, and interacting processes. These processes may have differing, overlapping, ill-defined, or even undefined objectives. Improving those processes requires discipline, a defined approach, and a plan for systematically considering the changes to be introduced.

Change is difficult for most organizations and individuals. A process may be inefficient and error-prone, but changing that process means abandoning the comfort and certainty of "the way we've always done business." Process improvement initiatives require an investment of time and intellectual energy. This investment, which comes on top of the existing activities needed to keep the enterprise running, may be difficult to sustain. In fact, failure to sustain the commitment to process improvement leads to a history of failed improvement efforts. This, in turn, makes the next improvement initiative even harder to implement. These additional issues make process improvement difficult:

- Lack of clearly stated business goals and objectives;
- Lack of management support;
- Lack of staff or budget;
- Everyday pressures to deliver products under development;
- Resistance to change;
- Desire to maintain the status quo;
- Fear of losing influence.

Despite these difficulties, once changes have been successfully implemented, stakeholders[1] usually refuse to return to the status quo. As an organization matures, change becomes a natural and desirable practice.

To address improvement obstacles, an organization needs to develop an improvement approach and a plan for systematically and incrementally introducing changes and new process technology.

First, an organization needs to define its process improvement goals, which are typically subsets of its business goals. Second, a problem-solving process and a framework to guide process improvement must be selected. Finally, resources must be allocated to execute and monitor the plan.

The problem-solving process, or approach, outlines the steps needed to systematically and incrementally introduce improvements and measure their effectiveness. The improvement framework is necessary to establish a model that will guide improvements and a means for measuring progress.

2.3 Typical process improvement approaches

Some process improvement approaches are generic problem-solving methods. Others, such as ISO 9004:2000 or Part 7 of ISO TR 15504, have been developed in conjunction with a specific standard or framework and later generalized in, for example, the IDEAL^{SM} model. Some approaches are based on Shewhart's PDCA cycle, while others have their roots in a specific

---

[1]. Stakeholders are defined as groups or individuals that are affected by or are in some way accountable for the outcome of an undertaking (CMMI®).

life-cycle model, such as the Software Productivity Consortium's evolutionary spiral process approach [2]. A common characteristic of most process improvement approaches is that they outline a series of steps that guide systematic implementation of improvements, measurement of success, and iterative adjustment of plans and activities.

The following sections describe the salient features of some of these approaches, concentrating on those aspects of process improvement that can be generalized. Implementation, described in later chapters, must take into consideration specific factors such as the organization's structure, current process maturity and capability, improvement goals, and available resources.

2.3.1 Plan-Do-Check-Act

The *Plan-Do-Check-Act* (PDCA) cycle is the problem-solving process developed by Walter Shewhart. It was also called the Shewhart cycle by W. Edwards Deming and the Deming cycle by others. Through the years, several authors, such as Deming, Juran, and Ishikawa, promoted it and added tools to help analyze information collected during PDCA execution and further fine-tune the PDCA approach.

PDCA is the basis of most process improvement approaches. Dr. Shewhart realized that a systematic approach is needed to successfully solve problems. First, one has to plan the process improvement approach, then perform planned work, check whether the improvements are working, and then act to modify the process based on the lessons learned. These steps are repeated until desired results are achieved.

PDCA is part of the overall *total quality management* (TQM) process. It is driven by quality planning processes to identify important areas. The process is domain independent and scalable. It applies to small issues and major initiatives in all functional areas. The four major steps are as follows:

1. Plan

   Identify the problem:
   - Select problems to be analyzed and establish a precise problem statement.
   - Set measurable goals for the problem solving effort.
   - Establish a process for coordinating with and gaining approval of leadership.

   Analyze the problem:
   - Identify the processes that impact the problem and select one.
   - List the steps in the process as it currently exists.

2.3 Typical process improvement approaches

- Identify potential cause of the problem.
- Collect and analyze data related to the problem.
- Verify or revise the original problem statement.
- Identify root causes of the problem.

2. Do

   Develop solutions:
   - Establish criteria for selecting a solution.
   - Generate potential solutions that address the root causes of the problem.
   - Select a solution.
   - Plan the solution implementation.

   Implement a solution:
   - Implement the chosen solution on a trial or pilot basis.

3. Check

   Evaluate the results:
   - Gather data on the solution.
   - Analyze the data on the solution.

4. Act

   Determine next steps:
   - If the desired goal was not achieved, repeat the PDCA process.
   - If the goal was achieved, identify systemic changes needed for full implementation.
   - Adopt the solution and monitor results.
   - Look for the next improvement opportunity.

Several books on process improvement [3–5] are based on the PDCA cycle. In addition, ISO 9001:2000 [6] refers to the PDCA "methodology" (sic) as the means for implementing all required processes from the high-level strategic processes to the product realization and other quality management system processes. ISO guidelines [7] address the use of the PDCA cycle throughout process implementation.

2.3.2 ISO TR 15504, Part 7

The *International Organization for Standardization* (ISO) and the *International Electrotechnical Commission* (IEC) formed a specialized technical committee to develop an international standard for software process assessment [8] that is currently in use for trial purposes. During its development, it was also known as *Software Process Improvement Capability Determination* (SPICE).

Although the committee's technical report describes *software* process assessment, it is sufficiently generic that it can be applied to any process assessment and improvement effort. This technical report has nine parts, as shown in Figure 2.1.

Part 7 provides an effective road map for process improvement. In the committee report, process improvement goes on continuously, starting with a process assessment and continuing until a desired result is reached and confirmed by the next assessment. Assessments provide the baselines used for developing the steps to be used in the next improvement cycle.

ISO TR 15504 recognizes the need for strong management leadership and commitment and the need for communication of objectives and results, team building efforts, continuous learning and evolution, and periodic reinforcement. The process improvement approach described in Part 7 is based on a set of process improvement principles:

- Use process assessment results when developing a process improvement strategy.

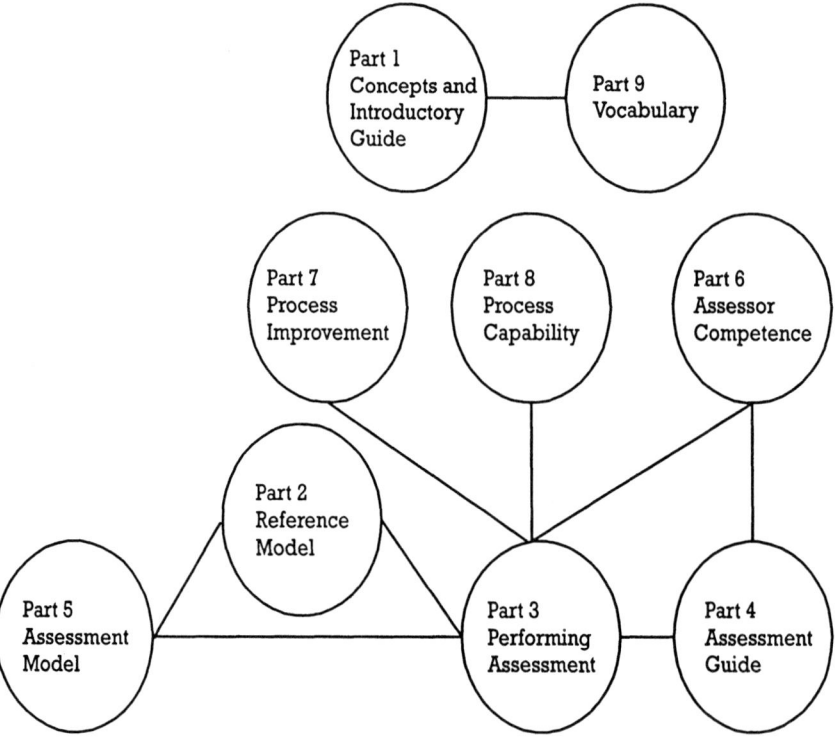

Figure 2.1 Relationships among ISO/IEC TR 15504 parts.

2.3 Typical process improvement approaches

- Process assessment describes an actual process capability that can be compared to a target capability.
- Process improvement is a continuous process.
- Process improvement should be implemented as a project.
- Use measurements for monitoring process improvement progress and for making corrections.
- Use process assessments to determine if desired process improvement results were met.
- Perform risk management by assessing implementation risk as well as the risk of failure in the improvement initiative.

As an international standard, ISO TR 15504 contains all the necessary tools for implementing process improvement including the reference model, process assessment guidelines, and process improvement planning guidelines. Although Part 7 is an integral part of the standard, it does not mandate the use of a specific process model or assessment methodology, thus enabling organizations to use any compatible framework or assessment method.

The process improvement approach has eight steps based on the process improvement principles just described. Those steps are shown in Figure 2.2 and listed here:

1. *Examine the organization's needs and business goals.* Each organization needs to establish its process improvement goals and link them to business objectives and goals. An additional benefit of stating process improvement goals in terms of business objectives is that senior management gets meaningful visibility into process improvement results.

2. *Initiate process improvement.* Experience shows that the most successful process improvement efforts are run as projects and are based on written plans. Process improvement plans specify the process improvement scope (in terms of organizational entities and processes to be included in the improvement effort), outline project phases, establish milestones, and identify risks and the management approach.

3. *Prepare for and conduct a process assessment.* To measure progress and the success of a process improvement initiative, a process baseline is required. Several assessment methods, associated with particular

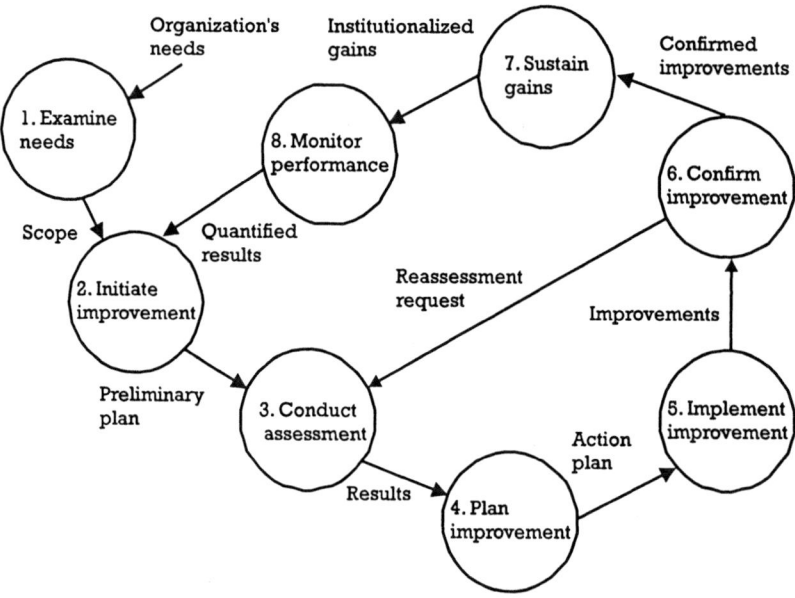

Figure 2.2 ISO TR 15504 software process improvement steps.

process models, are available. Common to all assessment methods is their ability to identify process improvement opportunities. Although the repeatability of assessment results may vary with the method's formality, even the most informal methods provide results that can be used for establishing a process improvement road map.

4. *Analyze assessment output and derive an action plan.* Upon analyzing assessment recommendations, the assessed organization develops detailed process improvement plans. Strategic plans respond to strategic business goals and priorities, whereas tactical plans outline detailed process improvement steps for implementing improvements that satisfy the strategic objectives.

5. *Implement improvements.* A process improvement infrastructure enables development of new processes and transfer of those processes to projects. Typically, a *process engineering group* (PEG) is formed to lead this effort. The PEG analyzes assessment results and fine-tunes the process improvement plan. Once the course of action is determined, the PEG will spawn *process action teams* (PATs) responsible for researching and implementing specific process improvement activities.

6. *Confirm improvements.* Periodically, the PEG measures and monitors process improvement progress, reports progress to the management committee, and institutes corrective actions as required. It reevaluates risks and devises mitigation actions to move the process improvement project toward its goal.

7. *Sustain improvement gains.* The PEG helps sustain process improvement gains and ensures that the organization does not revert to its previous state. The PEG supports transition of improvements to other projects and monitors its implementation.

8. *Monitor performance.* Process improvement requires a long-term commitment. It is not unusual for organizational goals to change over time, requiring changes in the process improvement goals. By measuring process improvement progress, senior management can redirect process improvement activities to best suit the current situation.

ISO TR 15504 also recognizes the importance of cultural issues and management leadership to the success of the process improvement effort and provides guidelines specifically for those issues. Guidelines for establishing effective communication and teamwork within the organization are also provided, including the following:

- The need to establish a set of values;
- Attitudes and behavior;
- The need for a recognition and reward system;
- Measurement;
- Education and training requirements.

2.3.3 IDEAL[SM]

In the early 1990s, when many organizations started process improvement efforts, there were no guidelines for initiating and executing the work. Although the CMM® for software and a compatible appraisal method existed, organizations were left to themselves to determine the most efficient way to implement process improvements. The CMM® itself, by virtue of its five maturity levels, contains a global high-level process improvement strategy. However, guidance is still required to achieve effective and efficient process institutionalization from the tactical point of view.

To help resolve this problem, the SEI developed the IDEAL^{SM} model as a life-cycle model for software process improvement [9]. It was intended to guide organizations in implementing software process improvement based on the CMM®. More recently, the SEI has published version 1.1 of the IDEAL^{SM} model, which has broader applicability. It provides "a usable, understandable approach to continuous improvement by outlining the steps necessary to establish a successful improvement program" [10].

Organizations that undergo software assessments and software capability evaluations obtain results that the SEI's assessment method—the *CMM® Based Appraisal for Internal Process Improvement* (CBA IPI)—very eloquently calls "improvement opportunities." However, without any guidance on how to implement the improvements, the sheer amount of work called for to introduce process improvement activities, address process improvement opportunities, and reach the desired process maturity level is overwhelming.

The IDEAL^{SM} model guides process improvement in a cyclical manner starting with a stimulus for improvement through execution and implementation of improvements. This model is based on the premise that improvement is a continuous process that requires incremental implementation, with periodic review of results, reimplementation of improvement steps based on those results, and execution of corrective actions.

Very early on, organizations realized that to be successful in process improvement, they needed an infrastructure to enable the introduction of changes in their processes and guide them toward the set goal. The IDEAL^{SM} model supports these needs through five phases: Initiating, Diagnosing, Establishing, Acting, and Learning, as depicted in Figure 2.3. These phases, discussed next, often overlap and may be executed in parallel.

Initiating phase

In the Initiating phase, goals for process improvement are established. Typically, those goals relate to the business goals of increased product quality, reduced cycle time, increased productivity, or a combination of these factors. Those goals provide the stimulus for change. As an organization advances through the IDEAL^{SM} phases, the goals can be refined and changed. To be effective, an organization defines the process improvement sponsorship and establishes the process improvement infrastructure in this phase. Establishing the organizational infrastructure, such as a PEG, a management council, and process working groups, is vital to the success of the overall effort. The infrastructure, just as in a construction project, provides the necessary foundation for the later phases. Therefore, the activities in this phase should be well understood and implemented with care.

2.3 Typical process improvement approaches

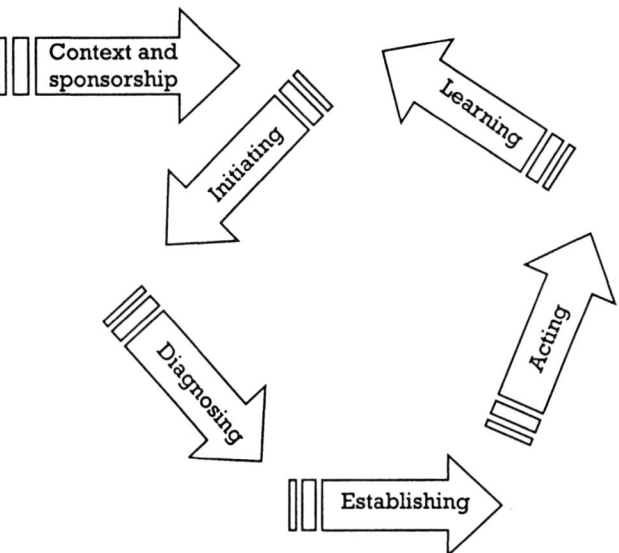

Figure 2.3 IDEAL^{SM} model.

Diagnosing phase

In the Diagnosing phase, a more complete understanding of improvement activities is developed. This phase establishes the basis for the work performed in later phases. The process as currently practiced is captured and documented. This current process is then compared to some process model, such as the CMM®, and gaps between the model and actual practices are identified. Typically, an assessment is used for that purpose, but other forms of gap analysis can be equally effective. These gaps then serve as a basis for process improvement and, in turn, development of the new and improved process.

Establishing phase

In the Establishing phase, a detailed process improvement plan is developed, based on organizational goals and objectives and the gaps identified in the previous phase. Priorities for the improvement efforts and project performance goals are determined; process improvement activities usually require the same resources needed for project activities. Diverting people to a process improvement initiative may impact product delivery schedules. The framework set up in the initiating phase should be able to mitigate those conflicts. The goals and objectives and the gaps identified in the diagnosing phase define the scope of the process improvement activities. A detailed process improvement plan, which includes tasks, schedule, milestones, deliverables, resources, responsibilities, measurements, tracking requirements, risks, and their mitigation, is now established.

Acting phase

In the Acting phase the planned work is implemented. Improvements are usually tested on pilot projects before they are introduced throughout the organization. On completion of the pilot implementations, organizations refine the solution, as necessary, and develop a plan for transitioning the piloted solution into projects. The transition plan takes into consideration the culture and readiness of the organization to accept this new process and the point in the life cycle of the selected projects where the improvements will be introduced.

Learning phase

The steps in the Learning phase concentrate on collecting lessons learned, determining what worked and what did not, and measuring the efficiency of the process improvement approach. Here, process improvement results are compared to the business needs identified in the initiating phase. Using this evaluation and any new business or process improvement goals, additional process improvement requirements are captured and proposals for the new changes to be introduced in the next improvement cycle are recommended.

Because process improvement requires significant effort, resources and expenditures, an additional activity—managing the process improvement program—is necessary in every phase to coordinate the process improvement activities. This activity is shown in Figure 2.4. Managing process improvement involves organizing the process improvement program, planning improvement activities, staffing the efforts, monitoring progress, and providing day-to-day direction.

A recent U.S. General Accounting Office study [11] suggests that IDEAL[SM] is considered to be a best practice and should be used by all Department of Defense services when performing process improvement, thus recognizing it as an approach of choice.

2.3.4 Evolutionary spiral process

The *Software Productivity Consortium* (SPC) has developed an approach that uses the evolutionary spiral process to manage process improvement [2].

2.3 Typical process improvement approaches

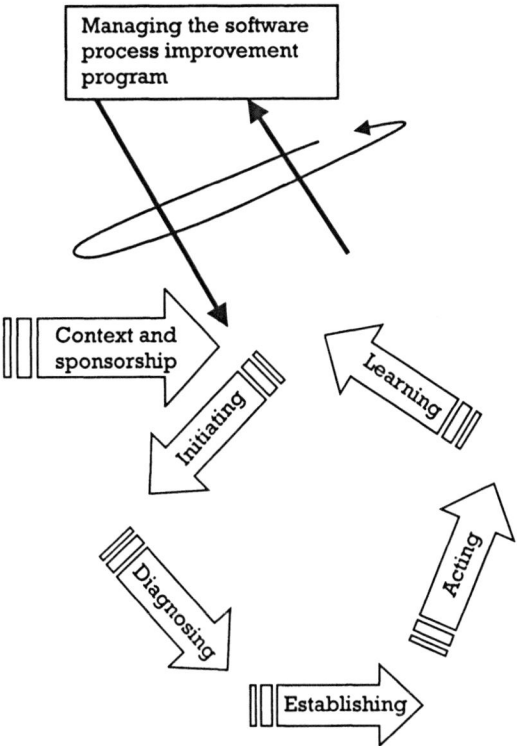

Figure 2.4 Managing process improvement based on the IDEAL^{SM} model.

Although it is written with software process improvement in mind, it can be generalized to include any process improvement effort. It is based on the premise that, just as in software, process improvement activities are seldom executed in a "waterfall" sequence in which activities have starting and ending points and when one ends another one starts. Many adverse impacts can influence each step in process improvement even when all of the process improvement requirements are known.

This method contains five major steps that are cyclically repeated until the goals and objectives are reached. Those five steps with their activities are as follows:

1. Understand context:
   - Build/reinforce sponsorship and foundation.
   - Define/update improvement strategies.
   - Identify objectives, alternatives, and constraints.
   - Assess/understand process.

2. Analyze risks and select strategy:
   - Analyze and resolve risks.
   - Select improvement strategy.
3. Plan improvements:
   - Define/update action plan.
4. Implement improvements:
   - Implement.
   - Manage and monitor.
5. Review and update:
   - Review progress.
   - Define/update program plan.

An advantage of the spiral model approach is that it recognizes the difficulties associated with static process improvement planning. Even when all process improvement requirements are known at the onset of the process improvement project, specific activities cannot be predicted far in advance. A process improvement project will encounter many adverse events throughout its implementation, such as loss of funding, lack (or loss) of qualified personnel, and changes in the organizational objectives and goals. Because the spiral approach is based on analysis and management of risk, the process improvement project will be able to mitigate identified risks, reevaluate its plan and optimally advance towards its goals.

2.3.5 ISO 9004:2000

ISO 9004:2000, *Quality Management Systems—Guidelines for Performance Improvements* [12] replaces ISO 9004-1:1994. It is the second part of what ISO 9000:2000 calls a "consistent pair" and is informative only. It emphasizes the process approach required by ISO 9000:2000 and reiterates the importance of following the set of quality management principles, both of which will be discussed later in this book. It follows the structure of ISO 9001:2000 and, for each section, provides guidelines for process improvement. Moreover, it suggests using the PDCA cycle throughout process implementation and specifically when implementing the quality management system general requirements of Section 4.1.

Unfortunately, although it elaborates each of the ISO 9001:2000 requirements, ISO 9004:2000 does not provide detailed guidance for improving processes. The elaborations and explanations are stated in the form of the requirements (using *should* rather than *shall*), which seems to add more requirements to those already existing in ISO 9001:2000. By reading ISO 9004:2000, it appears that an organization must address all processes at the same time in order to satisfy the ISO 9000:2000 requirements.

2.3.6 Brute force

When an organization recognizes the need for improvement but has not tied improvements to business goals, the typical improvement goal is usually phrased along the lines of "achieve ISO registration" or "reach CMM® level 2." Although the company recognizes that these frameworks have a demonstrated history of successfully improving productivity and product quality, analysis of specific business priorities may be missing.

In these cases, implementation is often by edict, usually accompanied by a schedule with an aggressive end date. The result is often no more than the mere appearance of change: Paperwork is generated and appropriate testimony is delivered, but business goes on as usual.

This is far from the optimal approach but if you find yourself in this situation, do not despair. Sharpen the definition of the objectives and add detail to the plans. Measure the time and effort expended and the results attained. Capitalize on the successes that are achieved. Those successes will help support continued progress.

2.4 Summary

Table 2.1 summarizes the features of four of the most prominent approaches described in this chapter. They all have similar structures and follow basic PDCA steps augmented by approach-specific activities (such as risk management in the spiral approach or performance monitoring in the ISO approach). Some approaches, such as the spiral approach, display more programmatic or management (control) features than other approaches, such as PDCA.

A major advantage of the IDEAL^{SM} model is that it is publicly available from the SEI. The spiral approach is proprietary to the SPC. The ISO approach, which exhibits excellent features, is described in the proprietary ISO document.

For this reason, we will use the IDEAL^{SM} model as a basis for our discussions. This model is versatile and can be implemented in any type of process improvement effort.

Table 2.1 Improvement Approaches

PDCA	ISO TR 15504	IDEAL^{SM}	Spiral Approach (SPC)
Plan Identify the problem	• Examine organization's needs and business goals • Initiate process improvement	*Initiating* • Stimulus for change • Set context • Build sponsorship • Charter infrastructure	• Understand context • Reinforce sponsorship and foundation • Define and update improvement strategies • Assess/understand process
Analyze the problem	• Prepare and conduct process assessment	*Diagnosing* • Characterize current and desired states • Develop recommendations	
Do Develop solutions	• Analyze results and derive action plan	*Establishing* • Set priorities • Develop approach • Plan actions	• Analyze risks and select strategy • Analyze and resolve risks • Select improvement strategy • Plan improvements • Define/update action plan
Implement solution	• Implement improvements	*Acting* • Create solution • Pilot/test solution • Implement solution	• Implement improvements • Manage and monitor
Check Evaluate the results	• Confirm improvements	*Learning* • Analyze and validate • Propose future actions	• Review and update • Review progress • Define/update program plan
Act Standardize the solution	• Sustain improvement gains • Monitor performance		

References

[1] McGibbon, T., *A Business Case for Software Process Improvement Revised: Measuring Return on Investment from Software Engineering and Management*, DoD Data and Analysis Center for Software (DACS), Rome, NY, September 1999.

[2] *Managing Process Improvement: A Guidebook for Implementing Change*, SPC-93105-CMC, Software Productivity Consortium, Herndon, VA, December 1993.

[3] Grady, R. B., *Successful Software Process Improvement*, Upper Saddle River, NJ: Prentice Hall, 1997.

[4] Arthur, L. J., *Improving Software Quality: An Insider's Guide to TQM*, New York: John Wiley & Sons, 1993.

[5] Potter, N., and M. Sakry, *Making Process Improvement Work: A Concise Action Guide for Software Managers and Practitioners*, Reading, MA: Addison-Wesley, 2002.

[6] *Quality management systems—Requirements, ISO 9001:2000*, Geneva, Switzerland: ISO, December 2000.

[7] *Guidance on the Process Approach to Quality Management Systems*, ISO/TC 176/SC 2/N544, Geneva, Switzerland: ISO, December 2000.

[8] *Information Technology—Software Process Assessment*, ISO/IEC TR 15504, Geneva, Switzerland: ISO, 1998.

[9] McFeeley, B., *IDEAL[SM]: A User's Guide for Software Process Improvement*, CMU/SEI-96-HB-001, Pittsburgh, PA: Software Engineering Institute, 1996.

[10] Gremba, J., and C. Myers, "The IDEAL[SM] Model: A Practical Guide for Improvement," *Bridge*, No. 3, 1997.

[11] *Software and Systems Process Improvement Programs Vary in Use of Best Practices*, GAO-01-116, Washington, D.C.: U.S. General Accounting Office, DOD Information Technology, March 2001.

[12] *Quality management systems—Guidelines for performance improvements, ISO 9004:2000*, Geneva, Switzerland: ISO, December 2000.

CHAPTER 3

Contents

3.1 Relationships between frameworks and process improvement approaches

3.2 ISO 9001:1994

3.3 CMM® for software

3.4 ISO TR 15504

3.5 EIA/IS-731

3.6 FAA-iCMM®

3.7 Summary

References

Framework Introduction

Frameworks support process improvement in the systems and software engineering domains. A framework is a set of assumptions, concepts, values, and practices that constitute a way of viewing reality. Frameworks provide ways to organize those elements so they can be managed and understood. Some of the most widely known frameworks are described in this chapter. Chapter 4 will focus on the current revisions of the two most widely accepted frameworks: ISO 9001:2000 and the CMMI®.

3.1 Relationships between frameworks and process improvement approaches

As shown in Figure 3.1, any framework can be used with any problem-solving process to develop an overall process improvement approach. Some approaches and frameworks make better matches than others.

Process improvement approaches require the development of plans that are based on organizational goals and objectives. Plans establish disciplined ways to manage process improvement projects and track improvement progress. Plans should address the following topics:

1. Goals and objectives;
2. Success criteria;
3. Requirements;

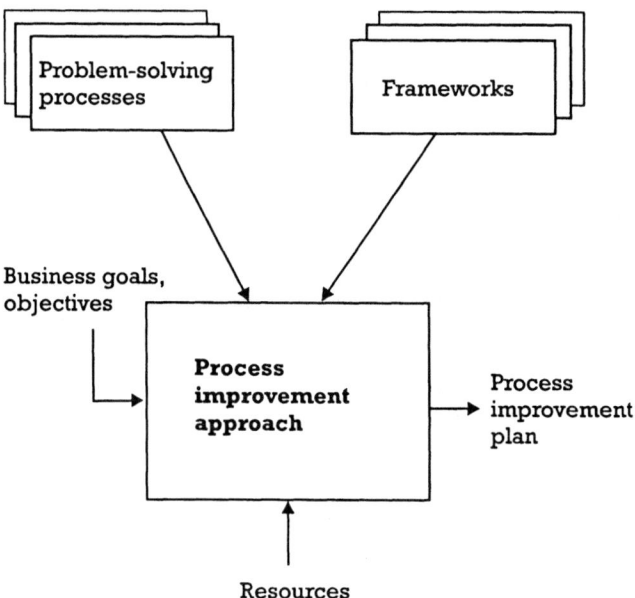

Figure 3.1 Relationship between process improvement approaches and frameworks.

4. Effort estimates;
5. Resource requirements;
6. Activities to be performed;
7. Schedule;
8. Measurements to be made;
9. Feedback.

As described in Chapter 2, most process improvement approaches are based on the PDCA cycle, which is used to determine the steps to be followed. A framework helps define the details to be included in each step. Those details are generally based on the best practices routinely followed by successful companies in similar situations. Any of the process improvement approaches described in Chapter 2 can be successfully used for process improvement with any framework described in this chapter and in Chapter 4.

For example, where a process improvement approach requires planning, a framework may provide guidance on what to include in the process improvement plan and may even provide a template for such a plan. Similarly, when an approach requires collection of performance measurements

3.1 Relationships between frameworks and process improvement approaches

to determine implementation success or failure, the framework may suggest a type of measurement best suited for that purpose.

When ISO 9001:1987 and ISO 9001:1994 were published, it was difficult to see how they could be applied to software. ISO 9000-3 was developed to show how to interpret ISO 9001 for software, but even with that supplementary document, there were virtually no guidelines for determining an implementation sequence. The latest approved revision of ISO 9000-3 [1] is consistent with ISO 9001:1994 [2]. As of this writing, a revision of ISO 9000-3 that corresponds to ISO 9001:2000 was being balloted.

In contrast, at approximately the same time, the CMM®-SW was published by the SEI, explicitly showing how an organization can advance its processes from chaotic to repeatable to defined, managed, and optimizing. The CMM® was based on the PDCA approach. Later, the SEI developed the IDEAL[SM] model to further strengthen the systematic continuous approach to process improvement. For more detail about the PDCA approach and the IDEAL[SM] model, refer to Chapter 2.

Attempts were made to relate (or map) ISO 9001:1994 and the CMM® and to identify their commonalties [3]. However, most organizations that implemented both frameworks, in sequence or simultaneously, did not sufficiently explore their commonalties, concentrating instead on their differences. ISO 9001:1994 did not explicitly require process improvement, whereas the CMM®-SW was based on the continuous process improvement approach, which was championed in Japan under the name *kaizen*.

Sometimes, a contract or the marketplace dictates framework selection. For example, European organizations will gravitate toward ISO registration while U.S. organizations, particularly those that contract with the federal government, will choose the CMM® or CMMI®. However, many organizations must serve many markets and cannot be limited to a single framework.

Overviews of several important and widely used frameworks for process improvement are presented in this section. The overviews are kept brief because detailed discussions are already available in many books and papers. We next discuss these frameworks:

- ISO 9001:1994;
- CMM®-SW;
- ISO TR 15504;
- EIA/IS-731;
- FAA iCMM®.

Two of the frameworks, ISO 9001:1994 and CMM®-SW, are being superseded by their recent revisions. The revised versions are described in Chapter 4 and their synergy is discussed in Chapter 5.

ISO TR 15504 is actually a process assessment standard that encourages the use of compatible process models and assessment techniques. The ISO TR 15504 architecture served as a basis for several models, such as EIA/IS-731, the FAA iCMM®, and the continuous representation of the CMMI®. EIA/IS-731 is a CMMI® predecessor model and has been incorporated into the CMMI®. The FAA iCMM® was developed before the CMMI® was issued, so its future application may be limited.

3.2 ISO 9001:1994

ISO 9000 is the world's most widely used quality management standard. It consists of a series of five related documents (ISO 9000, 9001, 9002, 9003, and 9004) issued by the ISO. The series forms a framework for quality management and improvement used by many industries for development, production, and service delivery.

Many excellent texts describing this standard in detail are available so only the most important features are discussed here. This discussion will help the reader understand the differences between the 1994 version and its 2000 revision, which is described in some detail in Chapter 4.

ISO 9000:1994, *Quality management and quality assurance standards—Guidelines for selection and use*, includes the characteristics and general philosophy behind the standards. Related standards in the ISO 9000 family cover specific aspects of quality management and quality assurance for those cases for which not all requirements of 9001 may be applicable, such as production or testing. Among the related standards are ISO 9002, *Model for quality assurance in production, installation and servicing*, and ISO 9003, *Model for quality assurance in final inspection and test*. ISO 9004, *Quality management and quality system elements—Guidelines*, provides guidance on quality management and quality system elements and is not intended for contractual use.

ISO 9001:1994, *Model for quality assurance in design, development, production, installation and servicing* [2], is a revision of the 1987 standard. No major architectural changes were introduced in that revision. It provides guidance for quality management and quality assurance in all industries and domains.

The ISO 9000 family specifies quality standards for virtually all activities and processes involved in designing, producing, and distributing products or services. ISO 9000 was intentionally written to be generic. Over the years, the quality management aspects of ISO 9001 have become well understood by its users, but process improvement has not been addressed consistently, particularly in the manufacturing sector.

ISO 9001:1994 requires organizations to document and use their processes for design, production, and distribution, collect quality records, and control product quality. Quality management is accomplished by managing the processes. Quality control is implemented through the quality manual that contains procedures and guidance for implementing the quality system. The quality manual enables identification, collection, storage, and retrieval of quality records and facilitates the implementation of corrective actions. Processes and potential corrective actions have to be analyzed and activities must be introduced to correct and improve those processes. Responsibility must be assigned for implementing and reviewing the quality system, implementing related improvements, and ensuring that corrective actions are being consistently evaluated, implemented and tracked. To accomplish those tasks, the quality system must be documented, the documentation must be controlled, and the organization's staff must be trained to use this documentation.

Those basic tenets are implemented in ISO 9001:1994 in the form of 20 clauses presented in Chapter 4 of the standard and shown in Table 3.1. (The first three chapters of the standard address the scope, normative references, and definitions.) The 20 clauses may be considered to be the "rules" that govern quality systems.

Most quality manuals written to satisfy this standard were based on these 20 clauses. In turn, most registrars assessing organizations for compliance to ISO 9001:1994 liked this approach because of its direct correspondence to the standard. In practice, such a quality manual structure may not be optimal and may not reflect the way people really perform. Departments that implemented quality system processes and wrote their procedures and work instructions to fit that structure have had difficulty keeping them current and training their staff in their use.

3.3 CMM® for software

The CMM® grew out of the U.S. Department of Defense's need to be able to predict the performance of its software contractors. The development of a process maturity framework began in the mid-1980s at the SEI. An initial description of the framework [4] and a questionnaire to help assess maturity [5] were published in 1987.

Several years of experience with the initial description and the questionnaire ultimately led to the 1991 publication of CMM® for software, version

Table 3.1 ISO 9001:1994 Clauses

Clause	Quality System Requirements	Description

4.1	Management responsibility
	• Quality policy
	• Organization
	  —Responsibility and authority
	  —Resources
	  —Management representative
	• Management review
		Establish policies, organization structure, resource requirements, and management responsibility.

4.2	Quality system • General • Quality system procedures • Quality planning	Define and document a quality system. Include procedures and plans for meeting quality requirements.
4.3	Contract review • General • Review • Amendment to contract	Define and document procedures for contract reviews and amendments.
4.4	Design control • General • Design and development planning • Organizational and technical interfaces • Design input • Design output • Design review • Design verification • Design validation • Design changes	Document procedures to control the product design and development process. Include planning, reviews, verification, and validation.
4.5	Document control • General • Document and data approval and issue • Document and data changes	Define procedures to maintain and control changes to documents and data.
4.6	Purchasing • General • Evaluation of subcontractors • Purchasing data • Verification of purchased product	Define procedures for managing subcontractors and controlling the purchasing process.
4.7	Control of customer-supplied product	Protect customer-supplied products and equipment.
4.8	Product identification and traceability	Identify and track products and work in process.
4.9	Process control	Monitor and control production and service processes.

3.3 CMM® for software

Table 3.1 ISO 9001:1994 Clauses *(continued)*

Clause	Quality System Requirements	Description
4.10	Inspection and testing • General • Receiving inspection and testing • In-process inspection and testing • Final inspection and testing • Inspection and test records	Inspect and test in-process material, incoming products, and final products.
4.11	Inspection, measuring, and test equipment • General • Control procedure	Define procedures to maintain and control equipment used for inspection and test.
4.12	Inspection and test status	Document and control the inspection status of all products.
4.13	Control of nonconforming product • General • Review and disposition of nonconforming product	Ensure that nonconforming products are segregated and that their disposition is controlled.
4.14	Corrective and preventive action • General • Corrective action • Preventive action	Define procedures to correct nonconformities and prevent their occurrence.
4.15	Handling, storage, packaging, and delivery • General • Handling • Storage • Packaging • Preservation • Delivery	Define procedures for handling, storing, packaging, and delivering products.
4.16	Control of quality records	Define procedures for maintaining quality records.
4.17	Internal quality audits	Define procedures for performing internal evaluations of the quality system.
4.18	Training	Define procedures for identifying training needs and delivering training.
4.19	Servicing	Define procedures for performing service on products.
4.20	Statistical techniques • Identification of need • Procedures	Establish statistical techniques for monitoring products and processes.

1.0, a framework that describes the key elements of an effective software process. After several years of use and industry feedback, the current and final CMM® for software, version 1.1, was published [6]. Note that the CMM® is not a theoretical model; it is based on actual performance of successful software development practices.

The CMM® is a *staged* model defining five levels of process maturity. Each level defines a maturity plateau, establishing the basis for continuing process evolution. The five levels are summarized in the CMM®, as shown in Table 3.2.

As each maturity level is implemented, visibility into software processes increases. Control advances from an ad hoc approach to one in which management is able to address problems and issues as they occur. With increasing maturity, greater insight into more granular process details becomes available. Process performance and product quality become more predictable. Eventually, instead of reacting to issues, processes and product quality can be quantitatively managed. As a staged model, it is a CMM® principle that this visibility and control comes through systematically implementing each maturity level in sequence.

3.3.1 CMM® structure

Each maturity level includes a number of *key process areas* (KPAs) and associated goals. The KPAs at each maturity level are shown in Figure 3.2. The

Table 3.2 CMM® Maturity Levels

Maturity Level	Description
1. Initial	The software process is characterized as ad hoc and occasionally even chaotic. Few processes are defined, and success depends on individual effort.
2. Repeatable	Basic project management processes are established to track cost, schedule, and functionality. The necessary process discipline is in place to repeat earlier successes on projects with similar applications.
3. Defined	The software process for both management and engineering activities is documented, standardized, and integrated into a standard software process for the organization. All projects use an approved, tailored version of the organization's standard software process for developing and maintaining software.
4. Managed	Detailed measures of the software process and product quality are collected. Both the software process and products are quantitatively understood and controlled.
5. Optimizing	Continuous process improvement is enabled by quantitative feedback from the process and from piloting innovative ideas and technologies.

3.3 CMM® for software

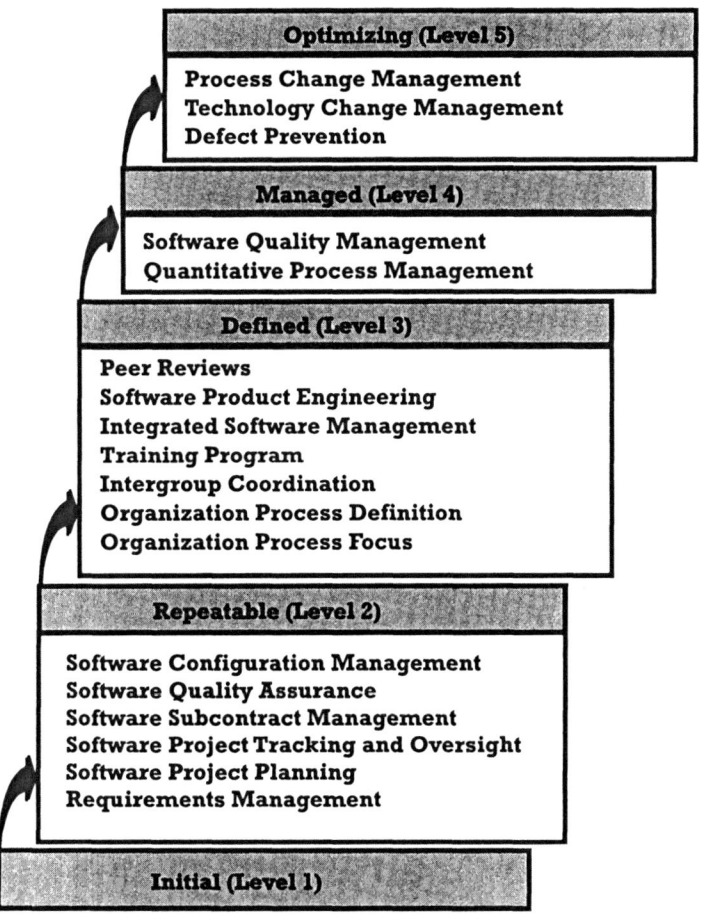

Figure 3.2 CMM® process maturity levels.

KPAs itemize the practices that will lead to the satisfaction of the goals. The goals signify the scope, boundaries, and intent of each KPA. By satisfying *all* of the goals of *all* of the KPAs at that level *and* below, a specified maturity level is achieved. Achievement of a maturity level is binary; there is no such status as "maturity level 2.5."

Every KPA organizes the key practices into five categories known as common features. The common features are summarized in Table 3.3.

The Commitment to Perform and Ability to Perform practices are prerequisites to the Activities Performed, whereas the Measurement and Analysis and Verifying Implementation practices ensure that the activities have been implemented. Taken together, those four common features are known as

Table 3.3 CMM® Common Features

Common Feature	Description
Commitment to Perform	Describes the actions the organization must take to ensure that the process is established and will endure. This typically involves establishing organizational policies and senior management sponsorship.
Ability to Perform	Describes the preconditions such as training and resources that must exist to implement the software process competently.
Activities Performed	Involves establishing plans and procedures, performing the work, tracking it, and taking corrective actions as necessary.
Measurement and Analysis	Addresses measurements to determine the status and effectiveness of the activities performed.
Verifying Implementation	Describes the steps to ensure that the activities are performed in compliance with established processes. Includes reviews and audits by management and software quality assurance.

the institutionalization common features. The CMM® architecture is shown in Figure 3.3.

A maturity level is achieved by satisfying all of the goals of all of the KPAs at that maturity level. The goals are satisfied by addressing the practices in all five common features for that KPA. The example in Figure 3.3 [7] shows how a practice (Activity 9) is traced though a common feature (Activities Performed) to a KPA goal (Software Project Planning Goal 1) and finally to a maturity level (Level 2: Repeatable).

3.3.2 Key process areas

In this section, we summarize the CMM® KPAs at each maturity level.

Maturity level 2: Repeatable

Organizations at level 2 can be summarized as being disciplined because planning and tracking of the software project is stable and earlier successes can be repeated. The project's processes are under the effective control of a project management system, following realistic plans based on the performance of previous projects.

The KPAs at maturity level 2 are as follows:

- *Requirements Management* (RM);
- *Software Project Planning* (SPP);

3.3 CMM® for software

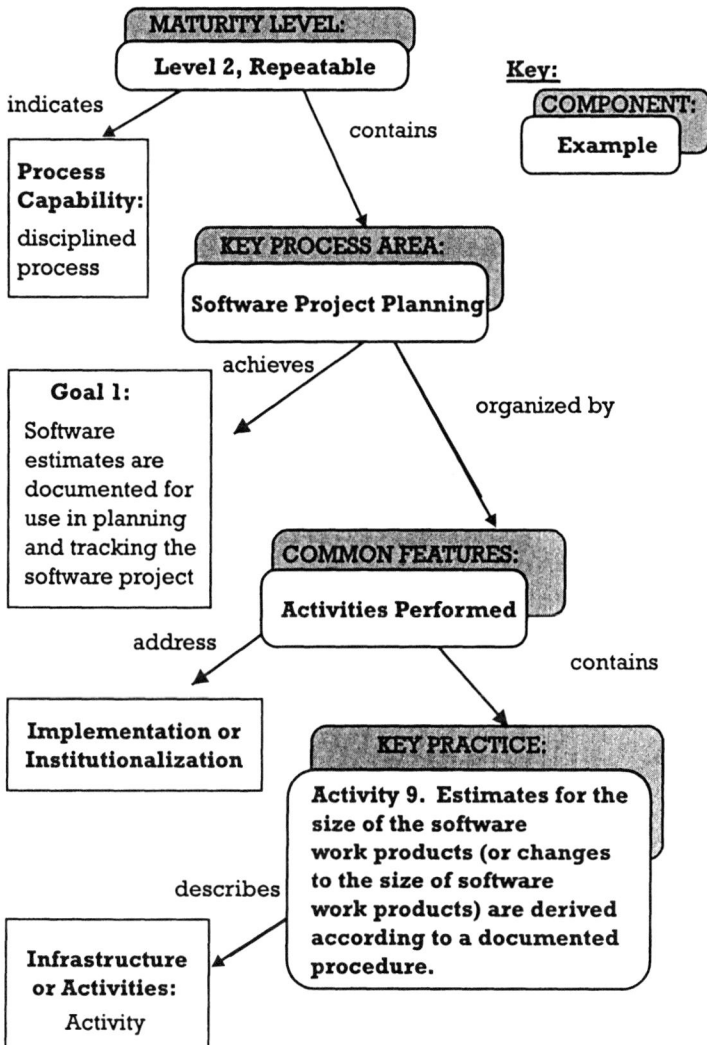

Figure 3.3 The CMM® architecture.

- *Software Project Tracking and Oversight* (SPTO);
- *Software Subcontract Management* (SSM);
- *Software Quality Assurance* (SQA);
- *Software Configuration Management* (SCM).

Maturity level 3: Defined

In level 3 organizations, software process capability is standard and consistent because both software engineering and management activities are stable and repeatable. Within established product lines, cost, schedule, and functionality are under control, and software quality is tracked. This process capability is based on a common, organization-wide understanding of the activities, roles, and responsibilities in a defined software process.

The KPAs at maturity level 3 are as follows:

- *Organization Process Focus* (OPF);
- *Organization Process Definition* (OPD);
- *Training Program* (TP);
- *Integrated Software Management* (ISM);
- *Software Product Engineering* (SPE);
- *Intergroup Coordination* (IC);
- *Peer Review* (PR).

Maturity level 4: Managed

In level 4 organizations, processes operate within measurable limits. This level of process capability allows an organization to predict trends in process and product quality within the quantitative bounds of these limits. When these limits are exceeded, action is taken to correct the situation. Software products are of predictably high quality.

The KPAs at maturity level 4 are as follows:

- *Quantitative Process Management* (QPM);
- *Software Quality Management* (SQM).

Maturity level 5: Optimizing

Level 5 organizations are continuously striving to improve process capability, thereby improving the performance of their projects and the quality of their products. Improvements are brought about through incremental advancements in the existing process and through innovations using new technologies and methods.

The KPAs at maturity level 5 are as follows:

- *Defect Prevention* (DP);
- *Technology Change Management* (TCM);
- *Process Change Management* (PCM).

3.4 ISO TR 15504

ISO TR 15504 [8] was written to provide a framework for conducting consistent assessments of process capability that would ensure an acceptable level of repeatability and reliability across various appraisal methods. It is intended to harmonize various assessment models and methods [9]. TR 15504 has both a reference model for software activities and a compatible embedded model for use in process assessments. It includes guidance on using assessments for process improvement and capability determination [10]. In its original format, TR 15504 was written from the supplier organization's point of view. As of this writing, efforts are still under way to extend this aspect to cover acquirer processes as well.

TR 15504 is compatible with several other standards, such as ISO 12207:1995 [11] and ISO 9001:1994. It is compatible with ISO 9001 in very general terms because both standards espouse the need for quality assurance in design, development, production, installation, and servicing of software products. Compatibility with ISO 12207 is much deeper because ISO 12207 provides an overall framework for software life-cycle processes.

Chapter 2 briefly discussed the process improvement aspects of ISO TR 15504, focusing on Part 7. Figure 2.1 shows all nine parts of the standard. Only Parts 2 and 3 are normative. All other parts are informative.

"Part 5: Assessment Model," called the *exemplar model*, is the most controversial part of the standard. The standard assumes that there will be many compliant models that satisfy, or map to, this reference model and thus may be used for assessments in accordance with the requirements of Part 3. Because Part 5 contains many details and elaboration of the mandatory processes and associated base practices, it is often used as a guideline for interpreting Part 2. Part 2 is a framework that allows assessments to use different models, but it can not be used by itself to support an assessment. Those models and methods must be mapped to the reference model to judge their compatibility. The controversial aspect of Part 5 stems from its inclusion in TR 15504 as an informative section. By publishing the assessment model as an integral part of the standard, it may become a de facto standard, despite being labeled *informative*. This then defeats the original intent of allowing various models to be used in appraisals.

TR 15504 uses a two-dimensional model for processes and process capability. Part 5 distinguishes between base practices ("if we are doing this, we meet the basic process requirements") and management practices ("if we do these we can determine how well we are doing the process") [9]. Base practices are associated with the process dimension of the model while the management practices are associated with the capability dimension. The six capability levels are shown in Table 3.4.

The process dimension is consistent with the international standard for software life-cycle processes [11].[1] Processes are divided into three categories, as shown in Table 3.5.

Specific process attributes, common to all processes, are required to achieve each capability level. These attributes, shown in Table 3.6, are the basic elements of the ISO TR 15504 assessment scheme.

During an assessment, these attributes are evaluated as follows:

- **N,** *not achieved:* Little or no evidence of achievement of the defined attribute (0–15%).

- **P,** *partially achieved:* Evidence of a systematic approach. Achievement of defined attribute; some aspects of the achievement may be unpredictable (16–50%).

Table 3.4 ISO TR 15504 Capability Levels

Capability Level	Description
0	Incomplete—The process is not generally performed or fails to achieve its process outcomes.
1	Performed—The purpose of the process is generally achieved. The process may not be rigorously planned and tracked, but actions are taken when required.
2	Managed—The work products of performed processes are developed according to standards and procedures and processes are planned and tracked.
3	Established—The managed process is performed using a defined process that is based on software engineering principles and is tailored for specific instantiations.
4	Predictable—The established process is performed consistently in practice. It is measured and measures are analyzed in order to control processes quantitatively.
5	Optimizing—The predictable process is optimized to meet current and future business needs.

---

1. ISO TR 15504 refers to ISO 12207:1995, rather than the ISO 12007:2001 revision.

3.4 ISO TR 15504

Table 3.5 ISO TR 15504 Process Dimension

Category	Process ID	Description
Primary life-cycle processes	CUS.1	Acquisition • Acquisition preparation • Supplier selection • Supplier management • Customer acceptance
	CUS.2	Supply
	CUS.3	Requirements elicitation
	CUS.4	Operation • Operational use • Customer support
	ENG.1	Development • System requirements analysis and design • Software requirements analysis • Software design • Software implementation • Software integration • Software testing • System integration and testing
	ENG.2	System and software maintenance
Supporting life-cycle processes	SUP.1	Documentation
	SUP.2	Configuration management
	SUP.3	Quality assurance
	SUP.4	Verification
	SUP.5	Validation
	SUP.6	Joint review
	SUP.7	Audit
	SUP.8	Problem resolution
	SUP.9	Measurement
	SUP.10	Reuse processes
Organizational life-cycle processes	MAN.1	Management • Project management
	MAN.2	Quality management
	MAN.3	Risk management
	ORG.1	Organizational alignment
	ORG.2	Improvement • Process establishment • Process assessment • Process improvement
	ORG.3	Human resource management
	ORG.4	Infrastructure

- **L,** *largely achieved:* There is evidence of sound systematic approach to and achievement of the defined attributes (51–85%). It has some variation in process implementation.

- **F,** *fully achieved:* There is evidence of complete and systematic achievement of the defined attributes (86–100%). No significant weaknesses.

Table 3.6 Capability Levels and Process Attributes

Capability Level	Process Attributes	Description
Level 1: Performed process	PA 1.1	Process performance attribute
Level 2: Managed process	PA 2.1	Performance management attribute
	PA 2.2	Work product management attribute
Level 3: Established process	PA 3.1	Process definition attribute
	PA 3.2	Process resource attribute
Level 4: Predictable process	PA 4.1	Process measurement attribute
	PA 4.2	Process control attribute
Level 5: Optimizing process	PA 5.1	Process change attribute
	PA 5.2	Continuous improvement attribute

The management practices are applicable to all processes. They are designed around the achievement of the principal management functions of planning, organizing, resourcing, and controlling. Attribute indicator sets are associated with each management practice and represent the types of evidence that substantiate judgments of the extent to which the management practice is performed [8]. The attribute indicator sets are listed here:

- Practice performance characteristics that provide guidance on the implementation of the practice;
- Resource and infrastructure characteristics that provide mechanisms for assisting in the management of the process;
- Associated processes from the process dimension that support the management practice.

An example of management practices for capability level 2 is given in Table 3.7.

The capability level achieved by a process is derived from the applicable attribute ratings for that process. For example, level 2 is determined by these rules:

Level 2	
Process performance [the performed process (CL 1) is now managed]	Fully satisfied
Process attribute 2.1, Performance management	Largely or fully satisfied
Process attribute 2.2, Work product management	Largely or fully satisfied

Table 3.7 Management Practices for Capability Level 2

Management Practice ID	Description
	Performance Management
1.1	Identify the objectives for the performance of the process (for example, time scale, cycle time, and resource usage).
1.2	Plan the performance of the process according to the identified objectives by identifying the activities of the process, the expected time schedule, and allocation of resources for each activity.
1.3	Plan and assign responsibility and authority for developing the process's work products.
1.4	Manage the execution of activities by continued tracking and replanning to produce work products that meet the defined objectives.
	Work Product Management
2.1	Identify work product requirements including both functional and nonfunctional aspects.
2.2	Manage the documentation, configuration management, and change control of the work products.
2.3	Identify and define any work product dependencies.
2.4	Manage the quality of work products to ensure that they meet their functional and nonfunctional requirements.

Since the CMMI® addresses both systems and software engineering, its scope is broader than Part 2 of ISO TR 15504. The ISO technical committee is now working to extend the scope of TR 15504 to include systems engineering so that the CMMI® and ISO TR 15504 will be harmonized.

3.5 EIA/IS-731

The Electronic Industries Alliance (EIA) issued EIA/IS-731, *Systems Engineering Capability Model* (SECM) [12], as an interim standard. The EIA, the *International Council on Systems Engineering* (INCOSE), and the *Enterprise Process Improvement Collaboration* (EPIC) collaborated on this project. They recognized that the CMMI® would encompass systems engineering and thus make the standard obsolete. Nevertheless, this standard provided guidance while the CMMI® was under development and was one of the source standards used in that development.

EIA/IS-731 has two parts: the SECM model, EIA/IS-731-1, and the SECM appraisal method, EIA/IS-731-2; our discussion will be limited to

EIA/IS-731-1. The standard is available to the public without charge and can be downloaded from the *Government Electronic and Information Technology Association* (GEIA) Web site.

EIA/IS-731 "applies to programs and organizations doing systems engineering: small or large; simple or complex; software intensive or not; precedented or unprecedented. It applies to systems that may contain hardware, software, personnel, facilities, data, materials, services, or techniques" [12].

EIA 731 complements EIA 632, *Processes for Engineering a System,* and IEEE Standard 1220-1994, *IEEE Trial-Use Standard for Application and Management of the Systems Engineering Process.* It has been made consistent with ISO 9001:1994 by covering all of its 20 clauses. The EIA/IS-731 architecture shown in Figure 3.4 is characterized as "continuous." It is aligned with the ISO TR 15504 architecture. EIA/IS-731 capability levels are shown in Table 3.8 [12].

A category is a natural grouping of focus areas. The three categories (technical, management, and environment) are shown in Table 3.9. A focus area is a set of related, unique *basic practices* (BPs) and *advanced practices* (APs)

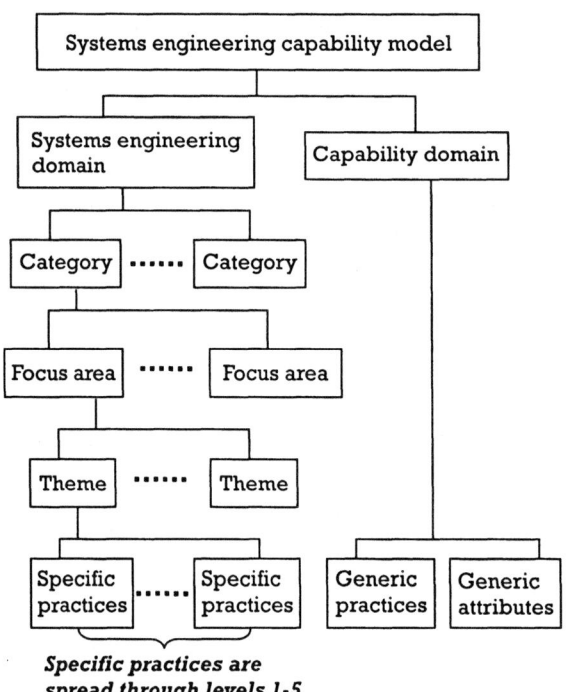

Figure 3.4 EIA/IS-731 architecture.

3.5 EIA/IS-731

Table 3.8 EIA/IS-731 Capability Levels

Capability Level	Process Attributes	Nonprocess Attributes
0: Initial	• General failure to perform activities • No easily identifiable work products • No proof that tasks are accomplished	• No assurance of success • Information is difficult to identify • Driving force for activities is indeterminate • No assurance of complexity management • No systems engineering focus • Activities and products of little effect or value
1: Performed	• Activities are done informally • Nonrigorous plans and tracking • Dependency on "heroes" • Work products are in evidence • General recognition of need for activity	• Information is paper based • Activities driven only by immediate contractual or customer requirements • *Systems engineering* (SE) focus limited to requirements • Activities are marginally effective • Work products are of marginal utility
2: Managed	• Policies define need for activities • Processes are program/project specific • Activities are planned, tracked, measured, and verified • Corrective actions are taken to ensure that the program/project specific process is followed • Work products are reviewed for adequacy • Defects are removed from products • Work products are controlled	• Key information managed electronically • Activities driven by benefit to customer • SE focus is requirements through design • Activities are adequately effective • Work products are of adequate utility

and, in some cases, *advanced attributes* (AAs) that address particular aspects of systems engineering. A theme is a subdivision of a focus area that defines a related set of specific practices to put those practices in context. A specific practice is an activity that is essential to accomplishing the purpose of a focus area or that helps accomplish the purpose of the focus area effectively and efficiently. Specific practices are associated with specific levels of capability within each focus area.

Table 3.8 EIA/IS-731 Capability Levels *(continued)*

Capability Level	Process Attributes	Nonprocess Attributes
3: Defined	• Processes are well defined • The organization has a standard SE process • Tailoring guidelines exist for the standard SE process • The standard SE process is tailored and used by each program/project • Tailoring is reviewed and approved • Data are collected on the performance of the tailored process • Qualitative process improvement is performed on both standard and tailored processes • Customer feedback is obtained	• Consistent program success • All information is managed electronically • Key information is integrated in a program database • Activities driven by benefit to program • SE focus is requirements through operation • Activities are significantly effective • Work products are of significant utility
4: Measured	• Metrics are derived from data on the tailored process • The tailored process is quantitatively understood • Performance of the tailored process can be predicted • Tailored process–induced defects are identified • Measurable quality goals are established for SE work products • Causal analyses are performed for the tailored process • Tailored processes are quantitatively improved • Standards process continues to be qualitatively improved	• All information fully integrated in a program database • Activities driven by SE benefit • SE focus on all phases of product life cycle • Activities are measurably effective • Work products are of measurably significant utility
5: Optimizing	• Process effectiveness goals are established for the program/project based on business objectives • Causal analyses are performed for the standard process • Standard processes are quantitatively improved • Improvements to the standard process are flowed down into each tailored process	• Activities driven by systems engineering and organizational benefit • Fully scalable complexity management • SE focus is product life cycle and strategic applications • Activities are optimally effective • Work products are of optimal utility

Table 3.9 EIA/IS-731 Focus Areas

Category	Focus Area ID	Description
SE technical	FA 1.1	Define stakeholder and system level requirements
	FA 1.2	Define technical problem
	FA 1.3	Define solution
	FA 1.4	Assess and select
	FA 1.5	Integrate system
	FA 1.6	Verify system
	FA 1.7	Validate system
SE management	FA 2.1	Plan and organize
	FA 2.2	Monitor and control
	FA 2.3	Integrate disciplines
	FA 2.4	Coordinate with suppliers
	FA 2.5	Manage risk
	FA 2.6	Manage data
	FA 2.7	Manage configurations
	FA 2.8	Ensure quality
SE environment	FA 3.1	Define and improve the SE process
	FA 3.2	Manage competency
	FA 3.3	Manage technology
	FA 3.4	Manage systems engineering support environment

Each *Focus Area* (FA) is defined by a set of unique *generic characteristics* (GCs), which serve as indicators of an organization's capability to perform systems engineering and are grouped into levels of maturity. Generic characteristics are comprised of process-oriented *generic practices* (GPs) and nonprocess-oriented *generic attributes* (GAs). Generic characteristics apply equally to the practices of every FA. Generic practices and their relationship to capability level are shown in Table 3.10.

GAs address the effectiveness of the process and the value of the products of the process. Both are viewed over a range related to the six capability levels. With increasing level, the worth of products and processes should increase. The two GAs are GA-1, implement an effective set of FA activities, and GA-2, produce a valuable set of FA products.

The effectiveness of the activities and the value of the work products are evaluated as marginal, adequate, significant, measurably significant, or optimal and are indicative of the level of performance. For example, effectiveness evaluated as *marginal* means that the effort could be removed without causing significant impact. At the other extreme, effectiveness evaluated as *optimal* means that maximum benefit for the effort expended is being received; more effort would result in diminishing returns [12].

Being "at a level" means doing all of the practices (generic and specific) at that level in a manner consistent with the descriptions of the GAs at that

Table 3.10 EIA/IS-731 Generic Practices

Capability Level	Generic Practice	Generic Description
0: Initial		There are no GPs at level 0.
1: Performed		There are no GPs at level 1.
2: Managed	GP 2.1	Follow recorded and approved plans and processes in implementing the focus area.
	GP 2.2	Verify compliance with approved plans and processes. Take appropriate action when performance deviates from plan or when processes are not followed.
3: Defined	GP 3.1	Standardize and record a well-defined FA process.
	GP 3.2	Tailor the organization's standards process using standard guidelines to meet specific program or organizational needs.
	GP 3.3	Implement and improve the FA activities (i.e., tailored process) per established and approved formal procedures.
	GP 3.4	Improve the organization's standards process using information from work product reviews and process compliance reviews.
4: Measured	GP 4.1	Collect and analyze metrics to determine the performance of the tailored FA activities.
	GP 4.2	Take appropriate action to align tailored FA performance and expectations.
5: Optimizing	GP 5.1	Identify those FA activities for which it is appropriate and inappropriate to quantify process repeatability.
	GP 5.2	Establish quantitative goals for improving the effectiveness of the standard process.
	GP 5.3	Improve the organization's standard process based on data and metrics collected from a continuing program of process compliance reviews and work product reviews.
	GP 5.4	Perform causal analysis of process and work product defects. Eliminate the causes of defects by changing the standard process.

level. For example, being at managed level 2 means performing all of the level 2 specific and generic practices and satisfying the generic attributes.

Each FA contains descriptions, comments, references to other process areas, themes with a list of typical work products, and a list of specific practices. Annex A to the standard, which is normative, contains tailoring guidelines. Tailoring helps an organization focus on those parts of the model from which it can most benefit. It involves eliminating higher-level practices in the model, when focusing on lower capability levels or eliminating parts of the model (such as FAs or themes) to align process improvement goals and activities with organizational objectives. When tailoring the model one should be aware that "tailoring out" may result in gaps that impact achievement of capability levels.

3.6 FAA-iCMM®

Version 1.0 of the iCMM® was first released in November 1997. The framework was subsequently revised and released as version 2.0 in 2001. Version 2 of the iCMM® includes features based on the experiences of users, lessons learned, and the need to maintain currency with newly developed or revised models and standards. It also includes material drawn from other sources not commonly addressed in such documents, including these:

- ISO 9001:2000 Quality management systems;
- EIA/IS-731 SE capability;
- Malcolm Baldrige National Quality Award/President's Quality Award criteria;
- CMMI®: CMMI®-SE/SW/IPPD and CMMI®-SE/SW/A;
- ISO/IEC TR 15504 Software process assessment;
- ISO/IEC 12207 Software life-cycle processes;
- ISO/IEC CD 15288 System life-cycle processes;
- iCMM® version 1.0, containing CMM®-SW, CMM®-SA, and CMM®-SE.

Its scope covers acquisition, supply, engineering, development, operation, evolution, support, and management of products and services throughout the life cycle from conception through operation and disposal. The iCMM® also contains an appraisal methodology called the *FAA-iCMM® Appraisal Method* (FAM).

The model is intended for application in organizations that focus on high-level issues (such as public responsibility, strategic direction, or system architecture), on low-level issues (such as task management, mechanism selection, or design implementation), or on both. A project can use the model to improve, as can a small organizational unit operating as a project, a large organizational unit comprising several units, or an overall enterprise [13].

The iCMM® architecture is referred to as "continuous with staging" because its process areas can be evaluated using either six capability or five maturity levels. The 23 process areas are grouped in three categories, as shown in Table 3.11.

A *capability level* addresses a set of practices that work together to provide a major enhancement in the capability to perform a process. GPs, shown in Table 3.12, characterize the capability dimension. A *GP* is a practice that enhances the capability to perform any process. They are grouped by capability level and contribute to achieving the goal at that level [13].

The descriptions make it clear that capability levels are cumulative. Each successive level is based on the previous level. Capability levels, goals, and generic practices provide guidance for process improvement that leads from the very elementary to quantitatively managed and optimizing.

The process dimension is characterized by categories, process areas, goals, and base practices. A *category* is a group of process areas addressing the same general type or area of activity. A *process area* (PA) is a group of related base practices that are essential for achieving the purpose of the PA. A *base practice* summarizes a fundamental characteristic of performing a process that meets the purpose of the PA. Base practices are mapped to *goals* [13].

Table 3.11 Process Areas

Group	PA ID	Process Area
Management processes	PA 00	Integrated Enterprise Management
	PA 11	Project Management
	PA 12	Supplier Agreement Management
	PA 13	Risk Management
	PA 14	Integrated Teaming
Life-cycle processes	PA 01	Needs
	PA 02	Requirements
	PA 03	Design
	PA 06	Design implementation
	PA 07	Integration
	PA 08	Evaluation
	PA 09	Deployment, Transition, and Disposal
	PA 10	Operation and Support
Support processes	PA 04	Alternatives Analysis
	PA 05	Outsourcing
	PA 15	Quality Assurance and Management
	PA 16	Configuration Management
	PA 17	Information Management
	PA 18	Measurement and Analysis
	PA 20	Process Definition
	PA 21	Process Improvement
	PA 22	Training
	PA 23	Innovation

3.6 FAA-iCMM®

Table 3.12 Generic Practices

Capability Level	Description, Goals, and Generic Practices
Level 0: Incomplete	An incomplete process is either not performed or partially performed. One or more of the goals of the process area are not achieved. (There are no goals and no GPs at this level.)
Level 1: Performed	A performed process is a process that achieves the goals of the process area. Base practices of the process area are generally performed. Goal: The process achieves the goals of the process area. GPs: 1.1 Identify work scope 1.2 Perform the process
Level 2: Managed (planned and tracked)	A managed process is a performed (capability level 1) process that is also planned and tracked. The process is managed to ensure its institutionalization, and to ensure the achievement of specific objectives for the process, such as customer satisfaction, cost, schedule, and quality objectives. Goal: The process is institutionalized as a managed (planned and tracked) process. GPs: 2.1 Establish organizational policy 2.2 Document the process 2.3 Plan the process 2.4 Provide adequate resources 2.5 Assign responsibility 2.6 Ensure skill and knowledge 2.7 Establish work product requirements 2.8 Consistently use and manage the process 2.9 Manage work products 2.10 Objectively assess process compliance 2.11 Objectively verify work products 2.12 Measure process performance 2.13 Review performance with higher level management 2.14 Take corrective action 2.15 Coordinate with participants and stakeholders
Level 3: Defined	A defined process is a managed (planned and tracked, capability level 2) process that is tailored from the organization's set of standard processes according to the organization's tailoring guidelines. Goal: The process is institutionalized as a defined process. GPs: 3.1 Standardize the process 3.2 Establish and use a defined process 3.3 Improve processes

Table 3.12 Generic Practices *(continued)*

Capability Level	Description, Goals, and Generic Practices
Level 4: Quantitatively managed	A quantitatively managed process is a defined (capability level 3) process that is controlled using statistical and other quantitative techniques. Quantitative objectives for process performance are used in managing process performance. Expected performance is within defined control limits. Goal: The process is institutionalized as a quantitatively managed process. *GP:* 4.1 Stabilize process performance
Level 5: Optimizing	An optimizing process is a quantitatively managed (capability level 4) process that is changed and adapted to meet relevant current and projected business objectives. Goal: The process is institutionalized as an optimizing process. *GP:* 5.1 Pursue process optimization

Staging groups process areas into a series of maturity levels or evolutionary plateaus as shown in Table 3.13. Staging provides guidance on which process areas might be pursued together and which process areas should be pursued first. In addition, it enables benchmarking against existing capability maturity models.

Two process areas are not included in the staging: PA 10, Operation and Support, and PA 17, Information Management. Their content does not correspond to any other model or standard. For those organizations that chose to consider these two process areas, PA 10 and PA 17 can be included at maturity levels 2 and 3, respectively.

The iCMM® predates the CMMI® by several years. It was written by and for the FAA. It is in the public domain and can be readily downloaded from the FAA Web site (http://www.faa.gov/aio). The iCMM® is a comprehensive model with an excellent discussion of its role in process improvement, process design, and process assessment. The iCMM® provides a supplement (which is also downloadable from the FAA Web site) that maps both the generic and base practices to the source models and standards listed earlier in this section. Although FAA experience and data show that the iCMM® is effective, it is not likely to have broad application because the CMMI® has overlapping coverage and greater general appeal.

3.7 Summary

This chapter has described several important models and standards. Each model or standard has an associated appraisal method, implying that the

3.7 Summary

Table 3.13 Process Areas by Maturity Level

Maturity Levels	Description and Process Areas
0 and 1	Default maturity level—no process areas
2	*Life-Cycle/Engineering Processes* PA 02 Requirements PA 08 Evaluation PA 09 Deployment, Transition, and Disposal *Management/Project Processes* PA 11 Project Management PA 12 Supplier Agreement Management *Supporting Processes* PA 05 Outsourcing PA 15 Quality Assurance and Management PA 16 Configuration Management PA 18 Measurement and Analysis
3	*Life-Cycle/Engineering Processes* PA 01 Needs PA 03 Design PA 06 Design Implementation PA 07 Integration *Management/Project Processes* PA 00 Integrated Enterprise Management PA 13 Risk Management PA 14 Integrated Teaming *Supporting Processes* PA 04 Alternatives Analysis PA 20 Process Definition PA 21 Process Improvement PA 22 Training
4	No process areas
5	*Supporting Processes* PA 23 Innovation

framework will be used not only for process improvement but also for benchmarking purposes. By studying the framework architectures, one can see where improvements were introduced and how the current state-of-the-art practice impacted their evolution or merger. Their comparison, on a per-practice level can be found in the FAA iCMM®.

In the next chapter, we concentrate on ISO 9001:2000 and the CMMI® because the synergy between the two forms a powerful process improvement framework.

References

[1] *Guidelines for the Application of ISO/IEC 9001 to the Development, Supply, and Maintenance of Software*, ISO/IEC 9000-3, Geneva, Switzerland: ISO, 1997.

[2] *Quality systems—Model for quality assurance in design, development, production, installation, and servicing*, ISO 9001:1994, Geneva, Switzerland: ISO, 1994.

[3] Paulk, M. C., *A Comparison of ISO 9001 and the Capability Maturity Model® for Software*, CMU/SEI-94-TR-12, Pittsburgh, PA: Software Engineering Institute, August 1994.

[4] Humphrey, W. S., *Characterizing the Software Process: A Maturity Framework*, CMU/SEI-87-TR-11, Pittsburgh, PA: Software Engineering Institute, 1987.

[5] Humphrey, W. S., and W. L. Sweet, *A Method for Assessing the Software Engineering Capability of Contractors*, CMU/SEI-TR-23, Pittsburgh, PA: Software Engineering Institute, 1987.

[6] Paulk, M. C., et al., *Capability Maturity Model® for Software, Version 1.1*, CMU/SEI-93-TR-24, DTIC Number ADA263403, Pittsburgh, PA: Software Engineering Institute, February 1993; and Paulk, M. C., et al., *Key Practices of the Capability Maturity Model® for Software, Version 1.1*, CMU/SEI-93-TR-25, DTIC Number ADA263432, Pittsburgh, PA: Software Engineering Institute, February 1993.

[7] *Tutorial: Introduction to CMM®*, Pittsburgh, PA: Software Engineering Institute, 1996.

[8] *Information Technology—Software Process Assessment*, ISO/IEC TR 15504, Geneva, Switzerland: ISO, 1998.

[9] *SPICE World*, Vol. 1, No. 1, PILOT, The InterSPICE Group, Inc., August 1999, http://www.spiceworld.hm.

[10] Rout, T., *SPICE and Other Flavours, Software Process Assessment Using ISO TR 15504*, Queensland, Australia: Software Quality Institute, Griffith University, 2001.

[11] *Information Technology—Software Lifecycle Processes*, ISO/IEC 12207:1995, Geneva, Switzerland: ISO, 1995.

[12] *Systems Engineering Capability Model*, EIA/IS-731, Washington, D.C.: Electronic Industry Alliance, 1998.

[13] Ibrahim, L., et al., *The Federal Aviation Administration Integrated Capability Maturity Model®* (FAA-iCMM®), Version 2.0, Washington, D.C.: Federal Aviation Administration, September 2001.

CHAPTER 4

Contents

4.1 ISO 9001:2000

4.2 CMMI®

References

Revised Frameworks: ISO 9001:2000 and the CMMI®

The previous chapter presented several of the most prominent process improvement frameworks. In this chapter, we provide an overview of ISO 9001:2000 [1] and the CMMI® [2, 3] using the framework definition given in Chapter 3. ISO 9001:2000 and the CMMI® v1.02 were issued at the end of 2000. CMMI® v1.1 was issued in December 2001. These two frameworks, individually and together, provide a comprehensive basis for process improvement.

ISO 9001:2000 outlines five areas that have to be considered for organizations to be successful in (1) defining processes for developing products, (2) satisfying customer requirements, and (3) keeping those processes under control. The CMMI® describes the steps an organization has to take to advance its systems and software engineering processes from an initial maturity level to a managed and eventually quantitatively managed level. When the two frameworks are considered simultaneously, the CMMI® provides a model for the essential practices necessary for the successful implementation of the five ISO areas and, in turn, the processes that convert customer requirements into products and services. The synergy between ISO 9001:2000 and the CMMI® will be further explored in Chapter 5.

4.1 ISO 9001:2000

In December 2000, a revised version of the ISO 9000 standard was issued after several years of worldwide rewrites, ballots, and approvals. This new and long awaited standard brought many changes to the old warhorse, ISO 9000:1994, including the withdrawal of ISO 9002 and ISO 9003. The new ISO family of standards forms a "coherent set of quality management system standards" [4] based on a consistent set of quality management principles. The following standards make up this new ISO family:

- ISO 9000, Fundamentals and vocabulary [4];
- ISO 9001, Requirements [1];
- ISO 9004, Guidelines for performance improvements [5];
- ISO 19011, Guidelines for quality and environmental management systems auditing.

The most notable change is in the spirit of this new standard: movement away from a prescriptive, procedure-based approach to modern quality management practices based on a systems engineering approach, process-oriented thinking, achievement of customer satisfaction, and continuous improvement. Another important change is in the increased emphasis on senior management commitment to customer satisfaction and continuous improvement.

The cancellation of the ISO 9002 and 9003 standards indicates the global appeal of the new ISO 9001 and 9004 standards. This "coherent pair" follows an identical structure to describe a framework applicable to all product categories and all organization sizes.

One of the more obvious differences between the 1994 and 2000 versions is a change to the structure. The new version has five parts instead of the 20 clauses found in the 1994 version. Although most of the 20 clauses map to these five parts, the emphasis of the new standard has changed significantly. Because the new standard's structure is less prescriptive, organizations have greater freedom in its implementation. Features of the new standard and some of the major differences between the two versions are described later.

Because, as of this writing, there are more than 400,000 ISO 9001:1994 registered organizations in the world, there is a need to support an orderly transition to the new version of the standard. Both standards are valid during the 3 years following the December 2000 publication of ISO 9001:2000. After this 3-year period, registration to the 1994 version of standards is not possible and certificates based on that version will become invalid. The timing for adopting the new standard depends on organizational business objectives, the current state of process implementation in the organization, and marketplace requirements.

The revision of the standard most certainly affects many organizations and their registrations or certifications. Depending on the structure of an organization's *quality management system* (QMS), the impact can range from negligible to major. If the QMS documentation was based on organizational business objectives, reflected organizational processes, and was successfully implemented, changes to the QMS could be minimal. On the other hand, if the QMS was written to satisfy the 20 ISO clauses and did not reflect the way the organization really operates, satisfying the new requirements will be a major undertaking. Guideline documents, such as ISO 9000-3, which provided guidance for applying ISO 9001 to software, are also being withdrawn and no replacement yet exists (although as of this writing ISO 9000-3 is being balloted).

4.1.1 Quality management principles

The ISO 9000:2000 standard is based on a set of quality management principles. Although they are not explicitly called for in the normative portion of the standard, they can be traced to each major clause. They are defined in [4] and restated in [5]. In this section, we discuss each of the eight principles shown in Table 4.1.

What do these principles mean and why are they important? No single principle will ensure success. They must all be implemented to get the benefits of the standard. They are based on the experiences of many organizations and reflect a consensus of all the standard's stakeholders. It is interesting to note that none of the principles contains the word *quality* in its title [6].

Principle 1: customer focus

An organization must understand its customers and their needs. Customers can be defined not only as purchasers but also as users of products or services

Table 4.1 Quality Management Principles

Principle	Description
1	Customer focus
2	Leadership
3	Involvement of people
4	Process approach
5	System approach to management
6	Continual improvement
7	Factual approach to decision making
8	Mutually beneficial supplier relationships

inside or outside the organization. Merely satisfying customer requirements may not be enough to achieve success in the marketplace—the requirements may have to be exceeded. By understanding the customer's requirements, an organization may better position itself in the marketplace, respond faster to changes in requirements and trends, and develop stronger customer loyalty. The essence of this principle is that an understanding of customer requirements should be propagated through the whole organization, from marketing and sales to production and support. Understanding the customer's needs also means having quantitative knowledge of customer satisfaction, balancing customer requirements with other organizational needs (such as profit, investments in new technology, and supplier relationships) and then taking steps to address those needs.

Principle 2: leadership

Leadership is reflected in organizational direction, motivation, and communication of goals and objectives through all organizational levels. Periodically, management must reevaluate its goals and objectives and then communicate them to the staff. Successful management provides clear vision, sets challenging goals and objectives, creates shared values, provides required resources, and encourages and recognizes staff contributions. Understanding corporate goals and objectives helps motivate improved performance.

Principle 3: involvement of people

People must be recognized for their contributions and must be involved in decision making. Achieving organizational goals and objectives requires these tasks to be accomplished:

- Motivating and involving staff at all levels;
- Fostering innovation and creativity;
- Encouraging participation in continuous improvement;
- Holding people accountable for their performance.

Performance constraints must be identified and resolved. New opportunities that will lead to the satisfaction of organizational goals and objectives need to be identified. Free sharing of knowledge and open discussion of problems will foster staff resolve to seek solutions that may have been hidden.

Principle 4: process approach

Any activity or set of activities that transforms inputs to outputs can be considered a process [4]. In any organization, many processes interact in various ways during the product life cycle. The output of one process may feed another process or processes. Thus, work products produced by one process may impact the work products of the downstream processes. When consuming resources, a process must add value to the input. If it does not add value, it should be changed or even eliminated. The process has to be captured, documented, planned, given adequate resources, measured, and improved. The purpose of the process and responsibility for its implementation must be clearly defined. The impact of the process on the final product, customers, and other stakeholders must be understood.

Principle 5: system approach to management

A system is a set of interrelated or interacting elements or processes. Therefore, an organization can be considered to be a system of interrelated and interacting processes. From identification of customer requirements to delivery of the final product, the processes interact, transforming inputs into outputs, consuming resources, and adding value. Therefore, each process may affect other processes in the system. To succeed, an organization must be able to analyze its processes and their interactions, determine if they are efficient and effective, and make corrections when required. At the same time, the roles and responsibilities associated with each process must be understood and optimized to achieve corporate goals and objectives.

Principle 6: continual improvement

ISO 9000:2000 emphasizes continual[1] improvement. A companion standard, ISO 9004, is dedicated to the principle of continual improvement. This principle requires an organization to set continual improvement as one of its permanent objectives; note, however, that ISO does not provide guidelines for achieving this objective. Continual improvement can reduce rework and scrap, reduce variation, and improve the ability to react quickly to emerging development opportunities. It is up to each company to determine where and when improvements will occur—at the component, department, or division levels, or across the whole organization. Each organization must

---

1. ISO uses the word *continual* versus *continuous*. *Continual* means repeated regularly, recurring, whereas *continuous* means without interruption. We will use these two terms interchangeably, with the emphasis where appropriate.

determine improvement goals, triggering mechanisms, and improvement cycle times. Improvement activities must be tracked and effectiveness must be measured.

Principle 7: factual approach to decision making

To be able to base decisions on facts, processes have to be measured and those measurements must then be used for quantitative decision making. Measurement data must be accurate, valid, and reliable. Appropriate methods must be used to analyze that data. Statistical methods, for example, enable users to distinguish between the common and special causes of variation in processes and thus are valuable guides to process improvement. Collection and analysis of measurements are intrinsic requirements of a process-based approach. The goal–question–metric paradigm is one of the proven approaches for implementing an effective measurement program.

Principle 8: mutually beneficial supplier relationships

No organization operates alone. The *supply chain* must be taken into account when developing a product. This principle is focused on increased benefits for both the organization and its suppliers. Such relationships have to consider both short- and long-term benefits in the potential marketplace. To realize the benefits, an organization has to carefully select its suppliers, monitor their performance, communicate its plans, and encourage them to improve their effectiveness.

To successfully implement ISO 9001:2000, these quality management principles must be understood. The organization's reason for implementing the standard should not be to receive registration or certification, but rather to improve the way it builds its products and satisfies its customers. An understanding of quality management principles leads to an appreciation of the processes mandated by the ISO standard and a clear vision of what is needed to implement them.

What happened to product quality? Quality is defined by ISO 9000:2000 as the degree to which a set of inherent distinguishing features (such as functionality or reliability) fulfills requirements. While requirements for the QMS are outlined in the standard, it is the customer who defines requirements for the product, including its expected quality. These customer requirements, explicit or implicit, are transformed and implemented via the product realization process, which includes verification that the product meets the customer's requirements. In a successful organization, every management level has responsibility for satisfying the requirements of its stakeholders.

4.1.2 Process approach and system approach to management

Because the process approach and systems approach to management are two of the fundamental principles on which the standard is built, we will discuss some of their important features. Historically speaking, ISO 9001:1994 was considered procedure oriented and was judged by many to be overly prescriptive. The new standard has moved away from this prescriptive approach by espousing a more generic, process-oriented approach.

Organizations develop products and delivers services using certain processes. The complexity of those products and services may require many interdisciplinary processes to transform customer requirements, inputs, and constraints into a product, or more generally, into a system solution. These interrelated processes form a system, defined as "a set or arrangement of elements [people, products (hardware and software) and processes (facilities, equipment, material, and procedures)] that are related and whose behavior satisfies customer/operational needs, and provides for the life cycle sustainment of the products" [7].

The system and process approach is shown in Figure 4.1. Each of the processes shown in this figure can be decomposed into their components until an atomic process that cannot be decomposed further is reached. Each component process has inputs and outputs, activities to be performed, resource requirements, and measurements that will be used to manage and control the process. In a large system, a complex network of interrelated processes may be required.

Once the processes comprised in the QMS are identified, they are documented, their dependencies are determined, and the processes are implemented. They then can be improved using one of the approaches described in Chapter 2. ISO 9001 specifically invokes the PDCA cycle.

From a top-level representation of processes, customer focus is made visible and customer satisfaction can more readily be achieved. It is also apparent that processes may affect one another through their interaction. Processes have to be managed collectively to achieve desired organizational goals and objectives and satisfy the customer. Operating an organization using a system approach makes it easier to measure process effectiveness to recognize and address the need for process improvements.

One of the most challenging requirements in the ISO 9000 standard is the introduction of the management process. It is the management process that governs all other processes, plans their execution, and ensures that

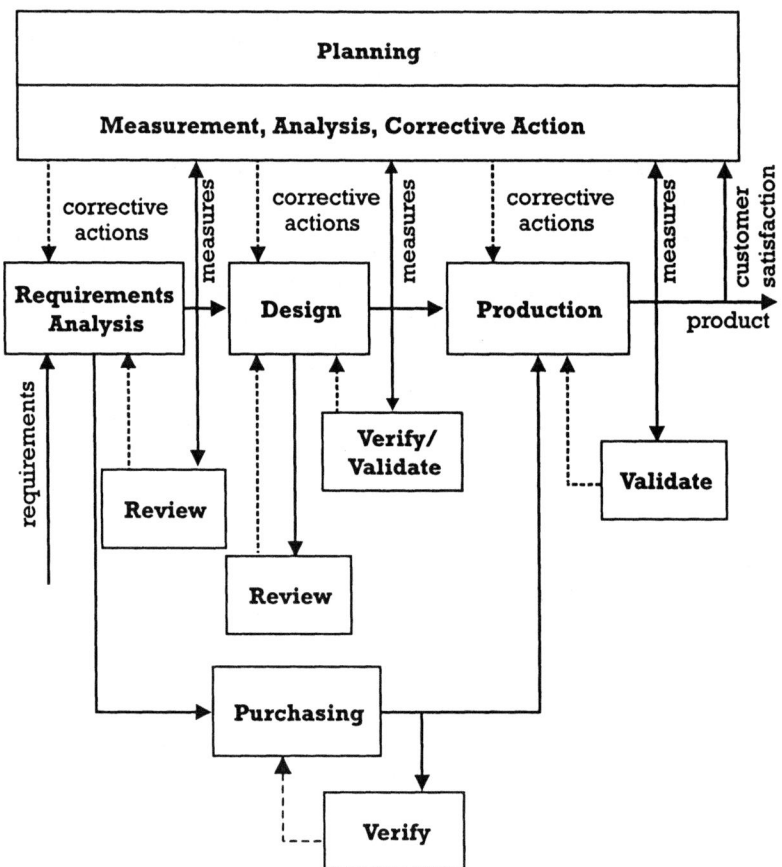

Figure 4.1 System and process approach.

resources are available, staff trained, and processes monitored, measured, controlled, and improved.

The system management approach may be difficult for many organizations to enact because processes may not line up with the organizational entities or functions. However, by hierarchically decomposing processes into their constituent parts, process ownership can be identified by mapping processes onto organizational functions. The desired process orientation can usually be achieved without adversely affecting an existing organizational structure, but sometimes the mapping exercise will reveal a suboptimal—or even dysfunctional—organization.

4.1.3 ISO 9001:2000 requirements

In the following sections we present five parts of ISO 9001:2000 (Parts 4 through 8) and discuss their features. The description given here is sufficient

4.1 ISO 9001:2000

for understanding other sections of this book and is not intended to be a comprehensive description of the standard. For more details on the ISO 9000:2000 standard or for detailed explanations and interpretations, please see the references at the end of this chapter. Hoyle [6] is recommended in particular because he provides a great deal of information and an extensive explanation of the standard. Reference [8] provides an excellent overview of the differences between the 1994 and 2000 versions of ISO 9001.

4.1.3.1 Quality management system (QMS)

ISO defines the QMS as a set of interrelated and interacting processes. Section 4 of ISO 9001:2000 contains the essential requirements for establishing, documenting, implementing, maintaining, and continually improving the QMS. These functions are shown in Figure 4.2.

The QMS is documented by these means:

- Publishing a quality manual;

- Specifying a quality policy and quality objectives;

- Developing and documenting the procedures required by the standard;

- Developing and controlling the documentation necessary to plan and manage the company's processes;

- Collecting records required by the standard.

The extent of the QMS documentation depends on the size of the organization, complexity and interactions of the processes, and the competency of

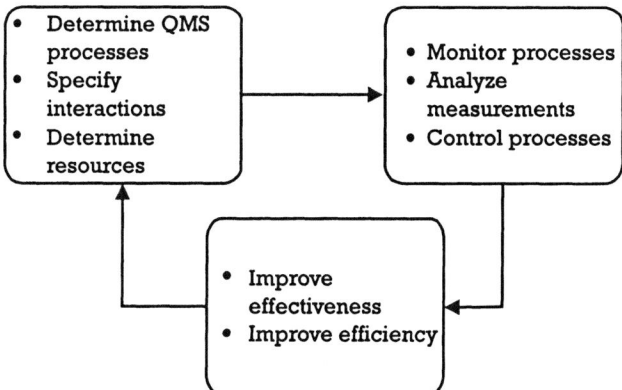

Figure 4.2 QMS requirements.

the personnel. No matter how terse or verbose the QMS documentation, it must be sufficient to implement effective and efficient planning, operation, and process management. Documents needed for management and control of the QMS have to be controlled, regularly reviewed, and updated. Records generated by executing the process have to be collected and controlled to provide evidence that requirements have been met.

A notable feature of the standard is the minimal amount of prescribed documentation. ISO 9001:2000 has explicit requirements for only six documented procedures: (1) document control, (2) control of records, (3) conducting audits, (4) nonconformity control, (5) corrective action, and (6) preventive action. Although very sparsely worded, this section of ISO 9001 has significant implications and impacts the entire QMS. First, an organization has to determine the scope of the QMS—decide what is included and excluded from the QMS. If dictated by the nature of the organization or product, some requirements in Part 7 of the standard may be excluded from the QMS documentation as long as the ability to meet customer requirements is not affected. Such exclusions must be identified and justified.

Then, the organization must document its processes, including the interactions, for example, among management, human resource, and product realization processes. Many organizations will find it much easier to document their product realization processes than their management or human resource processes. In many cases, identification of a *critical process chain* will be needed to completely describe how these processes are used to satisfy customer requirements and to ensure process efficiency and effectiveness.

After processes are documented, they must be implemented. In some cases, a process already exists in the organization and will only have to be captured and documented. Invariably, however, some aspects of some processes will not yet have been implemented, such as measurement collection and analysis. For such processes to be effective, staff will require training to understand what is needed to develop and implement the missing steps, to collect records, and then, after analyzing the data, to make necessary corrections. The measurement and analysis process is often poorly understood, and many organizations will need to devote significant time and effort to achieve effective implementation.

The relationships between management and measurement processes will also have to be understood and captured in the QMS so that questions like these can be answered:

- How long will it take to execute a process?
- What kinds of resources are needed: physical, human, financial?

- Which tools are needed to execute the process?
- If we increase resources, can we achieve goals and objectives?
- What are the constraints?
- How can we improve efficiency?
- Do we need more training?

Documentation is essential for understanding the impact of one process on another. This is particularly important at the lower process levels where the interactions among subprocesses may be more pronounced and effects of one on another more prominent. ISO 9001 does not explicitly specify the extent of the required documentation and does not provide guidelines for the type of documents that may be helpful when describing the process. In the following chapters, we will show how the synergy between the CMMI® and ISO 9001 can be used for that purpose.

4.1.3.2 Management responsibility

Section 5 of ISO 9001:2000 addresses management responsibility, particularly the responsibility of *top management*. As indicated earlier, publication and implementation of the QMS is an important strategic decision. The commitment to issue and follow this document is the responsibility of top management. The standard requires top management to provide evidence of its commitment to following the QMS and to continually improving its effectiveness. Top management develops and publishes a quality policy that must consider customer focus, responsibility, authority, communication, QMS planning, and reviews.

We now discuss each of those items in the order of their appearance in the standard. Numbers in parentheses denote major clauses in the standard. The subclauses are also indicated in the text.

Management commitment (5.1) The standard uses the term *top management* throughout this section. Top management is the "person or group of people who direct and control an organization at the highest level" [4]. In contrast, the 1994 standard used the term "management with executive responsibility" [9], which implies that lower level management, for example, at the department level, may have sufficient authority to take actions required by the standard.

Now, top management is required to show evidence of its commitment by these means:

- Communicating the importance of meeting customer requirements;
- Establishing the quality policy and quality objectives;
- Conducting reviews;
- Ensuring availability of resources.

In addition, top management is expected to accomplish these goals:

- Provide customer focus.
- Plan the QMS, based on the quality policy and objectives.
- Ensure that responsibilities and authorities are defined and communicated through the organization.
- Name a management representative with the responsibility for establishing, implementing, and maintaining QMS.
- Communicate the effectiveness of the QMS throughout the organization.

Customer focus (5.2) How will top management implement customer focus? An organization has to understand its customers' needs to determine the current and future needs of the marketplace. Sometimes, through a contract or a statement of work, the requirements are specified and the task is "merely" to implement those requirements. On the other hand, there may be many more consumers for a product that has certain desirable features. This section of ISO 9001:2000 establishes top management's responsibility for enabling the organization to implement customer focus and points to other sections that specifically address customer requirements and customer satisfaction.

Quality policy (5.3) It is important to note that establishing a quality policy and quality objectives is a two-step process. First, a policy that reflects the mission and vision of the organization is developed to provide a focus for action. The policy establishes a framework for defining the quality objectives that amplify the policy and provides a link between the policy goals and business objectives. When conditions change (for example, due to marketplace shifts, technology improvements, or reorganizations) the quality policy and objectives may have to change too. Again, top management has the responsibility for communicating these changes to the organization to obtain buy-in and coordination at all levels.

Planning (5.4)

    5.4.1   Quality objectives

    5.4.2   Quality management system planning

Top management has the responsibility for planning the QMS. Planning must address quality objectives and all processes included in the QMS. The QMS may need to be replanned to address changes in quality objectives or changes that may be required to improve some processes in the QMS.

A point to note here is that without resources the QMS has no meaning. Who in the organization can ensure that the necessary resources are available for establishing, implementing, maintaining, and improving the QMS but top management? Top management must also be able to plan for additional resources if those resources will be required in the future.

Responsibility, authority, and communication (5.5)

    5.5.1   Responsibility and authority

    5.5.2   Management representative

    5.5.3   Internal communication

For an organization to function efficiently, responsibilities and authorities must be clearly defined and communicated throughout the organization. Top management has to appoint a manager with the responsibility and authority to ensure that the QMS is established, implemented, maintained, and improved. This management representative is also responsible for making the organization aware of customer requirements and customer satisfaction measures. Appointing such a high-level manager with responsibility and authority for the QMS provides top management with visibility into its execution and improvement.

The requirement for communicating the effectiveness of the QMS through the organization is emphasized in the standard. In this context, effectiveness of the QMS is a measure of how well the QMS is achieving quality objectives. Awareness of QMS effectiveness makes the staff better positioned to seek and implement process improvements to satisfy the quality objectives.

Management review (5.6)

    5.6.1   General

    5.6.2   Review input

    5.6.3   Review output

Finally, top management is required to periodically review the QMS to ensure its suitability, adequacy, and effectiveness. Based on the results of the reviews, quality goals and objectives may be revised, plans for the QMS implementation modified, and process improvement opportunities identified.

4.1.3.3 Resource management

Section 6 of the standard addresses resource management. Without resources, organizational goals and objectives cannot be met. Resources can be identified in several forms such as materials, equipment, supplies, staff, buildings, or financial. In a typical organization, different divisions, departments, and functions control these resources. Projects then use the resources, as required, to develop their products. Resource management processes interact with every other process in the organization.

Provision of resources (6.1)   Implementation of resource management depends on the organizational structure. For example, in matrix organizations, the home departments manage resources used by projects while in program/project organizations, programs or projects completely control and manage required resources. Hybrid structure organizations employ combinations of these approaches. Regardless of the organizational structure, resources have to be identified, planned, acquired, deployed, trained (in the case of human resources), and maintained—in a word, managed. The standard emphasizes that the required resources have to be available for implementing, maintaining, and improving the QMS as well as for meeting customer requirements and enhancing their satisfaction.

Human resources (6.2)

    6.2.1   General

    6.2.2   Competence, awareness, and training

It is often said that people are the most important organizational resource. The standard requires that the people whose work may affect product quality are competent. This means that they either possess the required education, skills, and experience or will be trained to acquire those skills. The standard requires organizations to provide training, evaluate training effectiveness, and maintain records of staff education, skills, experience, and training. Further, the standard requires the demonstration of competence. That is, people must be able to perform required tasks rather than merely have knowledge about how to perform those tasks. In addition, the standard requires that people be aware of the relevance and importance of their contributions to the achievement of the organizational goals and objectives.

Infrastructure (6.3) Infrastructure is defined as a "set of facilities, equipment and services needed for the operation of an organization" [4]. The standard requires an organization to provide and maintain the means needed for successful implementation of the QMS. Infrastructure includes buildings, workspace, equipment, and supporting services. From the process point of view, the infrastructure is needed for implementing, executing, maintaining, and improving organizational processes and thus it encompasses the whole organization and the impact of its processes.

Work environment (6.4) Hoyle [6] defines the work environment as a "set of conditions (physical, social, psychological, or environmental) under which work is performed." The standard recognizes the impact that the work environment may have on successful process implementation and thus requires organizations to manage it as one of its resources.

4.1.3.4 Product realization

Product realization is the largest section of the standard, requiring the specification of processes that transform customer requirements into products. With the exception of the requirement for planning product realization processes, this section has changed very little from the 1994 standard.

Planning of product realization (7.1) Processes needed to develop products or deliver services must be identified. The sequencing of these processes and the means for their control must also be planned. Specific quality objectives drive the development of the plans.

Customer-related processes (7.2)

    7.2.1   Determination of requirements related to the product

    7.2.2   Review of requirements related to the product

    7.2.3   Customer communication

The customer-related processes addressed here start by identifying the applicable requirements. Obviously, the requirements explicitly identified by the customer are included, but this category also includes implied requirements, regulatory requirements, and self-imposed requirements of the quality management system.

Reviewing the requirements ensures that they are understood and that the organization has the capability and capacity to meet those requirements. Records of reviews, assumptions, and conclusions must be maintained and communicated to the customer.

Design and development (7.3)

    7.3.1   Design and development planning

    7.3.2   Design and development inputs

    7.3.3   Design and development outputs

    7.3.4   Design and development review

    7.3.5   Design and development verification

    7.3.6   Design and development validation

    7.3.7   Control of design and development changes

The design and development clauses cover a broad range of processes needed to realize the product. They begin with determination of the steps needed for design and development, including designation of responsibility and authority for each step.

Required inputs and planned outputs must be defined. During design and development, the outputs of each step are reviewed to ensure that appropriate progress is being made toward satisfying requirements and that activities are proceeding in accordance with plans.

Changes made during these activities must be controlled, recorded, and communicated. Changes may result from new customer requirements, discovery of errors, or altered business circumstances, but they are virtually inevitable.

Purchasing (7.4)

    7.4.1 Purchasing process

    7.4.2 Purchasing information

    7.4.3 Verification of purchased product

The selection of vendors is made using a systematic process. Potential suppliers are evaluated according to their ability to meet requirements. Evaluation and selection criteria must be defined to ensure that selection is not made strictly on the basis of price when other criteria are important.

Interestingly, the standard directs that the degree to which the supplier is controlled should depend on the impact of that supplier's product on design and development activities and the final product.

Purchasing activities also include verification that the purchased product meets its requirements.

Production and service provision (7.5)

    7.5.1 Control of production and service provision

    7.5.2 Validation of processes for production and service provision

    7.5.3 Identification and traceability

    7.5.4 Customer property

    7.5.5 Preservation of product

The infrastructure for controlling production must be in place. This infrastructure includes, for example, procedures, work instructions, equipment, measuring devices, and product information.

Raw material, parts, work-in-progress, and finished goods must be identified and traceable. Customer-provided equipment, information, or data must be identified and safeguarded.

Control of monitoring and measuring devices (7.6) Requirements for monitoring and measurement must be specified. The devices used for these measurements must be identified, calibrated, and maintained.

4.1.3.5 Measurement, analysis, and improvement

Measurement is a key element of successful management in every well-established engineering discipline [10]. ISO 9001:2000 has requirements for planning and implementing measurement, analysis, and improvement processes throughout the QMS (8.1). Many clauses in this section refer to clauses in earlier sections, especially Section 4, Quality management system, and Section 7, Product realization. Through measurement and analysis, one can quantitatively determine the status of a process, detect changes in its performance, and then implement corrective actions as necessary. The standard requires an organization to plan and implement measurement, analysis, and improvement processes to demonstrate and ensure conformity of its products to customer requirements and to continually improve the QMS. Although the standard does not prescribe the analysis techniques, statistical methods provide effective tools.

Monitoring and measurement (8.2)

- 8.2.1 Customer satisfaction
- 8.2.2 Internal audit
- 8.2.3 Monitoring and measurement of processes
- 8.2.4 Monitoring and measurement of product

The standard requires an organization to develop methods for measuring and monitoring the customer's perception of how the product satisfied the customer's requirements. Methods may include customer surveys, sales reports (for example, repeat orders or demand), or data obtained from the field, such as failures, complaints, and compliments.

The standard also requires an organization to perform internal audits to determine if the QMS has been fully and adequately implemented. These audits determine, for example, if necessary processes have been defined and implemented, required resources have been allocated, quality goals and objectives have been identified, and that the QMS is being continually improved. The audit uses a documented procedure (note that this is one of the few required procedures) and is conducted by impartial auditors. The nonconformances identified in the audit should be corrected and their implementation verified.

ISO 9001:2000 requires that both processes and products be monitored and measured and that associated measurement records be maintained. QMS processes have to be instrumented in such a way that they can be monitored, measured, and compared against expected results and objectives. In accordance with the steps identified in the planning process (Section 7.1), products are monitored and measured to ensure that they satisfy their requirements. Product measurements are integral parts of product realization, specifically product verification and validation. Here, we reconfirm that process and product measurements are an integral part of the other QMS processes.

Control of nonconforming product (8.3)   An organization must ensure that products that do not meet requirements are not delivered to the customer or otherwise improperly used. The applicable requirements include not only the explicitly specified customer requirements, but also the requirements of the organization's quality system and the customer's intended use of the product.

The nonconforming product must be identified to prevent its accidental use. The cause(s) of the nonconformity must be found and eliminated. One of the few documented procedures in the standard is required here. The procedure must specify the processes for detecting the nonconformance, performing the causal analysis, identifying the product, and determining the disposition of the product (e.g., rework or scrap).

Analysis of data (8.4)   Data are collected by processes defined throughout the quality system, particularly in clauses 8.1 and 8.2 of this section. Without analysis, however, those data are of little use. Applicable analyses include, for example, those that examine the following:

- Effectiveness of the quality system;
- Effects of changes to the quality system;
- Customer satisfaction;
- Product quality;
- Product performance;
- Supplier performance.

Improvement (8.5)

    8.5.1   Continual improvement

    8.5.2   Corrective action

    8.5.3   Preventive action

This section clearly supports the ISO 9000:2000 continual improvement principle. Action must be taken to correct nonconformances and prevent their future occurrence.

Supporting activities include examining the types and number of problems, determining their causes, evaluating the need for change, identifying and planning corrective and preventive actions, and measuring the effect of those activities.

4.2 CMMI®

The success of the CMM® led to a proliferation of capability maturity models: software, systems engineering, software acquisition, people, and security—just to name a few that are used by practitioners and are often required by acquisition authorities. Another look at the frameworks quagmire shown in Chapter 1 will suffice to convey this message. Implementing more than one CMM® means confronting multiple definitions, jargon, and overlapping process areas. Furthermore, each of the CMM®s has a unique and time-consuming associated appraisal method. Thus, among the CMMI® goals were these:

- Reduce the cost of implementing process improvements when several disciplines have to be considered.
- Enhance understanding.
- Eliminate duplication and inconsistencies among the models.
- Develop common components.
- Ensure consistency with the emerging ISO TR 15504 standard.

CMM® integration was necessary for more reasons than model efficiency. Software is an integral part of so many products that addressing its interaction with systems engineering is not optional—it is required. Even standards that carry the software name in their title, such as IEEE 12207 and 1074, address systems analysis and design as a part of the life cycle. What was once known as a *software* life cycle is now rapidly becoming a *product* life cycle.

In late 1998, the U.S. government directed the SEI to start working on CMM® integration. Development of CMM® v2.0 was halted and resources were channeled to the CMM® integration effort. The CMMI® project was born. In the beginning, the process improvement community showed some resistance to this project. Some members of the community felt that they had been left out of the decision-making process and questioned the wisdom of abandoning the nearly completed work on CMM® v2.0. Subsequently, the SEI and the CMMI® project did an excellent job of including industry, government, and academic process improvement stakeholders in the development and review of the CMMI® product suite. The CMMI® product suite consists of the CMMI® models, training materials, and the appraisal method. Table 4.2 shows the chronology of CMMI® releases.

The SEI has developed a schedule for "sunsetting," or retiring, the software CMM® (Table 4.3). Because many organizations have significant investments in the CMM® and CMM®-based process improvement, there is a need for a systematic migration from the CMM® v1.1 for software to the CMMI®. To a lesser extent, this is also true for transition from EIA/IS 731 to the CMMI®. The software CMM® v1.1 will no longer be updated.

The CMMI® is intended to alleviate the problems of using multiple models, maximize the strengths of each model, and still preserve organizational investments in legacy process improvements based on the software and systems engineering CMM®s. In the following sections we will describe what is new in the CMMI® and describe its structure.

Table 4.2 CMMI® Releases

Model	Date
CMMI® version 1.0	August 2000
CMMI® version 1.01	November 2000
CMMI® version 1.02	December 2000
CMMI® SE/SW version 1.1	December 2001
CMMI® SE/SW/IPPD version 1.1	December 2001
CMMI® SE/SW/IPPD/SS version 1.1	March 2002
CMMI® SW version 1.1	August 2002

Table 4.3 CMM® Sunset Schedule

Activity	Date
CMM® v1.1 training	Ends December 2003
CMM® assessments (CBA-IPI and SCE) are recorded by the SEI	Ends December 2005
CMMI® appraisals (SCAMPI[SM])	Started in 1999. Version 1.1 of the method was issued in December 2001.

4.2.1 New to CMMI® version 1.1

The CMMI® was developed based on the following models:

- CMM® v2.0 (draft C) for software;
- EIA Interim Standard 731, System Engineering Capability Model (SECM);
- Integrated Product Development Model, draft v0.98a (IPD-CMM®);
- Software Acquisition CMM®, v.1.02 (SA-CMM®).

Although the CMM® v1.1 is not officially listed as a CMMI® predecessor model, for software organizations, the transition to CMMI® will be from CMM® v1.1, rather than from the unpublished CMM® v2.0c.

The CMMI® uses a systems approach to product development and emphasizes process improvement for products (or services). The CMMI® has two representations: *staged* and *continuous*, and several bodies of knowledge or disciplines: systems engineering, software engineering, and *integrated product and process development* (IPPD).[2] Although one can select either the software or systems engineering discipline, IPPD is not a separate discipline. It requires other disciplines to be present in order to be implemented. This is discussed in more detail in the following sections.

Because the staged representation, similar to the CMM® v1.1, addresses the process maturity of an organization, it answers the question "What will be the most likely outcome of the next project we undertake?" [11]. The staged representation is concerned with organizational maturity.

The continuous representation, similar to EIA 731, deals with improvement of a single process area and answers the question "What is a good order in which to approach improvement of this process area?" The continuous representation addresses the capability levels of process areas.

Both representations contain the same components,[3] using the same wording. A major difference between the representations is in the approach to process improvement: If an organization strives to achieve organizational maturity, it may select the staged representation. In contrast, if the organization is interested in specific process capabilities it will select the continuous representation. *Equivalent staging*, described later in this chapter, was developed to allow comparisons of benchmarking conducted using the continuous

---

2. Additional bodies of knowledge may be added to the CMMI® later. Its architecture was developed to accommodate new disciplines. The CMMI® described in this book is CMMI®-SE/SW/IPPD, v1.1.
3. The component descriptions are the same with some well-defined variations that are explained later.

and staged representations. Both representations converge and can be seen as different paths leading to the same goals.

4.2.2 Model representations

The two representations (continuous [2] and staged [3]) have essentially the same content. Users of the CMM® for software may be more comfortable with the staged representation because it follows a similar structure. Similarly, the users of EIA 731 or ISO TR 15504 may be more comfortable with the continuous representation because its architecture is similar to those models.

Both representations contain common PAs. This is a change in terminology from *key process areas* in the CMM® and focus areas in EIA 731. PAs are the major building blocks for evaluation and improvement, consisting of related practices that collectively satisfy a set of goals. In the staged representation, PAs are grouped into maturity levels. In the continuous representation, the same PAs are grouped into categories. Figures 4.3 and 4.4 show the staged and continuous CMMI® structures, respectively. The staged representation shown in Figure 4.3 is quite similar to that shown for the CMM® in Chapter 3. A major difference, however, is seen in the grouping of common features into generic goals.

Table 4.4 compares features of the continuous and staged representations. As the table shows, an organization may have several reasons for selecting one representation over another, but the prevailing reason for selecting one over another is usually the relative familiarity with the representation architecture.

We will show later in the book that there are advantages to using a "hybrid" staged–continuous approach for process improvement.

4.2.3 Maturity versus capability levels

Maturity levels are used in the staged representation, whereas capability levels are used in the continuous representation. In the CMMI®, *maturity level* has the same definition as in the CMM® v1.1: "A maturity level is a well-defined evolutionary plateau on the path to becoming a mature organization" [3]. A *capability level* is "a well-defined evolutionary plateau describing the capability of a process area" [2]. By carefully reading these two definitions, we can see the major difference between the two representations. A maturity level is associated with the process maturity of an organization, whereas a capability level is associated with a single PA.

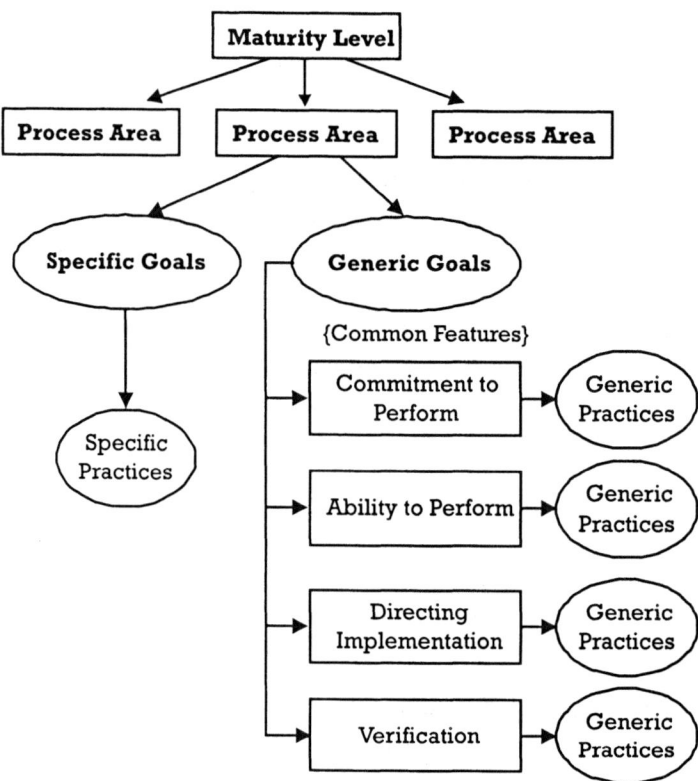

Figure 4.3 Staged representation.

As in the legacy CMM®, the staged representation distinguishes five maturity levels; each level builds on the achievements of the lower levels. In the CMMI®, the maturity level names are different from those used in the CMM®. Table 4.5 shows PAs for the staged representation grouped by maturity levels.

The continuous representation distinguishes six capability levels. Capability levels are cumulative, where each higher capability level includes the attributes of the lower levels. Table 4.6 shows PAs for the continuous representation grouped into categories.

Maturity levels and capability levels are related through what the CMMI® calls *equivalent staging*. In some cases, it may be desirable to relate both representations by converting capability levels into maturity levels using the conversion table shown in the CMMI® appendix [2]. Based on this table, to achieve maturity level 2, all relevant PAs must achieve at least capability level 2. Similarly, to achieve maturity level 3, all PAs that belong to maturity levels 2 and 3 must achieve at least capability level 3, and so on.

4.2 CMMI®

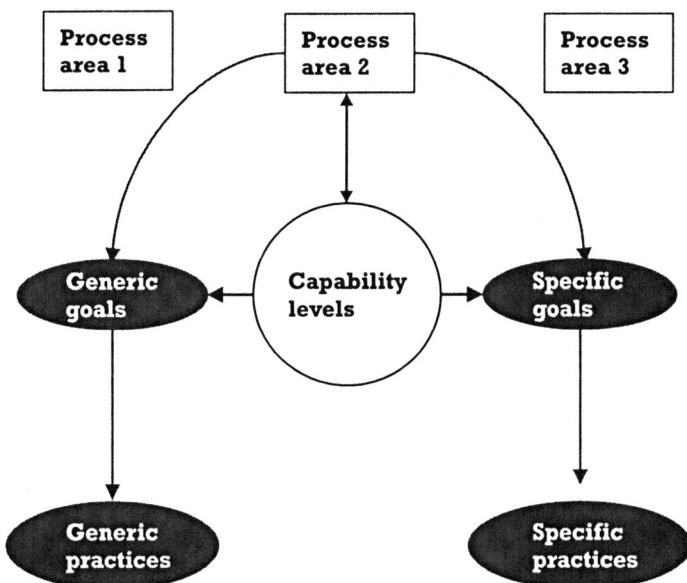

Figure 4.4 Continuous representation.

Table 4.4 Comparison of the Continuous and Staged Representations

Continuous Representation	Staged Representation
Can select the order of improvement that best meets the organization's objectives.	Order of improvement is determined by maturity levels.
Benchmarking and comparison among organizations are done on a per PA basis.	Benchmarking and comparison among organizations are done on a maturity level basis.
Migration from EIA/IS-731 is straightforward.	Migration from the SW-CMM® is straightforward.
It can be easily compared to ISO/IEC 15504.	

4.2.4 Institutionalization

An addition to the CMMI® is the introduction of *generic goals* (GGs). A generic goal describes the institutionalization required to achieve a capability or maturity level. Generic goals are also required model components used in appraisals to determine satisfaction of the PA. Each generic goal is associated with a set of *generic practices* (GPs) that provide descriptions of the activities required for institutionalizing processes in a particular PA. The GPs also

Table 4.5 Staged Representation

Maturity Level	Focus	PAs
Initial (1)		
Managed (2)	Basic project management	Requirements Management Project Planning Project Monitoring and Control Supplier Agreement Management Measurement and Analysis Process and Product Quality Assurance Configuration Management
Defined (3)	Process standardization	Requirements Development Technical Solution Product Integration Verification Validation Organizational Process Focus Organizational Process Definition Organizational Training Integrated Project Management Risk Management Decision Analysis and Resolution Organizational Environment for Integration Integrated Teaming
Quantitatively managed (4)	Quantitative management	Organizational Process Performance Quantitative Project Management
Optimizing (5)	Continuous process improvement	Organizational Innovation and Deployment Causal Analysis and Resolution

contain subpractices that provide implementation guidance. GPs are categorized by capability level in the continuous representation and by common feature in the staged representation.

Each PA contains unique *specific goals* (SGs) and *specific practices* (SPs). Each specific goal contains a set of specific practices that describe a set of activities important to achieving that specific goal. The specific practices may contain subpractices that provide implementation guidance. Most specific practices also identify typical work products as examples of the practice's outputs.

In the continuous representation, some specific practices are denoted as *advanced practices* in contrast to the *base practices*. A base practice is associated with capability level 1, whereas advanced practices are associated with capability level 2 or higher. The numbering scheme in the CMMI® clearly identifies these practices. If an advanced practice builds on the base practice, then the

Table 4.6 Continuous Representation

Category	PAs (Including IPPD)
Process management	Organizational Process Focus Organizational Process Definition Organizational Training Organizational Process Performance Organizational Innovation and Deployment
Project management	Project Planning Project Monitoring and Control Supplier Agreement Management Integrated Project Management Integrated Teaming Risk Management Quantitative Project Management
Engineering	Requirements Management Requirements Development Technical Solution Product Integration Verification Validation
Support	Configuration Management Process and Product Quality Assurance Measurement and Analysis Causal Analysis and Resolution Decision Analysis and Resolution Organizational Environment for Integration

advanced practice is included in the staged model but the base practice is not. The base practice is presented in the staged representation as informative material after the specific practices. The specific goals are required model elements that are used in appraisals to determine PA satisfaction.

Generic goals and GPs are central to process institutionalization. In the continuous representation the basis for institutionalization is established via the capability level 2 GPs. GPs at capability levels 3, 4, and 5 extend the initial capability level 2 institutionalization. In the staged representation, institutionalization is achieved via common features. The staged representation's common features correspond to the continuous representation's capability level 2 and 3 generic practices.

GPs are applicable to all PAs—they do not belong to any specific PA.[4] When applied to a single PA, the GPs will help to institutionalize improved

---

4. In some PAs, GPs contain amplifications and examples specific to that PA.

processes in that area. When applied to multiple PAs, a GP will increase process stability and enable improvement across the organization.

Table 4.7 shows the continuous representation's generic goals and associated GPs.

Capability level 0 in the continuous representation denotes an incomplete process; the process is either not performed or is only partially performed. There are no specific or generic goals associated with capability level 0.

Capability level 1 in the continuous representation is associated with a performed process. A process at capability level 1 satisfies the specific goals of the PA. A critical distinction between capability level 0 and level 1 is that at capability level 1 all of the specific goals of each PA are satisfied. For example, the requirements development PA (level 3 in the staged representation and an engineering PA in the continuous representation) has three specific goals: (1) develop customer requirements, (2) develop product requirements, and (3) analyze and validate requirements. All associated specific practices (base practices) must be performed to satisfy the specific goals and thus achieve capability level 1 for the requirements development PA.

The staged representation addresses institutionalization through common features. Table 4.8 shows the generic goals and generic practices for the staged representation grouped into common features.

At maturity level 2, only GG 2 and the generic practices GP 2.x have to be implemented. For maturity level 3, both GG 2 and GG 3 and their associated generic practices (GP 2.x and GP 3.x) have to be implemented. This also means that to satisfy GG 3, PAs that belong to maturity level 2 in the staged representation will have to be revisited when an organization attempts to achieve maturity level 3.

Clearly, there are major differences in the way institutionalization is addressed in the staged and continuous representations. As we can see from Table 4.8, the staged representation does not explicitly address capability levels 4 and 5. Based on specific business goals and objectives, achieving maturity level 4 in the staged representation is equivalent to capability level 4 for selected subprocesses. Maturity levels 4 and 5 have only generic goal GG 3, meaning that they are described through capability level 3.

4.2.5 Generic Goals and Generic Practices

In the following sections, we discuss each generic goal and its associated generic practices.

Table 4.7 Continuous Representation: Generic Goals and Generic Practices

Generic Goal/ Practice	Description
GG 1	*Achieve Specific Goals* The process supports and enables achievement of the specific goals of the process area by transforming identifiable input work products to produce identifiable output work products.
GP 1.1	*Perform Base Practices* Perform the base practices of the process area to develop work products and provide services to achieve the specific goals of the process area.
GG 2	*Institutionalize a Managed Process* The process is institutionalized as a managed process.
GP 2.1	*Establish an Organizational Policy* Establish and maintain an organizational policy for planning and performing the process.
GP 2.2	*Plan the Process* Establish and maintain the plan for performing the process.
GP 2.3	*Provide Resources* Provide adequate resources for performing the process, developing the work products and providing the services of the process.
GP 2.4	*Assign Responsibility* Assign responsibility and authority for performing the process, developing the work products, and providing the services of the process.
GP 2.5	*Train People* Train the people performing or supporting the process as needed.
GP 2.6	*Manage Configurations* Place designated work products of the process under appropriate levels of configuration management.
GP 2.7	*Identify and Involve Relevant Stakeholders* Identify and involve the relevant stakeholders as planned.
GP 2.8	*Monitor and Control the Process* Monitor and control the process against the plan for performing the process and take appropriate corrective action if necessary.
GP 2.9	*Objectively Evaluate Adherence* Objectively evaluate adherence of the process against its process description, standards, and procedures and address noncompliance.
GP 2.10	*Review Status with Higher Level Management* Review the activities, status, and results of the process with higher level management and resolve issues.
GG 3	*Institutionalize a Defined Process* The process is institutionalized as a defined process.
GP 3.1	*Establish a Defined Process* Establish and maintain the description of a defined process.

Table 4.7 Continuous Representation: Generic Goals and Generic Practices *(continued)*

Generic Goal/ Practice	Description
GP 3.2	*Collect Improvement Information* Collect work products, measures, measurement results, and improvement information derived from planning and performing the process to support the future use and improvement of the organization's processes and process assets.
GG 4	*Institutionalize a Quantitatively Managed Process* The process is institutionalized as a quantitatively managed process.
GP 4.1	*Establish Quantitative Objectives for the Process* Establish and maintain quantitative objectives for the process that address quality and process performance based on customer needs and business objectives.
GP 4.2	*Stabilize Subprocess Performance* Stabilize the performance of one or more subprocesses to determine the ability of the process to achieve the established quantitative quality and process-performance objectives.
GG 5	*Institutionalize an Optimizing Process* The process is institutionalized as an optimizing process.
GP 5.1	*Ensure Continuous Process Improvement* Ensure continuous improvement of the process in fulfilling the relevant business objectives of the organization.
GP 5.2	*Correct Root Causes of Problems* Identify and correct the root causes of defects and other problems in the process.

Generic Goal GG 1: Achieve Specific Goals

The process supports and enables achievement of the specific goals of the process area by transforming identifiable input work products to produce identifiable output work products.

Generic Practice GP 1.1: Perform Base Practices

Perform the base practices of the process area to develop work products and provide services to achieve the specific goals of the process area.

Why is this important?

The base practices are those specific practices with practice numbers in the form SP x.y-1. This GP requires all base practices associated with the PA to be

Table 4.8 Staged Representations: Common Features

Generic Goal/ Practice	Description
GG 2	*Institutionalize a Managed Process* The process is institutionalized as a managed process.
GG 3	*Institutionalize a Defined Process* The process is institutionalized as a defined process.
	Commitment to Perform
GP 2.1	(CO 1) Establish an Organizational Policy Establish and maintain an organizational policy for planning and performing the process.
	Ability to Perform
GP 3.1	(AB 1) *Establish a Defined Process* Establish and maintain the description of a defined process.
GP 2.2	(AB 2) *Plan the Process* Establish and maintain the plan for performing the process.
GP 2.3	(AB 3) *Provide Resources* Provide adequate resources for performing the process, developing the work products and providing the services of the process.
GP 2.4	(AB 4) *Assign Responsibility* Assign responsibility and authority for performing the process, developing the work products, and providing the services of the process.
GP 2.5	(AB 5) *Train People* Train the people performing or supporting the process as needed.
	Directing Implementation
GP 2.6	(DI 1) *Manage Configurations* Place designated work products of the process under appropriate levels of configuration management.
GP 2.7	(DI 2) *Identify and Involve Relevant Stakeholders* Identify and involve the relevant stakeholders as planned.
GP 2.8	(DI 3) *Monitor and Control the Process* Monitor and control the process against the plan for performing the process and take appropriate corrective action.
GP 3.2	(DI 4) *Collect Improvement Information* Collect work products, measures, measurement results, and improvement information derived from planning and performing the process to support the future use and improvement of the organization's processes and process assets.
	Verifying Implementation
GP 2.9	(VE 1) *Objectively Evaluate Adherence* Objectively evaluate adherence of the process against its process description, standards, and procedures and address noncompliance.
GP 2.10	(VE 2) *Review Status with Higher Level Management* Review the activities, status, and results of the process with higher level management and resolve issues.

performed. It does not require those practices to be documented or formally performed.

There is no such requirement for the staged representation.

Generic Goal GG 2: Institutionalize a Managed Process

The process is institutionalized as a managed process.

A managed process is a performed process (capability level 1) with these characteristics:

- It is planned and executed in accordance with policy.
- Employs skilled people having adequate resources to produce controlled outputs.
- Involves relevant stakeholders.
- It is monitored, controlled, and reviewed.
- It is evaluated for adherence to its process description [4].

Within an organization, a managed process may be applicable to a project, group, or some function, and its implementation in each of those instances may be quite different. The objectives of the managed process may be related to each individual process or may be part of a broader process definition.

Generic Practice GP 2.1: Establish an Organizational Policy

Establish and maintain an organizational policy for planning and performing the process.

Why is this important?

An organization must define expectations for its processes and make those expectations visible to all stakeholders. Policies are guiding principles established by top management that influence and determine implementation decisions and generally change only in exceptional situations. Policies establish direction without becoming mired in details.

Generic Practice GP 2.2: Plan the Process

Establish and maintain the plan for performing the process.

Why is this important?

Process implementation takes both a description and a plan. The organization has to determine what steps are needed to perform a process and then plan its implementation. The objectives that govern process implementation may come from organizational or project objectives and have to be coordinated to make those needs compatible. Typically, a plan will contain or reference the following items:

- Process descriptions;
- Requirements for work products and services;
- Standards for work products and services;
- Specific objectives for the performance of the process (e.g., quality, timescale, cycle time, and resource usage);
- Dependencies among the activities, work products, and services;
- Resources (including funding, people, and tools) needed to perform the process;
- Assignment of responsibility and authority;
- Training needed for performing and supporting the process;
- Identification of work products to be placed under configuration management and the level of configuration management for each item;
- Definition of measurements needed to provide insight into process performance, work products, and services;
- Involvement of identified stakeholders;
- Activities for monitoring and controlling the process;
- Activities for objective evaluation of the process and work products;
- Activities for management review of the process and work products.

The plan has to be reviewed, revised as necessary, and accepted by the stakeholders. In general, one can think of this plan as a replacement for the CMM® v1.1 "... according to a documented procedure" construct. It is important to note that, for example, a project's *quality assurance* (QA) plan is not equivalent to the plan for performing quality assurance as defined in GP 2.2. The former is a project-level plan for performing specific QA activities, whereas the latter is the organization-level plan developed for implementing the organization's overall QA objectives.

The structure and the packaging of the plan are left to the organization. It may choose to document all of the processes in a separate process document and then refer to them from each plan or it may include process descriptions in each plan. A separate process document is usually the preferred approach because it makes process changes easier and reduces the documentation effort.

Generic Practice GP 2.3: Provide Resources

> Provide adequate resources for performing the process, developing the work products, and providing the services of the process.

Why is this important?

To implement and perform a process, adequate resources must be available when needed. Resources include funding, appropriate physical facilities, appropriate tools, skilled people, and training that will help the existing staff gain necessary knowledge and skills. Interpretation of "adequate resources" can be tricky. It means that resources are available to perform the process as defined by the organization under GP 2.2. Where resources cannot be made adequate, process objectives may have to be adjusted.

Generic Practice GP 2.4: Assign Responsibility

> Assign responsibility and authority for performing the process, developing the work products, and providing the services of the process.

Why is this important?

For an organization to perform effectively, responsibilities and authorities must be clearly defined, understood, and accepted. Responsibilities can be assigned in process plans or can be assigned dynamically as processes are executed. In all cases, they have to be clearly communicated to the affected stakeholders. This GP ensures that there are no "orphan" processes; somebody is assigned responsibility for the process, its documentation, implementation, and institutionalization. In some organizations, the assignee is called a *process owner*. In many cases, several individuals may be working on different aspects of process institutionalization, such as planning, documenting, or training. All such assignments should include a clear understanding of the division of responsibility and accountability.

Generic Practice GP 2.5: Train People

> Train the people performing or supporting the process as needed.

Why is this important?

This practice supports the principle that training in the purpose, objectives, and methods of a process is needed for its effective implementation. Training may be provided in many ways, such as mentoring, on-the-job training, or classroom training.

Not everyone needs the same level of training. People who document and execute the process may require more in-depth training than casual users. For casual users, orientation may be sufficient. For example, a *configuration management* (CM) group may require training in CM principles, identification methods, audits, and setting up a configuration library. Other project staff may only need an orientation on tool use and an overview of related interactions with the other project staff members.

Generic Practice GP 2.6: Manage Configurations

> Place designated work products of the process under appropriate levels of configuration management.

Why is this important?

The integrity of work products must be maintained throughout their useful life. Certain work products, such as process descriptions or plans, should be placed under configuration management and access to them should be controlled. Although it may be sufficient to implement only version control for some work products, others may require more rigorous and formal levels of configuration management. It is important to determine the appropriate CM level for each work product so developers are not overburdened with unnecessary CM control while still ensuring work product integrity. This generic practice is closely related to the Configuration Management PA.

Generic Practice GP 2.7: Identify and Involve Relevant Stakeholders

> Identify and involve the relevant stakeholders as planned.

Why is this important?

A stakeholder is ". . . a group or individual who is affected by or is in some way accountable for the outcome of an undertaking" [4]. Stakeholders may, for example, include project members, customers, end users, or suppliers. The term *relevant stakeholders* limits the scope of this practice to those who may be intimately involved in or affected by the process in question. It is important for the stakeholders to be involved in the appropriate aspects of process execution. This is especially important for activities involving external interactions such as planning activities, decision making, communications, coordination, reviews, and requirements definition. In this way, stakeholders are part of the process and their interactions are planned and coordinated at the specific points in the process instead of through random events.

Generic Practice GP 2.8: Monitor and Control the Process

> Monitor and control the process against the plan for performing the process and take appropriate corrective action.

Why is this important?

Processes must be monitored and controlled to ensure that they are performing as expected and that their objectives are being achieved. Monitoring and controlling includes collecting and analyzing measurements of actual performance against the plan, reviewing accomplishments and results of the implemented process against the plans, identifying and evaluating the effects of deviations from plans, and tracking corrective actions to closure when progress differs from the plan. This GP is closely related to the Project Monitoring and Control and Measurement and Analysis PAs.

Generic Practice GP 2.9: Objectively Evaluate Adherence

> Objectively evaluate adherence of the process against its process description, standards, and procedures, and address noncompliance.

Why is this important?

An underlying premise for process improvement activities is that the quality of products and services depends on the processes used to produce them. Thus, it is important to verify that desired processes are being followed. Objective evaluation compares the results of the performed process to standards, policies, and requirements rather than to subjective criteria. Objectivity is usually ensured by having people who are not directly involved in the process conduct the evaluation. This generic practice is closely related to the Process and Product Quality Assurance PA.

Generic Practice GP 2.10: Review Status with Higher Level Management

> Review the activities, status, and results of the process with higher level management and resolve issues.

Why is this important?

To be able to take appropriate actions, higher level management must be appraised of the progress of process definition, execution, implementation, and institutionalization. Visibility into selected processes is needed to enable them to resolve issues. Typically, the senior managers responsible for establishing policies are those who are the most interested in process implementation and institutionalization. Reviews are typically scheduled on a periodic basis, such as quarterly, but can also be driven by significant events.

Generic Goal GG 3: Institutionalize a Defined Process

The process is institutionalized as a defined process.

Explicit requirements for level 3 (and later, level 4 and 5) generic goals and practices are new in the CMMI®; no CMM® common features correspond to those generic practices. By introducing generic goals at levels 3, 4, and 5, the institutionalization steps at those levels are made more explicit.

Generic Practice GP 3.1: Establish a Defined Process

Establish and maintain the description of a defined process.

Why is this important?

This generic practice drives the description of processes tailored from the organization's standard processes. To implement this GP, the organization has to have a set of standard processes with associated tailoring guidelines. A defined process is a managed process that also clearly states the purpose, inputs, entry criteria, activities, roles, measures, verification steps, outputs, and exit criteria.

Although a managed process is applicable to a specific project or group, a defined process enables individual projects to capitalize on processes that have been proven across the organization. When an organization has a set of standard processes, it is better able to share its experiences and staff across the project boundaries. Because a defined process is usually documented in detail, it can be more easily measured. Collection and analysis of measurement information enable quantitative management and make improvement better understood. This generic practice depends on the Organizational Process Definition and Integrated Project Management PAs.

Generic Practice GP 3.2: Collect Improvement Information

Collect work products, measures, measurement results, and improvement information derived from planning and performing the process to support the future use and improvement of the organization's processes and process assets.

Why is this important?

To build on past successes, work products and measurements are collected and used in subsequent projects. These assets are the result of investment in process improvement and are expected to produce present and future value to the organization. Typically, process assets are collected periodically from the projects, evaluated for appropriateness and accuracy, and stored in a process asset library. Measurements resulting from process execution (such as process effectiveness, effort expended for various activities, defects injected and detected) are collected and stored in the organizational measurement repository. This generic practice depends on the Organizational Process Definition PA.

Generic Goal GG 4: Institutionalize a Quantitatively Managed Process[5]

The process is institutionalized as a quantitatively managed process.

A defined process that is controlled using statistical and other quantitative techniques is a quantitatively managed process. To quantitatively manage a process, the organization has to establish quantitative objectives for quality and process performance. Those objectives are understood in statistical terms. The sources of quality and process performance objectives are the organizational process capabilities, needs of customers and end users, and organizational business objectives. Subprocesses that significantly impact process performance or quality are statistically managed. Quantitatively managed processes allow prediction of future performance while defined processes are only qualitatively predictable. A quantitatively managed process is a defined process that also includes the following [2]:

- Identifying the subprocesses that are to be brought under statistical management;

---

5. This goal exists only in the continuous representation.

- Identifying and measuring product and process attributes that are important contributors to quality and process performance;
- Identifying and addressing special causes of subprocess variations;
- Managing each of the selected subprocesses, with the objective of bringing their performance within natural bounds;
- Predicting the ability of the process to satisfy established quantitative quality and process-performance objectives;
- Taking appropriate corrective actions when it is determined that the established quantitative quality and process-performance objectives will not be satisfied.

Generic Practice GP 4.1: Establish Quantitative Objectives for the Process

Establish and maintain quantitative objectives for the process that address quality and process performance based on customer needs and business objectives.

Why is this important?

To effectively define and improve the standard processes, an organization has to establish and maintain a set of quantitative quality and process performance objectives. These objectives are reviewed and agreed on by the relevant stakeholders. Note that the objectives may also cover intermediate objectives that are important in managing the organizational processes over time. This generic practice is closely related to the Quantitative Project Management PA.

Generic Practice GP 4.2: Stabilize Subprocess Performance

Stabilize the performance of one or more subprocesses to determine the ability of the process to achieve the established quantitative quality and process-performance objectives.

Why is this important?

To predict overall process performance and product quality, critical subprocesses must be stable. A stable process shows no significant special causes of variation. Processes or subprocesses that have intermediate quality and performance objectives have to be quantitatively understood so that the overall process may achieve the established objectives.

Generic Goal GG 5: Institutionalize an Optimizing Process[6]

The process is institutionalized as an optimizing process.

An optimizing process is a quantitatively managed process that is changed and adapted to meet business objectives. To achieve this goal, both incremental and innovative techniques are used. This process involves identifying and removing the root causes of process variation in a measurable fashion based on the quantitative understanding of the organization's process improvement objectives and their cost impact to the organization.

Generic Practice GP 5.1: Ensure Continuous Process Improvement

Ensure continuous improvement of the process in fulfilling the relevant business objectives of the organization.

Why is this important?

This generic practice focuses on continuous process improvement in relation to business goals. To implement this practice, an organization must identify process improvements that are expected to result in measurable and meaningful improvements in process performance. In addition, the organization should systematically implement processes and technology that will enable meeting quality and performance objectives of the process.

Generic Practice GP 5.2: Correct Root Causes of Problems

Identify and correct the root causes of defects and other problems in the process.

Why is this important?

To identify and correct root causes of problems, the organization should analyze defects and other detected problems and then prevent these defects and problems from occurring again in the future. This generic practice is closely related to the causal analysis and resolution PA.

4.2.6 Process Areas

This section describes the CMMI® PAs and their interactions. We continue to use the continuous representation as the presentation vehicle. The contin-

---

6. This goal exists only in the continuous representation.

uous representation defines four process categories: engineering, project management, process management, and support.

Although the PAs are grouped into categories, they interact in many ways and those interactions must be kept in mind when their features are discussed. Specific goals, associated specific practices, and a brief discussion of each PA's salient features are given next. For more details, refer to [2].

4.2.6.1 Engineering

The engineering PAs include these:

- *Requirements Management* (REQM);
- *Requirements Development* (RD);
- *Technical Solution* (TS);
- *Product Integration* (PI);
- *Verification* (VER);
- *Validation* (VAL).

These are the only PAs that contain both base and advanced specific practices. Base practices, denoted as SP x.y-1, are required if capability level 1 is to be satisfied. The advanced practices, denoted as SP x.y-2 or SP x.y-3, are associated with capability levels 2 and 3, respectively. As indicated earlier, base and advanced practices are not distinguished in the staged representation.

Requirements Management

> The purpose of *requirements management* is to manage the requirements of the project's products and product components and to identify inconsistencies between those requirements and the project's plans and work products.

SG 1	*Manage Requirements*
SP 1.1-1	Obtain an Understanding of Requirements
SP 1.2-2	Obtain Commitment to Requirements
SP 1.3-1	Manage Requirements Changes
SP 1.4-2	Maintain Bidirectional Traceability of Requirements
SP 1.5-1	Identify Inconsistencies Between Project Work and Requirements

Why is this important?

An understanding of a project's requirements is needed to be able to manage the project and ensure customer satisfaction. When requirements change, relevant stakeholders must evaluate the importance of the changes and their cost, schedule, and technical impact. REQM practices provide the basis for understanding customer and end-user expectations and balancing those expectations with implementation considerations.

Requirements have to be traced through intermediate work products to ensure that the delivered product matches the approved requirements and customer expectations. Traceability between requirements and products (and product components) has to be bidirectional. When requirements change, this bidirectional traceability allows the impact of the change to be identified.

This PA interacts with PAs in the Engineering (Requirements Development and Technical Solution), Project Management (Project Planning, Project Monitoring and Control, and Risk Management), and Support (Configuration Management) categories. Although the Requirements Development PA provides for requirements elicitation, analysis, and allocation to product components, the allocated requirements are managed in this PA. The Configuration Management PA controls the requirements once they have been baselined. The Project Planning PA uses requirements to develop project plans, and the Risk Management PA provides analysis of requirements changes and their impact on plans. The Project Management and Control PA keeps track of the requirements changes and provides feedback to the Project Planning PA.

The CMMI® continuous representation distinguishes between capability level 1 (CL 1) and capability level 2 (CL 2) in this PA. For CL 1, it is sufficient to obtain an understanding of requirements, manage them, and identify inconsistencies between work products. For CL 2, project participants make commitments to implement the requirements and bidirectional traceability among requirements and work products is maintained.

Requirements Development

> The purpose of *requirements development* is to produce and analyze customer, product, and product-component requirements.

SG 1	*Develop Customer Requirements*
SP 1.1-1	Collect Stakeholder Needs
SP 1.1-2	Elicit Needs
SP 1.2-1	Develop the Customer Requirements

SG 2	*Develop Product Requirements*
SP 2.1-1	Establish Product and Product-Component Requirements
SP 2.2-1	Allocate Product-Component Requirements
SP 2.3-1	Identify Interface Requirements
SG 3	*Analyze and Validate Requirements*
SP 3.1-1	Establish Operational Concepts and Scenarios
SP 3.2-1	Establish a Definition of Required Functionality
SP 3.3-1	Analyze Requirements
SP 3.4-3	Analyze Requirements to Achieve Balance
SP 3.5-1	Validate Requirements
SP 3.5-2	Validate Requirements with Comprehensive Methods

Why is this important?

Requirements Development is closely related to the Requirements Management, Technical Solution, Product Integration, Verification, Validation, Risk Management, and Configuration Management PAs.

This PA begins with identification of the customers' needs and requirements. These drive the definition of the products to be delivered. Finally, Requirements Development addresses the way the requirements work together by defining operational scenarios and required functionality.

Technical Solution

> The purpose of *technical solution* is to design, develop, and implement solutions to requirements. Solutions, designs, and implementations encompass products, product components, and product-related life-cycle processes either singly or in combinations as appropriate.

SG 1	*Select Product-Component Solutions*
SP 1.1-1	Develop Alternative Solutions and Selection Criteria
SP 1.1-2	Develop Detailed Alternative Solutions and Selection Criteria
SP 1.2-2	Evolve Operational Concepts and Scenarios
SP 1.3-1	Select Product-Component Solutions
SG 2	*Develop the Design*
SP 2.1-1	Design the Product or Product Component
SP 2.2-3	Establish a Technical Data Package
SP 2.3-1	Establish Interface Descriptions
SP 2.3-3	Design Interfaces Using Criteria
SP 2.4-3	Perform Make, Buy, or Reuse Analyses
SG 3	*Implement the Product Design*
SP 3.1-1	Implement the Design
SP 3.2-1	Develop Product Support Documentation

Why is this important?

The TS PA is driven by the Requirements Development PA. From the universe of potential approaches to addressing the requirements, alternatives must be evaluated and solutions selected. As the criteria for choosing specific approaches are refined, the operational concepts initially identified become more detailed.

Development of the design includes defining the product architecture, system modes and states, component interfaces, and product capabilities. Detailed design fleshes out the implementation, interfaces, data requirements, and performance. Finally, the design is implemented and end-user documentation is developed.

Product Integration

The purpose of *product integration* is to assemble the product from the product components, ensure that the product, as integrated, functions properly, and deliver the product.

SG 1	*Prepare for Product Integration*
SP 1.1-1	Determine Integration Sequence
SP 1.2-2	Establish the Product Integration Environment
SP 1.3-3	Establish Product Integration Procedures and Criteria
SG 2	*Ensure Interface Compatibility*
SP 2.1-1	Review Interface Descriptions for Completeness
SP 2.2-1	Manage Interfaces
SG 3	*Assemble Product Components and Deliver the Product*
SP 3.1-1	Confirm Readiness of Product Components for Integration
SP 3.2-1	Assemble Product Components
SP 3.3-1	Evaluate Assembled Product Components
SP 3.4-1	Package and Deliver the Product or Product Component

Why is this important?

Components must be assembled to create the product needed by the customer. The strategy for component integration must be planned and must answer questions such as these:

- How should integration be sequenced?
- What environment is needed?
- What are the success criteria?

Interfaces between components and between the product and the outside world must be reviewed. Interface definitions must be managed. As components are integrated, the assembled product is evaluated and eventually delivered to the customer.

Verification

The purpose of *verification* is to ensure that selected work products meet their specified requirements.

SG 1	*Prepare for Verification*
SP 1.1-1	Select Work Products for Verification
SP 1.2-2	Establish the Verification Environment
SP 1.3-3	Establish Verification Procedures and Criteria
SG 2	*Perform Peer Reviews*
SP 2.1-1	Prepare for Peer Reviews
SP 2.2-1	Conduct Peer Reviews
SP 2.3-2	Analyze Peer Review Data
SG 3	*Verify Selected Work Products*
SP 3.1-1	Perform Verification
SP 3.2-2	Analyze Verification Results and Identify Corrective Action

Why is this important?

To ensure that products satisfy their requirements, the appropriate verification techniques must be selected. Verification methods include analysis, test, inspection, demonstration, and peer review. As VER activities are performed, results are recorded and compared to established criteria. Peer reviews are one well-known and effective verification technique. In fact, peer reviews are a KPA in their own right in the CMM®. Here, the technique is integrated with other verification methods.

Validation

The purpose of *validation* is to demonstrate that a product or product component fulfills its intended use when placed in its intended environment.

SG 1	*Prepare for Validation*
SP 1.1-1	Select Products for Validation
SP 1.2-2	Establish the Validation Environment
SP 1.3-3	Establish Validation Procedures and Criteria

SG 2	Validate Product or Product Components
SP 2.1-1	Perform Validation
SP 2.2-1	Analyze Validation Results

Why is this important?

The VAL PA is closely related to the VER PA. Whereas verification ensures that a product satisfies its requirements, validation demonstrates that the product can meet its intended use.

4.2.6.2 Project Management

The Project Management PAs are:

- *Project Planning* (PP);
- *Project Monitoring and Control* (PMC);
- *Supplier Agreement Management* (SAM);
- *Integrated Project Management* (IPM);
- *Integrated Teaming* (IT);
- *Risk Management* (RSKM);
- *Quantitative Project Management* (QPM).

Project Planning

The purpose of *project planning* is to establish and maintain plans that define project activities.

SG 1	Establish Estimates
SP 1.1-1	Estimate the Scope of the Project
SP 1.2-1	Establish Estimates of Work Product and Task Attributes
SP 1.3-1	Define Project Life Cycle
SP 1.4-1	Determine Estimates of Effort and Cost
SG 2	Develop a Project Plan
SP 2.1-1	Establish the Budget and Schedule
SP 2.2-1	Identify Project Risks
SP 2.3-1	Plan for Data Management
SP 2.4-1	Plan for Project Resources
SP 2.5-1	Plan for Needed Knowledge and Skills

SP 2.6-1	Plan Stakeholder Involvement
SP 2.7-1	Establish the Project Plan
SG 3	*Obtain Commitment to the Plan*
SP 3.1-1	Review Plans that Affect the Project
SP 3.2-1	Reconcile Work and Resource Levels
SP 3.3-1	Obtain Plan Commitment

Why is this important?

Project planning begins by establishing the scope of the project through a work breakdown structure. The selected project life cycle and the attributes of tasks and work products are used to develop estimates of effort and cost. The estimates, risks, constraints, and resource requirements are used to develop the plans and schedules. Plans are then reviewed by stakeholders and commitments are obtained from those responsible for implementing the plans.

Specific practices SP 2.5 and SP 2.6 support generic practices GP 2.5 and GP 2.7, respectively, in all other PAs.

Project Monitoring and Control

> The purpose of *project monitoring and control* is to provide an understanding of the project's progress so that appropriate corrective actions can be taken when the project's performance deviates significantly from the plan.

SG 1	*Monitor Project Against Plan*
SP 1.1-1	Monitor Project Planning Parameters
SP 1.2-1	Monitor Commitments
SP 1.3-1	Monitor Project Risks
SP 1.4-1	Monitor Data Management
SP 1.5-1	Monitor Stakeholder Involvement
SP 1.6-1	Conduct Progress Reviews
SP 1.7-1	Conduct Milestone Reviews
SG 2	*Manage Corrective Action to Closure*
SP 2.1-1	Analyze Issues
SP 2.2-1	Take Corrective Action
SP 2.3-1	Manage Corrective Action

Why is this important?

This PA is driven by the plans developed in the Project Planning PA. The PMC PA provides insight into the actual progress being made against those plans. By monitoring progress and the effect of changing conditions, corrective actions can be taken.

Monitoring does not focus solely on schedule progress. It also addresses areas such as risks, requirements changes, planning parameters (for example, size or complexity), staffing, and dependencies.

Specific practices SP 1.1 through SP 1.5 support generic practices GP 2.6 and GP 2.7 in all PAs.

Supplier Agreement Management

> The purpose of *supplier agreement management* is to manage the acquisition of products from suppliers for which there exists a formal agreement.

SG 1	*Establish Supplier Agreements*
SP 1.1-1	Determine Acquisition Type
SP 1.2-1	Select Suppliers
SP 1.3-1	Establish Supplier Agreements
SG 2	*Satisfy Supplier Agreements*
SP 2.1-1	Review COTS Products
SP 2.2-1	Execute the Supplier Agreement
SP 2.3-1	Accept the Acquired Product
SP 2.4-1	Transition Products

Why is this important?

The SAM PA starts with the decision to acquire products and services rather than to produce them. This decision may be driven by one or more other PAs, primarily the Technical Solution and Project Planning PAs.

First, qualified suppliers are identified and agreements are established. Then the supplier's performance is monitored and the products evaluated, accepted, and integrated into the project.

Integrated Project Management

> The purpose of *integrated project management* is to establish and manage the project and the involvement of the relevant stakeholders according to an integrated and defined process that is tailored from the organization's set of standard processes.

SG 1	*Use the Project's Defined Process*
SP 1.1-1	Establish the Project's Defined Process
SP 1.2-1	Use Organizational Process Assets for Planning Project Activities
SP 1.3-1	Integrate Plans
SP 1.4-1	Manage the Project Using the Integrated Plans
SP 1.5-1	Contribute to the Organizational Process Assets
SG 2	*Coordinate and Collaborate with Relevant Stakeholders*
SP 2.1-1	Manage Stakeholder Involvement
SP 2.2-1	Manage Dependencies
SP 2.3-1	Resolve Coordination Issues
SG 3	*Use the Project's Shared Vision for IPPD*
SP 3.1-1	Define Project's Shared-Vision Context
SP 3.2-1	Establish the Project's Shared Vision
SG 4	*Organize Integrated Teams for IPPD*
SP 4.1-1	Determine Integrated Team Structure for the Project
SP 4.2-1	Develop a Preliminary Distribution of Requirements to Integrated Teams
SP 4.3-1	Establish Integrated Teams

Why is this important?

The IPM PA describes the way in which the successful practices that form an organization's standard process are tailored to fit the needs of each project. The activities of planning and managing a project are connected through this PA to other activities in the project's defined process.

The PA also addresses coordination of the interactions and dependencies among stakeholders. IPPD is a systematic approach that achieves a timely collaboration of relevant stakeholders throughout the life of the product to better satisfy customer needs, expectations, and requirements [2]. IPPD is not a discipline by itself, in contrast, for example, to systems engineering. It is implemented with other disciplines, which are augmented with the IPPD-specific practices. In this PA, a shared vision is established to provide context for organizing integrated teams. An integrated team partitions responsibilities and requirements to team members with the right expertise and abilities, and fosters communication among the team members who are working toward the shared vision.

This PA is required for an effective implementation of GP 3.1 and GP 3.2 across all PAs.

Risk Management

> The purpose of *risk management* is to identify potential problems before they occur, so that risk-handling activities can be planned and invoked as needed

across the life of the product or project to mitigate adverse impacts on achieving objectives.

SG 1	Prepare for Risk Management
SP 1.1-1	Determine Risk Sources and Categories
SP 1.2-1	Define Risk Parameters
SP 1.3-1	Establish a Risk Management Strategy
SG 2	Identify and Analyze Risks
SP 2.1-1	Identify Risks
SP 2.2-1	Evaluate, Categorize, and Prioritize Risks
SG 3	Mitigate Risks
SP 3.1-1	Develop Risk Mitigation Plans
SP 3.2-1	Implement Risk Mitigation Plans

Why is this important?

The RSKM PA expands on the Project Planning specific practice SP 2.2, *Identify Project Risks,* and Project Monitoring and Control specific practice SP 1.3, *Monitor Project Risks.* In this PA, the approach is more sophisticated. A risk management strategy is defined and risks are identified, analyzed, and prioritized. Plans for mitigating risk are developed and implemented when needed.

Integrated Teaming

The purpose of *integrated teaming* is to form and sustain an integrated team for the development of work products.

SG 1	Establish Team Composition
SP 1.1-1	Identify Team Tasks
SP 1.2-1	Identify Needed Knowledge and Skills
SP 1.3-1	Assign Appropriate Team Members
SG 2	Govern Team Operation
SP 2.1-1	Establish a Shared Vision
SP 2.2-1	Establish a Team Charter
SP 2.3-1	Define Roles and Responsibilities
SP 2.4-1	Establish Operating Procedures
SP 2.5-1	Collaborate among Interfacing Teams

Why is this important?

The IT PA focuses on establishing and operating an integrated team. The integrated team is a self-managed entity, composed of skilled stakeholders having specific roles and responsibilities and the power to make decisions regarding the product being developed. The team works toward clear and commonly understood objectives and tasks. Team members maintain their connections with the functional organizations that may be required to provide additional product development support. The shared vision fosters a common understanding of the product and the team's mission and purpose, and guides the activities of the team. The team must understand its place in the organization and the project.

Quantitative Project Management

> The purpose of *quantitative project management* is to quantitatively manage the project's defined process to achieve the project's established quality and process-performance objectives.

SG 1	*Quantitatively Manage the Project*
SP 1.1-1	Establish the Project's Objectives
SP 1.2-1	Compose the Defined Process
SP 1.3-1	Select the Subprocesses that Will Be Statistically Managed
SP 1.4-1	Manage Project Performance
SG 2	*Statistically Manage Subprocess Performance*
SP 2.1-1	Select Measures and Analytic Techniques
SP 2.2-1	Apply Statistical Methods to Understand Variation
SP 2.3-1	Monitor Performance of the Selected Subprocesses
SP 2.4-1	Record Statistical Management Data

Why is this important?

The QPM PA focuses on managing product quality and process performance by using quantitative methods. To begin, the project's objectives must be identified and prioritized. Choices must be made to determine which customer, project, and organizational needs and desires are most important. This, in turn, leads to identification of the subprocesses that will be statistically managed.

In conjunction with the Organizational Process Performance PA, the selected subprocesses are then monitored so that special causes of variation can be identified and corrective action can be taken.

4.2.6.3 Process Management

This process category contains the following PAs:

- *Organizational Process Focus* (OPF);
- *Organizational Process Definition* (OPD);
- *Organizational Training* (OT);
- *Organizational Process Performance* (OPP);
- *Organizational Innovation and Deployment* (OID).

These PAs contain activities associated with process definition, deployment, planning, appraisal, resourcing, training, measuring, monitoring, verifying, improving, and innovating.

Organizational Process Focus

> The purpose of *organizational process focus* is to plan and implement organizational process improvement based on a thorough understanding of the current strengths and weaknesses of the organization's processes and process assets.

SG 1	Determine Process-Improvement Opportunities
SP 1.1-1	Establish Organizational Process Needs
SP 1.2-1	Appraise the Organization's Processes
SP 1.3-1	Identify the Organization's Process Improvements
SG 2	Plan and Implement Process-Improvement Activities
SP 2.1-1	Establish Process Action Plans
SP 2.2-1	Implement Process Action Plans
SP 2.3-1	Deploy Organizational Process Assets
SP 2.4-1	Incorporate Process-Related Experiences into the Organizational Process Assets

Why is this important?

The OPF PA addresses three of the most important aspects of process improvement: (1) establishing responsibility for process improvement, (2) understanding which areas need improvement, and (3) developing and executing the improvement plan.

It is here where existing processes are evaluated (typically by using a framework such as the CMMI® or ISO 9000) and the process needs (derived from business objectives) are identified. These steps allow the most important improvements to be identified and prioritized. Next, *process action plans* or *process improvement plans* are developed to spell out the activities to be performed and their associated resources, responsibilities, and authorities.

This PA also addresses the collection and deployment of actual results of process implementation, such as measurements and work products. Use of these "lessons learned" allows effective organizational learning to take place.

Through implementation of GP 2.4, this PA addresses the need to assign responsibility for process improvement. That responsibility is typically vested in the management steering committee and engineering process group.

Organizational Process Definition

> The purpose of *organizational process definition* is to establish and maintain a usable set of organizational process assets.

SG 1	Establish Organizational Process Assets
SP 1.1-1	Establish Standard Processes
SP 1.2-1	Establish Life-Cycle Model Descriptions
SP 1.3-1	Establish Tailoring Criteria and Guidelines
SP 1.4-1	Establish the Organization's Measurement Repository
SP 1.5-1	Establish the Organization's Process Asset Library

Why is this important?

Use of a standard set of processes allows for consistent and predictable performance. The OPD PA is concerned with development and deployment of those standard processes. Whereas some organizations may generally develop the same type of product repeatedly, others engage in a variety of businesses and products and may need more flexibility in adapting the standard processes to fit specific needs. Although this flexibility is needed, too much freedom may mean that the benefits of standardization are lost. Therefore, as part of the standard process definitions, guidance is provided on selection of life-cycle models and the tailoring of processes and process elements.

This PA also addresses establishing and maintaining a library of process assets and a measurement repository. This PA enables GP 3.1 and GP 3.2 across all other PAs.

Organizational Training

The purpose of *organizational training* is to develop the skills and knowledge of people so they can perform their roles effectively and efficiently.

SG 1	*Establish an Organizational Training Capability*
SP 1.1-1	Establish the Strategic Training Needs
SP 1.2-1	Determine Which Training Needs Are the Responsibility of the Organization
SP 1.3-1	Establish an Organizational Training Tactical Plan
SP 1.4-1	Establish Training Capability
SG 2	*Provide Necessary Training*
SP 2.1-1	Deliver Training
SP 2.2-1	Establish Training Records
SP 2.3-1	Assess Training Effectiveness

Why is this important?

A prerequisite for effective performance is ensuring that people have the skills and knowledge they need. Some training can be provided on a "spot" basis; that is, it is delivered to address an immediate, local need. The OT PA is concerned with systematically identifying and addressing the training needed to support strategic and tactical business needs.

As an organizational process, decisions must be made concerning the scope of the training program. Not all training and training services need to be supported by an organization-level program, but the division of responsibility must be explicit. For example, where specific training is needed by only a few people, it may be left to a project to plan, acquire, and deliver the training, leaving only the maintenance of training records to the organization.

In all cases, however, the effectiveness of the training must be evaluated to determine if the training is meeting the goal of making or keeping people competent to perform their tasks.

This PA enables GP 2.5 across all other PAs.

Organizational Process Performance

The purpose of *organizational process performance* is to establish and maintain a quantitative understanding of the performance of the organization's set of standard processes in support of quality and process-performance objectives, and to provide the process performance data, baselines, and models to quantitatively manage the organization's projects.

SG 1	Establish Performance Baselines and Models
SP 1.1-1	Select Processes
SP 1.2-1	Establish Process Performance Measures
SP 1.3-1	Establish Quality and Process-Performance Objectives
SP 1.4-1	Establish Process Performance Baselines
SP 1.5-1	Establish Process Performance Models

Why is this important?

Once processes are defined, institutionalized, and measured, an organization is in a position to quantitatively characterize the results expected from executing those processes. It is not practical or sensible to do this for all processes, so an organization must first decide which processes or process elements should be included in the analysis. The selection of processes will typically be driven by understanding which processes have the strongest relationships to business goals.

Baselines describing the expected range of results for the selected processes can then be established. In general, a single baseline will not be adequate; different results will usually be obtained when the standard processes are tailored to fit different project environments.

Organizational Innovation and Deployment

> The purpose of *organizational innovation and deployment* is to select and deploy incremental and innovative improvements that measurably improve the organization's processes and technologies. The improvements support the organization's quality and process-performance objectives as derived from the organization's business objectives.

SG 1	Select Improvements
SP 1.1-1	Collect and Analyze Improvement Proposals
SP 1.2-1	Identify and Analyze Innovations
SP 1.3-1	Pilot Improvements
SP 1.4-1	Select Improvements for Deployment
SG 2	Deploy Improvements
SP 2.1-1	Plan the Deployment
SP 2.2-1	Manage the Deployment
SP 2.3-1	Measure Improvement Effects

Why is this important?

Continual improvement works best when all people in an enterprise are encouraged to suggest changes. With the OID PA, improvement proposals are collected and systematically analyzed to determine which suggestions are likely to improve quality and process performance and are in concert with business goals and strategic plans. The selected proposals are then implemented on a pilot basis. Building on the OPP PA, successful pilots are then analyzed to determine which improvements should be deployed.

Deployment must then be planned, managed, and measured. Deployment generally involves changes to the organization's set of standard processes and to organizational training. Measurement of actual results of effective improvements leads to changes in the process performance baselines.

4.2.6.4 Support

The support category contains the following PAs:

- *Configuration Management* (CM);
- *Process and Product Quality Assurance* (PPQA);
- *Measurement and Analysis* (MA);
- *Decision Analysis and Resolution* (DAR);
- *Causal Analysis and Resolution* (CAR);
- *Organizational Environment for Integration* (OEI).

As we will see next, the support PAs address processes that are needed for implementing many generic practices across all PAs.

Configuration Management

> The purpose of *configuration management* is to establish and maintain the integrity of work products using configuration identification, configuration control, configuration status accounting, and configuration audits.

SG 1	Establish Baselines
SP 1.1-1	Identify Configuration Items
SP 1.2-1	Establish a Configuration Management System
SP 1.3-1	Create or Release Baselines
SG 2	Track and Control Changes
SP 2.1-1	Track Change Requests
SP 2.2-1	Control Configuration Items

SG 3	Establish Integrity
SP 3.1-1	Establish Configuration Management Records
SP 3.2-1	Perform Configuration Audits

Why is this important?

The CM PA addresses the understanding of how system components are related and the control of changes to those components. Not all work products require the same level of control, so a first step in implementing the CM PA is identifying the work products to be placed under configuration management. A configuration management system or library must be established to store and retrieve the configuration items as they are developed.

Changes to items that are under configuration management are made only after review and evaluation of change requests. Records of changes to configuration items are maintained and the system is periodically audited.

This PA supports implementation of GP 2.6 in all other PAs.

Process and Product Quality Assurance

The purpose of *process and product quality assurance* is to provide staff and management with objective insight into processes and associated work products.

SG 1	Objectively Evaluate Processes and Work Products
SP 1.1-1	Objectively Evaluate Processes
SP 1.2-1	Objectively Evaluate Work Products and Services
SG 2	Provide Objective Insight
SP 2.1-1	Communicate and Ensure Resolution of Noncompliance Issues
SP 2.2-1	Establish Records

Why is this important?

A fundamental precept of process improvement is that the quality of the products produced depends on the processes used to produce them. The PPQA PA addresses objective evaluation of actual activities performed and work products produced against processes and standards. Noncompliances are communicated to management and staff and resolution is tracked. By establishing records of PPQA activities and findings, trends may be discovered and improvement actions identified.

This PA supports implementation of GP 2.9 in all other PAs.

Measurement and Analysis

The purpose of *measurement and analysis* is to develop and sustain a measurement capability that is used to support management information needs.

SG 1	Align Measurement and Analysis Activities
SP 1.1-1	Establish Measurement Objectives
SP 1.2-1	Specify Measures
SP 1.3-1	Specify Data Collection and Storage Procedures
SP 1.4-1	Specify Analysis Procedures
SG 2	Provide Measurement Results
SP 2.1-1	Collect Measurement Data
SP 2.2-1	Analyze Measurement Data
SP 2.3-1	Store Data and Results
SP 2.4-1	Communicate Results

Why is this important?

The MA PA is closely tied to several other PAs. In fact, through the generic practices, it interacts with all PAs. The first specific goal of this PA is to ensure that measurement and analysis activities are aligned with information needs. Measurements will initially be concentrated at the project level, but may also address organization-level objectives. The PA recognizes that a useful measurement capability does not just happen: Responsibility must be assigned and collection, storage, and analysis procedures must be established. The second specific goal addresses the need to analyze data and communicate results to stakeholders so that appropriate actions may be taken.

This PA supports implementation of GP 2.8 in all other PAs.

Decision Analysis and Resolution

The purpose of *decision analysis and resolution* is to analyze possible decisions using a formal evaluation process that evaluates identified alternatives against established criteria.

SG 1	Evaluate Alternatives
SP 1.1-1	Establish Guidelines for Decision Analysis
SP 1.2-1	Establish Evaluation Criteria
SP 1.3-1	Identify Alternative Solutions
SP 1.4-1	Select Evaluation Methods
SP 1.5-1	Evaluate Alternatives
SP 1.6-1	Select Solutions

Why is this important?

DAR addresses a formal decision-making process that need not—and should not—be applied to all issues. Thus, the first specific practice establishes guidelines for determining when a formal decision analysis process is appropriate.

For those decisions that are properly in the scope of a formal process, evaluation criteria and evaluation methods must be determined. The range of alternative solutions is then identified, usually by involving stakeholders with diverse backgrounds, opinions, and goals. The alternatives are evaluated against the defined criteria and a solution is selected. Documentation of the rationale for that selection and the rejection of others allows the analysis to be reused and the assumptions to be reevaluated as part of ongoing risk management activities.

This PA supports all other PAs that require a formal evaluation process.

Causal Analysis and Resolution

> The purpose of *causal analysis and resolution* is to identify causes of defects and other problems and take action to prevent them from occurring in the future.

SG 1	*Determine Causes of Defects*
SP 1.1-1	Select Defect Data for Analysis
SP 1.2-1	Analyze Causes
SG 2	*Address Causes of Defects*
SP 2.1-1	Implement the Action Proposals
SP 2.2-1	Evaluate the Effect of Changes
SP 2.3-1	Record Data

Why is this important?

CAR goes beyond defect detection and correction. This PA involves identifying the reasons problems and defects occur and taking action to remove those reasons. Effective application of CAR practices requires an organization to have processes that are quantitatively understood and managed.

Defects (or other problems) must first be selected for analysis by using, for example, Pareto analyses. The root causes of the selected defects are then determined by using, for example, Ishikawa diagrams. Proposals for removal of the root cause(s) are then evaluated and implemented and the results are measured.

This PA supports all other PAs that require understanding and removal of process variation.

Organizational Environment for Integration

The purpose of *organizational environment for integration* is to provide an IPPD infrastructure and manage people for integration.

SG 1	*Provide IPPD Infrastructure*
SP 1.1-1	Establish the Organization's Shared Vision
SP 1.2-1	Establish an Integrated Work Environment
SP 1.3-1	Identify IPPD-Unique Skill Requirements
SG 2	*Manage People for Integration*
SP 2.1-1	Establish Leadership Mechanisms
SP 2.2-1	Establish Incentives for Integration
SP 2.3-1	Establish Mechanisms to Balance Team and Home Organization Responsibilities

Why is this important?

An integrated product team and its individual members need the appropriate infrastructure and tools to operate efficiently and effectively. An infrastructure such as that provided by using the OEI PA includes an organizational set of standard processes, organizational processes assets (including a library, database, and various tools), trained staff, and a workplace that provides resources to maximize productivity.

References

[1] *Quality Management Systems—Requirements, ISO 9001:2000*, Geneva, Switzerland: ISO, December 2000.

[2] CMMI® Product Team, *Capability Maturity Model Integration® (CMMI®)*, v1.1, Continuous Representation, CMU/SEI-2002-TR-003, Pittsburgh, PA: Software Engineering Institute, December 2001.

[3] CMMI® Product Team, *Capability Maturity Model Integration® (CMMI®)*, v1.1, Staged Representation, CMU/SEI-2002-TR-004, Pittsburgh, PA: Software Engineering Institute, December 2001.

[4] *Quality management systems—Fundamentals and vocabulary, ISO 9000:2000*, Geneva, Switzerland: ISO, December 2000.

[5] *Quality management systems—Guidelines for performance improvements, ISO 9004:2000*, Geneva, Switzerland: ISO, December 2000.

[6] Hoyle, D., *ISO 9000 Quality Systems Handbook*, 4th ed., Woburn, MA: Butterworth-Heinemann, 2001.

[7] *IEEE Standard for Application and Management of the Systems Engineering Process*, IEEE Std 1220-1998, New York: IEEE, 1998.

[8] Cianfrani, C. A., J. J. Tsiakals, and J. E. West, *ISO 9001:2000 Explained*, 2nd ed., Milwaukee, WI: ASQ Quality Press, 2001.

[9] *Quality Systems—Model for Quality Assurance in Design, Development, Production, Installation, and Servicing, ISO 9001:1994*, Geneva, Switzerland: ISO, 1994.

[10] *Practical Software and Systems Measurement: A Foundation for Objective Project Management*, Version 4.0b, Picatinny Arsenal, NJ, October 2000.

[11] "Intermediate Concepts of the CMMI® Models," SEI training workshop handouts, Pittsburgh, PA: Software Engineering Institute, June 2001.

CHAPTER 5

ISO 9001:2000 and CMMI® Synergy

Contents

5.1 Commonalities

5.2 Differences

5.3 Strengths

5.4 Weaknesses

5.5 Synergy

5.6 Summary of ISO requirements not covered by the CMMI®

References

Chapters 3 and 4 presented several major frameworks for process improvement. The two most widely used frameworks are the CMM®-SW and ISO 9001:1994. As of this writing, more than 1,600 organizations and 9,000 projects have conducted and reported formal CMM® appraisals and more than 400,000 organizations are registered under ISO 9001:1994. Unfortunately, there are no data to show the number of organizations in both groups and the number of the ISO registered organizations with active process improvement programs. Nevertheless, since the publication of the revised standards in late 2000, significant interest has been seen in certification and registration under ISO 9001:2000 and in transition from the CMM® to the CMMI®. The ISO Web site shows that more than 43% of all the certificates they awarded in 2001 were certificates of conformity to ISO 9001:2000.

Any company interested in using both standards must ask if they are compatible. The answer is a resounding *yes*. However, it is less clear how an organization that has already invested in one or both of the legacy standards can transition to the revised standards. In this chapter we show how ISO 9001:2000 and the CMMI® are synergistic. Chapters 6 and 7 will show how this synergy can be used to develop a consistent process improvement strategy that will lead to ISO certification and achievement of targeted CMMI® maturity or capability levels.

A high-level comparison of those two standards is shown in Table 5.1 [1]. This comparison points to both similarities and

121

Table 5.1 High-Level Comparison of ISO 9001:2000 and CMMI® Features

ISO 9001:2000	CMMI®
Standard	Model
Broad direction	Detailed
One set of requirements to be satisfied	Progressive steps (levels)
No guidelines for implementation	Institutionalization and implementation guidance
Requires interpretation for an organization with many programs	Accommodates organizations with many programs

differences. Fortunately, the synergy between the frameworks can be exploited and the weaknesses of one can be supplemented by the strengths of the other.

ISO 9001 is an international standard, widely accepted around the world. Certification represents a "badge" of quality and is often a mandatory business requirement. On the other hand, the CMMI® is a model. Its predecessor model, the CMM® v1.1 for software, was and is widely used and has become a de facto software industry standard. It is expected that the CMMI® as its successor will be similarly widely accepted. As a model, the CMMI® intent is different from that of the ISO standard. While ISO 9001 is structured in clauses and uses *shall* statements, the CMMI® is not prescriptive and has no *shall* statements. Appraisals against ISO 9001 are primarily used to judge compliance with its clauses. The CMMI® is based on real-world experiences and the consensus of experienced professionals that will help an organization develop its products with fewer errors, within budget, and on time. CMMI®-based appraisals are primarily used to guide process improvement. ISO 9004:2000 provides guidance for continual process improvement based on ISO 9001:2000, but it is not used for certification or contractual purposes. Thus, the intent of ISO 9004:2000 is closer to that of the CMMI® than to its counterpart ISO 9001:2000.

ISO 9001:2000 can be applied to any organization regardless of its size or the field in which it operates. On the other hand, the CMMI® specifically focuses on organizations that develop products and systems containing software.

Looking at the size of these two documents, we realize that ISO is very sparse, totaling just a little more than 20 pages, whereas the CMMI® is published in two representations, each more than 700 pages long. ISO does not provide guidelines for interpretation and does not elaborate its statements. The CMMI® provides details needed for its understanding, provides typical work products expected from each practice, and many elaboration statements that provide hints for its implementation. Nevertheless, many users will find both ISO and the CMMI® inadequate for guiding implementation, regardless of their relative size.

Another major difference between ISO and the CMMI® (also shared by their predecessor models) is in the approach used to achieve their goals. Whereas the CMMI® provides a road map for achieving process capability or maturity levels, ISO requires all of its requirements to be fulfilled before certification can be issued.

With its eight sections and 20-plus pages, ISO provides virtually no guidelines for its implementation. Although several notes are provided that elucidate the requirements, in general, the ISO standard simply sets forth requirements to be fulfilled. The requirements flow from the eight ISO 9000 management principles and thus provide a direct link to the best practices for achieving customer satisfaction and product quality. The CMMI® is structured to guide gradual process improvement, moving an organization from an initial, possibly chaotic state, to statistically controlled processes that will enable the development of high-quality products that are delivered on time and within budget. In addition, the CMMI® is based on the premise that if processes are institutionalized, they will endure even when the circumstances around it are not optimal.

The CMMI® builds process capability and maturity around projects that develop products. Initially, these projects may improve their own processes, while at the higher capability or maturity levels the whole organization benefits from process improvements. This concept is not visible in ISO 9001, which addresses the whole enterprise. Products may be developed by various projects within and outside this enterprise, but interactions among projects are not explicitly addressed.

The CMM® and the CMMI® stress the need for stable management processes before technical processes can be systematically addressed. ISO makes no such distinction—it requires both management and production processes to be implemented at the same time. ISO addresses purchasing of products and services from the outside the enterprise but does not address interactions within that enterprise.

So after contrasting the ISO 9001:2000 and CMMI® approaches and philosophies, one may ask—where is the synergy?

Both ISO and the CMMI® are based on principles of systems engineering and a process approach. Systems engineering is "an interdisciplinary approach governing the total technical and managerial effort required to transform a set of customer needs, expectations, and constraints into a product solution and support that solution throughout the product's life" [2]. A process has inputs and outputs, activities that consume resources, and has requirements for measurement and analysis of its performance to guide its management and improvement. In other words, a process is a building block for the system. Whereas ISO requires this process approach at a very high level, the CMMI® decomposes those processes and shows how individual subprocesses can be managed to fulfill top-level requirements.

Figure 5.1 relates ISO sections to CMMI® PAs and generic practices. Viewed in this way, we can consider the CMMI® to be a framework within the ISO framework. In other words, ISO provides the *what to do* direction,

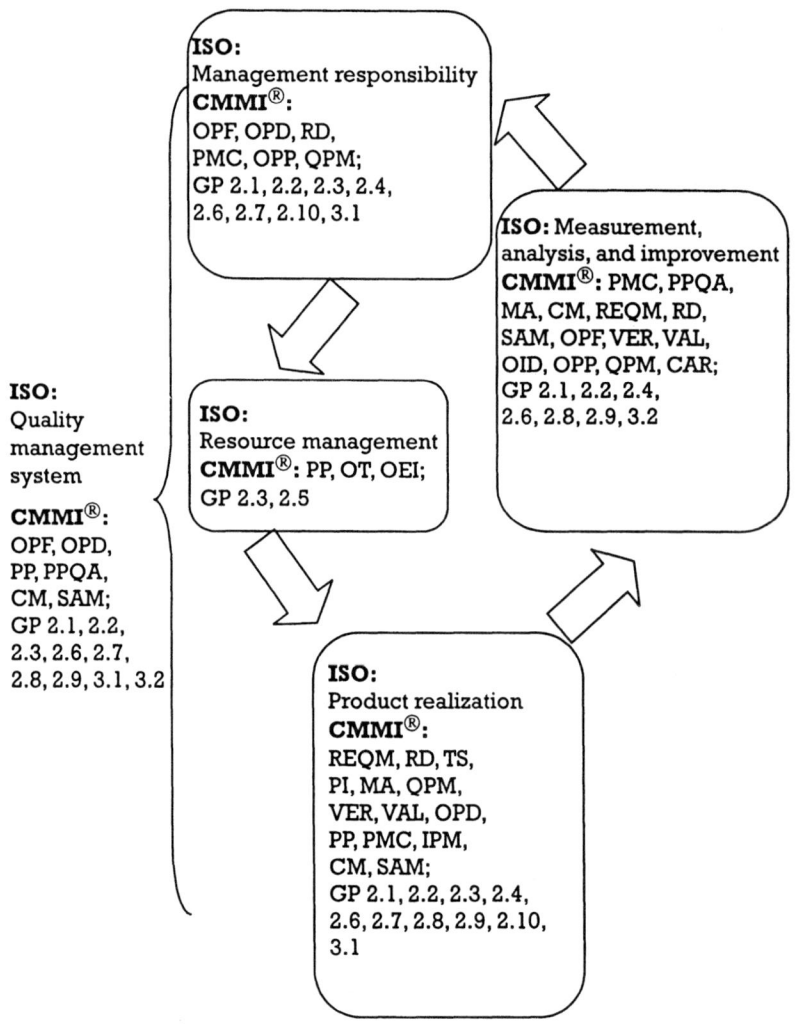

Figure 5.1 ISO–CMMI® relationships.

while the CMMI® elaborates these *what's* in more detail without mandating the *how's*.

To better understand the commonalties and synergy between these two standards, let us first discuss the terminology they use. Terms that are essentially equivalent in both standards (such as system or process) are not discussed. Table 5.2 lists selected ISO and the CMMI® terminology. Detailed definitions are given in [2, 3]. Further discussion of some terms is given below and later in this chapter when commonalties and differences between the two standards are addressed.

Quality management system (QMS), Quality Manual In the ISO standard, the QMS is described as a set of interrelated and interacting processes that include product and customer satisfaction requirements. In other words, the QMS has to satisfy an organization's quality policy and quality objectives. In this case, the organization is the whole enterprise or a major part of the enterprise. In the CMMI®, the organization is "an administrative structure in which people collectively manage one or more projects as a whole, and whose projects share a senior manager and operate under the same policies" [2]. Furthermore, the CMMI® defines an enterprise as "the larger entity not always reached by the word 'organization'" [2]. If we now want to apply the ISO 9001:2000 standard to such an organization, as a subset of an enterprise, we have two options: (1) Apply ISO to the whole enterprise and treat this particular organization as a part of the enterprise, or (2) apply ISO to the organization itself. In most practical instances, case (1) is an extension of case (2). An organization that develops a product containing software may be part of a larger enterprise developing other products that may or may not include software. Such an organization will:

- Depend on the whole enterprise;
- Share management responsibility with other parts of the enterprise;
- Use the resource management capability of the whole enterprise;
- Follow a common quality policy.

At the same time, the organization may have, for example, its own quality objectives, product realization processes, and measurement and analysis processes. In this book, we describe case (2), in which each organization is assumed to have its own QMS, as shown in Figure 5.2. This will enable us to better explain the synergy between ISO and the CMMI® without the loss of generality.

Table 5.2 High-Level Comparison of ISO 9001:2000 and CMMI® Terminology

ISO 9000:2000	CMMI®	Comment
Top management	Higher level management; senior management	Similar; pertains to a management role in the organization.
Quality management system, quality manual	Organization's set of standard processes	The QMS is the set of processes an organization follows to reach its objectives. The QMS is documented in a quality manual. An organization's set of standard processes contains definitions that guide all activities in an organization.
Quality plan	Project plan, software development plan, system engineering management plan, data management plan	ISO terminology is much broader and less specific than CMMI® terminology. The project plan can be construed to contain the project's defined process, based on tailoring of the organization's standard process.
Customer, interested party	Customer, stakeholder	The CMMI® term *stakeholder* is much broader and less specific than ISO terminology.
Documented procedure	Plan for performing the process	Planning the process produces the process description, which includes or references relevant standards and procedures.
Record	Work product, record, evidence	Similar meanings; captures results of activities and supports compliance verification.
Quality management	Quality management	ISO uses the term in a very broad sense. CMMI® usage focuses on quantitative management.

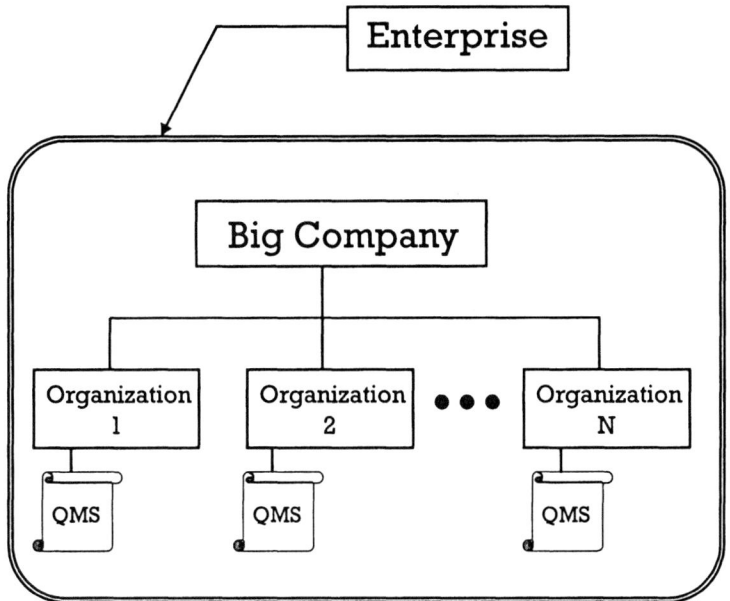

Figure 5.2 Each organization has a QMS.

The quality manual, described in Chapter 4, documents (1) the scope of the QMS, (2) procedures for the QMS, and (3) descriptions of processes and their interactions. In CMMI® terms, the ISO quality manual is thus roughly equivalent to the organization's set of standard processes—a collection of documents that describe organizational policies, processes and process elements, description of approved life-cycle models, tailoring guidelines, standards, and procedures.

Quality Plan The ISO standard requires a quality plan that also includes plans for product realization. The product realization plan addresses these topics:

- Quality objectives;
- Product requirements;
- Processes needed to develop the product;
- Documentation and resources needed;
- Verification;
- Validation;

- Monitoring;

- Inspection and test activities performed;

- Collection of associated records.

All of this is aimed at ensuring that the product satisfies customer requirements. Additional information is provided in ISO 10005, *Quality management—Guidelines for quality plans* [4]. ISO 9001, however, is mute on the concept of tailoring the QMS (the organization's standard process) to develop this plan.

The CMMI® adds this powerful idea: An organization has a standard process (QMS) that is systematically tailored to produce a project's defined process (quality plan). From the CMMI® point of view, the ISO quality plan reflects the project's defined process and includes the project plan, systems engineering management plan, software development plan, and system master schedule. For organizations at higher capability or maturity levels, this means that an "integrated plan" has to be developed (as defined in the IPM PA). An integrated plan:

- Incorporates project needs, objectives, and requirements;

- Addresses customers and users;

- Integrates other plans that affect the project, such as QA and CM plans;

- Defines the risk management strategy;

- Incorporates the project's defined process.

Quality management ISO defines quality management as "coordinated activities to direct and control an organization with regard to quality" [3]. These are the activities for setting up quality policies and quality objectives, establishing a quality plan, quality assurance and quality control, and implementing quality improvements. The CMMI® uses *quality management* terminology much more narrowly, primarily as part of quantitative management activities.

The ISO sense of quality management—based on the principles espoused in ISO 9000, especially process approach, systems approach, and continual improvement—are found throughout the CMMI®.

5.1 Commonalities

Quite frequently, when an organization attempts to implement more than one standard, it relies on correspondence tables or mappings. Some mappings are published and some are homegrown. Some tables even appear as appendices to the formal standards. For example, Annex B of ISO 9001:2000 shows the correspondence between ISO 9001:1994 and ISO 9001:2000 clauses. Some organizations have developed databases that contain comparisons of multiple models and standards. Figure 5.3 shows some mappings that can be established between pairs of standards and models.

Although the cross-references help to quickly visualize commonalties and differences between a pair of standards, they fall short of illuminating the underlying principles of those standards. Moreover, all such mappings are subject to the interpretations of their creators and cannot be viewed in absolute terms. To successfully implement multiple standards, a process engineer has to be familiar with each standard and understand their underlying principles. We too provide several mappings in this book. They are

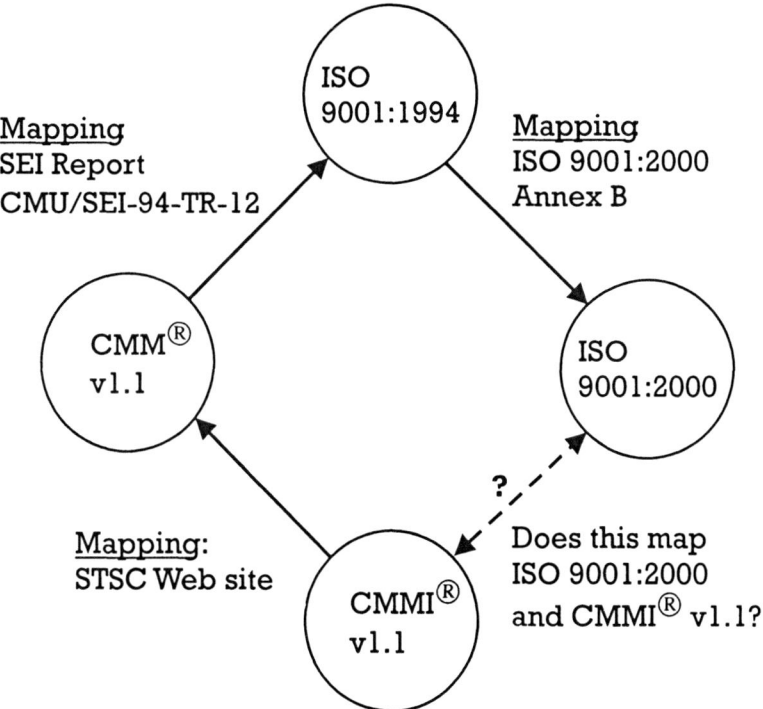

Figure 5.3 Standards mapping.

included only for convenience in comparing frameworks and not as a tool for implementation. In this book, we strive to capture the essence of ISO 9001:2000 and the CMMI® and explain and interpret their similarities and differences.

Because ISO 9001:2000 is based on the eight ISO 9000:2000 quality management principles described in Chapter 4, let us explore the similarities between those principles and the CMMI®. One would expect many of the quality management principles to correspond to CMMI® generic practices since the generic practices provide a foundation for process institutionalization. The comparison is given next. (The CMMI® differs from the ISO approach to principles 1 and 8, but all principles are listed here for completeness.)

1. *Customer focus.* In the CMMI®, customer focus is addressed through generic practice GP 2.7, *Identify and Involve Relevant Stakeholders,* and specific practice SP 2.6, *Plan Stakeholder Involvement,* in the Project Planning PA. As we will discuss later, customer focus is also addressed in the Requirements Development and Technical Solution PAs. This principle is much more strongly represented in ISO than in the CMMI®.

2. *Leadership.* Leadership is covered in several generic practices: GP 2.1, *Establish an Organizational Policy,* GP 2.4, *Assign Responsibility,* and GP 2.10, *Review Status with Higher Level Management.* In addition, the OPF PA supports aspects of leadership.

3. *Involvement of people.* The involvement of people is addressed in the CMMI® through implementation of generic practices GP 2.3, *Provide Resources,* GP 2.5, *Train People,* and GP 2.7, *Identify and Involve Relevant Stakeholders.*

4. *Process approach.* The process approach is amply supported by generic practices GP 2.2, *Plan the Process,* and GP 3.1, *Establish a Defined Process.* It is also explicitly supported by the OPD and IPM PAs and implicitly supported by all other PAs.

5. *System approach.* The system approach is addressed explicitly with GP 3.1, as well as by all the PAs.

6. *Continual improvement.* Continual improvement is the focus of the CMMI®. Simply stated, the whole CMMI®, with its capability or maturity levels, provides a foundation for continual improvement.

7. *Factual approach to decision making.* The CMMI® supports this principle through generic practice GP 2.8, *Monitor and Control the Process,* and through several PAs. Specifically, strong support is provided through the PMC, MA, IPM, and DAR PAs.

8. *Mutually beneficial supplier relationships.* The CMMI® addresses suppliers, especially in the SAM PA, from the control point of view rather than from the collaboration point of view.

5.2 Differences

As indicated in the previous section, many similarities exist between ISO 9001 and the CMMI®, but there are also several major differences. We often refer to the CMMI® as a standard, but it is only a de facto standard. It is a widely accepted model for applying systems and software engineering principles to product development that can be also used to measure process improvement progress. ISO 9001:2000 is intended for broad implementation in variety of industries and uses, whereas the CMMI® is specifically intended to apply to systems engineering, software engineering, and, more recently, to software acquisition.

A major difference between these two standards is in their language. Whereas ISO is clearly prescriptive, the CMMI® does not list its requirements using *shall* statements. For example, ISO specifies its requirement for the QMS as "The organization shall a) identify the processes needed for the QMS . . . ," whereas the corresponding CMMI® OPD specific practice SP 1.1 states: "Establish and maintain the organization's set of standard processes" and goes on to list nine subpractices describing the details needed to successfully implement this practice.

Another major difference is found in the compactness of the ISO language, which uses phrases such as "establish and maintain" or "determine and provide." For example, in the ISO standard, "The organization shall determine and provide . . ." addresses two distinct actions: first determining resource requirements, and then providing those resources. In the CMMI®, this ISO requirement maps to project planning ("determine") and then to GP 2.3 in all PAs to ensure that the resources are available ("provide").

Because of their differing targets and intent, the amount of detail they exhibit is also vastly different. As a model, the CMMI® covers details necessary for developing complex systems. On the other hand, ISO simply outlines a set of requirements necessary for developing high-quality products and satisfying customer requirements. The details of satisfying these requirements are left to the user, but to achieve ISO registration, *all* of its requirements have to be satisfied. ISO 9004:2000 provides very high-level guidelines for implementing process improvement, but no details are given on how to approach this task, where to start, and how to sustain improvements when the process improvement goals are finally reached. In contrast, the CMMI® has five levels of process maturity and six levels of process capability that guide an organization in progressively attaining its goals. The CMMI® generic and specific practices provide an orderly progression, enabling specific activities to become established in changing organizations. ISO 9001:2000 does not provide guidelines for implementing its requirements in small organizations or in very large multiproject organizations, or for that matter for products that contain software. The CMMI®, on the other hand, distinguishes between localized process improvement and organization-wide process improvement.

5.3 Strengths

Each standard has strengths that may help to offset the other standard's weaknesses. Some important ISO 9001:2000 strengths are as follows:

- Broad applicability;
- Affects most functional areas of an organization;
- International recognition and appeal;
- Freedom of implementation.

An obvious strength of the ISO 9001:2000 standard is its broad applicability. It can be applied to any industry or environment and still provide sensible requirements for implementing a QMS. ISO 9001:2000 affects most organizational entities, such as management, human resources, production, engineering, and quality. Interaction among these entities is needed to ensure that customer requirements are satisfactorily implemented. ISO standards have an international appeal as a mark of excellence awarded to companies that are ISO registered.

Because the standard is so sparsely worded, organizations have considerable freedom in interpreting the requirements. Documentation types and levels of detail can largely be addressed as the organization sees fit.

Selected CMMI® strengths include (1) inclusion of institutionalization practices, (2) a "road map" for improvement through maturity and capability levels, and (3) recognition of organizational versus project-defined processes. If one were to select a single major contribution that the CMM® and CMMI®

have brought to the field of process improvement, it would be the notion of *institutionalization*. Institutionalization is defined in the CMM® and CMMI® as:

> The building and reinforcement and corporate culture that support methods, practices, and procedures, so that they are the ongoing way of doing business, even after those who originally defined them are gone.

As previously noted, institutionalization in the CMMI® is further strengthened through the institutionalization goal in every PA. It indicates a set of prerequisites needed for implementing specific practices and ensuring that those practices are implemented.

Process improvement plans often specify a targeted maturity or capability level. The CMMI®, with its maturity levels and the notion that maturity levels cannot be skipped, outlines a strategy for attaining that goal. It becomes clear that an organization must first stabilize its management activities before introducing advanced technology into processes. The CMMI® continuous representation allows greater freedom of process improvement implementation than the staged representation. However, although one can select a PA to improve, it may be more advantageous to first establish the enabling PAs and then capitalize on them to implement the selected PA. The concept of "enabling PAs" further enhances the notion of systematic process improvement: Start with those PAs, institutionalize them, and then build the enduring process improvement infrastructure. In general, the CMMI® provides sufficient guidelines for systematically implementing process improvement. We will address this in the next chapter.

As an organization climbs the process improvement ladder, it will usually include an increasing number of projects under the process improvement umbrella. Projects benefit from the experiences and lessons learned by others by collecting those lessons learned in an organizational process asset library and database. They all benefit by tailoring the family of standard processes for their own purposes. Participating projects are obligated to provide their own experience to this library and database. This transition from "individual learning" to "local learning" to "organizational learning" [5] is one of the great concepts in process improvement, but unfortunately it is not articulated in the ISO standards.

5.4 Weaknesses

Although both standards have many strengths, they also exhibit a few weaknesses. ISO 9001:2000 is very general, provides no interpretation for how to apply it to entities smaller than the enterprise, and provides no guidelines for implementation in various industries.

The CMMI® may be too detailed for some organizations, may be considered prescriptive, requires major investment to be fully implemented, and may be difficult to understand. Where the CMMI® is too detailed, requiring large expenditures for its full implementation, ISO is too general, requiring guidelines for its specific implementation. Lack of specific guidelines when implementing the ISO standard causes some organizations to spend a lot of time developing and implementing their QMS. The use of the QMS is often not sustained after registration is achieved or between reregistrations. This weakness contrasts with the CMMI® institutionalization focus, which enables organizations to sustain process improvement achievements. Similarly, whereas the ISO standard lacks details, the CMMI® may be too detailed.

Because of the ISO standard's wide applicability, there are few guidelines for its implementation in some specific industries or fields. In addition, there are no guidelines for implementing it in a division or at a site of an enterprise. For ISO 9001:1994, another standard, ISO 9000-3, was published as an informative guide to interpret ISO 9001 for software. Subsequently, an assessment tool (TickIT) was developed to facilitate benchmarking an organization's software processes with respect to ISO 9001:1994.

ISO 9004:2000 is dedicated to process improvement. It follows the structure of ISO 9001 and provides some explanation of what is expected, but it falls short of delivering a road map for implementing process improvement.[1] When reading ISO 9004, one does not know which areas to address first and which to address next. This is where the CMMI® is helpful.

5.5 Synergy

Based on the preceding discussion, one can see where ISO and the CMMI® complement each other and how the strengths of one can remedy weaknesses of the other. ISO 9001:2000 and the CMMI® are both based on the process approach and systems thinking. This facilitates their comparison and is a major contribution to their synergy. We now take a closer look at their synergy and show how they work together to provide guidance for process improvement.

It is important to emphasize that this chapter simply points out the synergy between ISO and the CMMI®. Later chapters address the practical

---

1. As of this writing, ISO 9000-3:2000 is being balloted and has not been released.

5.5 Synergy

implementation of this synergy. In this section, we discuss, at a high level, how the CMMI® satisfies specific ISO requirements. For more details on the generic and specific CMMI® practices, refer to Chapter 4.

5.5.1 Institutionalization

Because one of the most important features of the CMMI® is the concept of institutionalization, we start our discussion of the synergy between the two standards by comparing the CMMI® generic practices with the clauses of ISO 9001:2000.

Let us first consider ISO 9001:2000 Section 4, *Quality Management System*. Section 4 requires an organization to establish, document, maintain, and improve a set of interrelated processes that will enable it to develop a quality product and satisfy customer requirements. The CMMI® will help such an organization by providing the necessary guidelines for establishing a QMS.

What does this mean in terms of CMMI®? As discussed in Chapter 4, GPs, by their nature, apply to all PAs and specifically enable institutionalization. Therefore, it is appropriate to compare the CMMI® generic practices to ISO Sections 4.0, *Quality Management System*, and 4.1, *General Requirements*, as shown in Table 5.3. CMMI® GPs support this clause in establishing, documenting, implementing, maintaining, and continually improving a QMS. GP 2.1, *Establish an Organizational Policy*, requires an organization's management to define expectations for the relevant processes and make those expectations visible. Specifically, GP 2.1 of the OPD PA requires organizations to define expectations for establishing and maintaining the *organization's set of standard processes* (OSSPs) and making them available across the organization. As

Table 5.3 Comparison of ISO Part 4 and CMMI® Generic Practices

ISO 9001:2000		CMMI® Generic Practices
4.1	General requirements	GP 2.1 Establish an Organizational Policy
		GP 2.2 Plan the Process
		GP 2.3 Provide Resources
		GP 2.6 Manage Configurations
		GP 2.7 Identify and Involve Relevant Stakeholders
		GP 2.8 Monitor and Control the Process
		GP 2.9 Objectively Evaluate Adherence
		GP 3.1 Establish a Defined Process
		GP 3.2 Collect Improvement Information
4.2	Documentation requirements	GP 2.1 Establish an Organizational Policy
		GP 2.2 Plan the Process
		GP 2.6 Manage Configurations

discussed earlier, an OSSP may be considered equivalent to a QMS. By implementing GP 2.1 across all PAs, an organization will be on its way to satisfying the requirements for a QMS.

CMMI® GP 2.6 supports the ISO requirements for the control of documents (ISO clause 4.2.3) and control of records (ISO clause 4.2.4). Note that the CMMI® Level 3 generic practices, GP 3.1, *Establish a Defined Process,* and GP 3.2, *Collect Improvement Information,* are not initially required by the CMMI®. Process improvement can be started without them and they can be introduced after an organization has already attained some process improvement capability. However, awareness of these practices certainly helps while establishing the OSSP. In addition, these GPs are required for satisfying the ISO requirements. In the next chapter, we will see how one can capitalize on their early implementation.

The only GPs not mapped to ISO Section 4 are GP 2.4, *Assign Responsibility,* GP 2.5, *Train People,* and GP 2.10, *Review Status with Higher Level Management.* These three practices are not explicitly addressed in Section 4 but are expected by other ISO sections.

Let us now compare ISO Sections 5 through 8 to the CMMI® generic practices. Table 5.4 summarizes this comparison and shows a very strong relationship between the generic practices and the ISO sections. This is particularly significant because it indicates that the generic practices can be used to establish, improve, and institutionalize the QMS.

ISO 9001:2000 primarily addresses issues that concern the whole organization in Sections 5 and 6 and it addresses product issues in Sections 7 and 8. The CMMI® distinguishes between the organizational and project process aspects and carefully builds organizational processes on the strengths of the project processes. ISO does not address the relationship between the OSSP and project process at all. Therefore when interpreting the CMMI® we have to be careful when applying GPs and SPs from organizational and project PAs.

It is interesting to note that all CMMI® generic practices are mapped to one or more ISO clauses. The message of this comparison is that institutionalizing the processes required by the CMMI® leads to a stable and strong process infrastructure that will also satisfy the ISO requirements.

5.5.2 Process areas and specific practices

We now compare ISO requirements to CMMI® PAs and specific practices. For that purpose, we use ISO sections and discuss how the CMMI® can be used to implement this section.

5.5 Synergy

Table 5.4 Comparison of ISO Sections 5–8 and CMMI® Generic Practices

ISO 9001:2000		CMMI® Generic Practices
5.0	Management responsibility	GP 2.1 Establish an Organizational Policy GP 2.2 Plan the Process GP 2.3 Provide Resources GP 2.4 Assign Responsibility GP 2.6 Manage Configurations GP 2.7 Identify and Involve Relevant Stakeholders GP 2.10 Review Status with Higher Level Management GP 3.1 Establish a Defined Process
6.0	Resource management	GP 2.3 Provide Resources GP 2.5 Train People
7.0	Product realization	GP 2.1 Establish an Organizational Policy GP 2.2 Plan the Process GP 2.3 Provide Resources GP 2.4 Assign Responsibility GP 2.6 Manage Configuration GP 2.7 Identify and Involve Relevant Stakeholders GP 2.8 Monitor and Control the Process GP 2.9 Objectively Evaluate Adherence GP 2.10 Review Status with Higher Level Management GP 3.1 Establish a Defined Process
8.0	Measurement, analysis, and improvement	GP 2.1 Establish an Organizational Policy GP 2.2 Plan the Process GP 2.4 Assign Responsibility GP 2.6 Manage Configuration GP 2.8 Monitor and Control the Process GP 2.9 Objectively Evaluate Adherence GP 3.2 Collect Improvement Information

5.5.2.1 QMS

As described in Chapter 4, ISO Section 4, *Quality Management System*, contains the basic requirements for establishing, documenting, implementing, maintaining, and improving the QMS. Most other ISO sections refer to this section. Therefore, it is important to understand this section in depth when comparing it to the CMMI®.

What does this mean in terms of CMMI®? Most ISO Section 4 requirements are satisfied by the OPD PA. The OPD PA goes further than ISO: It requires organizations to define a set of life-cycle models to be used by projects when they tailor the OSSP. It also requires an organizational measurement repository and a process asset library, which is different from the ISO requirement for controlling records (ISO 4.2.4). Although OPD is a maturity level 3 PA (in the staged representation), implementation of its specific practices will enable an organization at any level to implement maturity level 2 PAs more effectively.

The previous chapter discussed CMMI® generic practices and their contribution to implementing processes that will satisfy ISO requirements. Implementing GP 2.2, *Plan the Process*, for each PA seems to lead to an organizational set of processes. Although such processes may satisfy ISO requirements, they would not meet all of the CMMI® requirements for defining an organization's standard processes. Process elements comprised in the OSSP must include definitions of process element relationships, such as ordering, dependencies, and interfaces.

ISO requires processes to be managed in accordance with the QMS requirements. This is equivalent to CMMI® GP 2.1, which requires an organization to establish, publish, and maintain organizational policies and set the associated expectations for those policies.

In ISO 9001, several requirements that deal with outsourcing are introduced in Section 4 and expanded in Section 7. Outsourcing includes, for example, purchasing of services, labor, or computer maintenance, and control of the suppliers. By implementing SAM generic practices GP 2.2, 2.7, 2.8, and 2.9, and specific practices SP 1.3, *Establish Supplier Agreements*, and SP 2.2, *Execute the Supplier Agreement*, these ISO requirements will be satisfied.

Implementation of GP 2.6, *Manage Configurations*, for each relevant PA (supported by the CM PA) satisfies the document control requirements of Section 4.2.3. Here, *relevant* means those PAs that are relevant to ISO 9001 implementation.

ISO 9001, Section 4.2.4, requires the control of records. This control is implemented by establishing a *documented procedure* to address identification, storage, protection, retrieval, retention time, and disposition of records. This is one of only six required procedures in the whole ISO standard. Implementing project planning SP 2.3, *Plan for Data Management*, will ensure that all required documents, including records, are identified and controlled. This practice is much broader than that required by ISO.

5.5.2.2 Management responsibility

Implementation of the QMS is a management responsibility. It is not, however, sufficient for management to merely express its commitment to quality. Management must provide ongoing evidence that it is committed to the QMS and its continual improvement. It is interesting to note that all clauses in this section commence with the phrase "Top management shall . . ." [6], thus emphasizing management responsibility. The customer focus theme

5.5 Synergy

runs through this section, requiring an organization to not only satisfy requirements but also to enhance customer satisfaction. Furthermore, it requires the following to happen:

- A quality policy must be established.
- Quality objectives must be established in relevant functions and at various levels.
- A QMS must be planned and maintained.
- Responsibilities and authorities must be identified.
- The QMS must be reviewed and improved to ensure its effectiveness.

What does this mean in terms of CMMI®? The CMMI® establishes a framework equivalent to the ISO requirements for management responsibility, commitment, and review through GP 2.1, *Establish Organizational Policy*; GP 2.3, *Provide Resources*; GP 2.4, *Assign Responsibility*; and GP 2.10, *Review Status with Higher Level Management*. However, the CMMI® does not explicitly require senior management to establish a quality policy and objectives and tie them together into an encompassing whole—this is left to the "organization." In the CMMI®, senior management is responsible for defining organizational expectations, guiding principles, and direction and for reviewing the processes. Specifically, if an organization implements OPD GP 2.1, *Establish Policy*, it will satisfy the ISO requirements for management commitment.

Quality objectives are addressed in the OPP PA in SP 1.3, *Establish Quality and Process-Performance Objectives*, and GP 4.1, *Establish Quantitative Objectives for the Process*. OPP is a level 4 PA in the staged representation and is one of the advanced process management PAs. GP 4.1 is a capability level 4 generic practice. This indicates that from the CMMI® point of view, these important concepts can be deferred until an organization attempts to achieve level 4 maturity or implement level 4 capability in selected PAs. This may not satisfy the ISO requirements. In other words, every organization must address this ISO requirement regardless of CMMI® maturity level.

There is no explicit CMMI® requirement to name a management representative responsible for ensuring that the QMS is established, implemented, maintained, and improved (ISO clause 5.5.2). The closest match to this clause is GP 2.4, *Assign Responsibility*, in the OPF PA, which addresses process improvement products and services. The typical implementation of this practice establishes a management council and an engineering process group to provide guidance for improvements, which may include quality goals and objectives. A typical management council reviews and approves the OSSP, which is by our definition equivalent to the QMS.

Customer focus is achieved in the CMMI® by implementing GP 2.7, *Identify and Involve Relevant Stakeholders*, in every PA. Customer focus is also provided by the RD PA:

- SP 1.1-1, *Collect Stakeholder Needs*[2];
- SP 1.1-2, *Elicit Needs*;
- SP 1.2-1, *Develop the Customer Requirements*;
- SP 2.1-1, *Establish Product and Product-Component Requirements*;
- SP 3.3, *Analyze Requirements*;
- SP 3.4, *Analyze Requirements to Achieve Balance*;
- SP 3.5, *Validate Requirements with Comprehensive Methods*.

In the CMMI®, stakeholders include both internal and external customers and end users.

As far as process improvements are concerned, the CMMI® OPF PA (particularly SP 1.2, *Appraise the Organization's Processes*, and SP 1.3, *Identify the Organization's Process Improvement*) corresponds to ISO clause 5.6.1.

As indicated earlier, an organization should establish measurable quality objectives regardless of the CMMI® requirements. Further, the management council must be visible and its chair must have responsibility for the OSSP. Ensuring that the OSSP is implemented, maintained, improved, and communicated will satisfy not only the letter of the ISO requirements but also the spirit.

Although GP 2.10 requires senior management to periodically review processes, the CMMI® does not specifically list review inputs and outputs as ISO does in Section 5.6. PMC specific practices SP 1.6, *Conduct Progress Reviews*, and SP 1.7, *Conduct Milestone Reviews*, as well as SG 2, *Manage Corrective Actions to Closure*, can be used as guidelines. Engineering process groups generally provide senior management with expected review inputs and outputs. For example, typical review topics associated with the state of process improvement include these:

- Results of appraisals;
- Actions required for process improvement;

---

2. Recall that a number after a dash in the SP title in the continuous representation denotes the capability level to which that SP pertains.

- Customer feedback on process performance;
- Status of outstanding problem reports;
- Actions required for the resolution of problem reports.

Similarly, the outputs of these reviews are in these forms:

- Action items for resolving the reviewed problems;
- Plans and schedules for resolving problems;
- Resources needed for their resolution.

Reviews can be made effective by specifically outlining senior management inputs and outputs and by maintaining review action items.

5.5.2.3 Resource management

Organizations require resources for developing, implementing, monitoring, and improving the QMS and for addressing customer requirements and customer satisfaction. Resource management functions are needed by every other process, so they are generally distributed throughout the organization and receive senior management attention. ISO distinguishes human resources and infrastructure resources, such as buildings, equipment, supporting services, and the work environment.

What does this mean in terms of CMMI®? In the CMMI®, GP 2.3, *Provide Resources*, when applied to all relevant PAs, satisfies the ISO requirement for providing needed resources. This GP addresses human and other resources, such as development tools. The OT PA, as a whole, and GP 2.5, *Train People*, when applied to all relevant PAs, address ISO clause 6.2.2. Evaluation of training effectiveness, that is, determination of the achievement of "competence,"[3] is covered by SP 2.3, *Assess Training Requirements*, in the OT PA. Planning for necessary training is addressed in PP SP 2.5, *Plan for Needed Knowledge and Skills*.

The infrastructure and work environment requirements are mostly satisfied by the OEI PA (an IPPD PA), particularly SP 1.2, *Establish an Integrated Work Environment*, and by the PP SP 2.4, *Plan Project Resources*. Although

---

3. Competence is defined as the ability to demonstrate use of education, skills, and behaviors to achieve the results required for the job [6].

OEI SP 1.2 describes the need for establishing an IPPD environment, it is sufficiently broad to be used as a guideline for responding to the infrastructure and work environment requirements identified in this ISO section. The CMMI® states:

> An integrated work environment includes the physical infrastructure (e.g., facilities, tools, equipment, and support needed to effectively use them) that people need to perform their jobs effectively. Properly functioning environments help people communicate clearly and efficiently about the product, processes, people needs, and organization. An integrated work environment helps integrate the business and technical functions and the interfaces among teams, projects, and organization. [2]

5.5.2.4 Product realization

This is largest section in the ISO standard. It is subdivided into several processes: planning, customer-related processes, design and development, purchasing, production and service provision, and control of monitoring and measuring devices. Figure 5.4 shows at a very high level how product realization interacts with all other ISO processes. We now address each ISO product realization subprocess and compare it to the CMMI®.

What does this mean in terms of CMMI®?

Planning

As noted earlier, from the CMMI® point of view this ISO section addresses each project's defined processes. Therefore, the PP specific practices satisfy most of the ISO requirements. Implementing GP 2.2, *Plan the Process*, in each relevant PA will provide sufficient planning to satisfy the ISO requirements. However, the CMMI® goes beyond the ISO requirements by recognizing that for a plan to be effective, "those responsible for implementing and supporting the plan" are required to make a commitment to that plan (PP SG 3).

An organization will also benefit by implementing the IPM PA, particularly SP 1.1, *Establish the Project's Defined Process*; SP 1.2, *Use Organizational Process Assets to Plan Project Activities*; and SP 1.3, *Integrate Plans*. Although IPM is a maturity level 3 (staged) PA and requires the organization to have an OSSP, these practices will enable consistent implementation of processes across the organization. Similarly, implementing GP 3.1, *Establish a Defined Process*, in all relevant PAs will help organizations satisfy this ISO requirement. It is interesting to note that the QPM PA may provide additional input to this ISO requirement, but may be too difficult to implement in lower maturity organizations.

5.5 Synergy

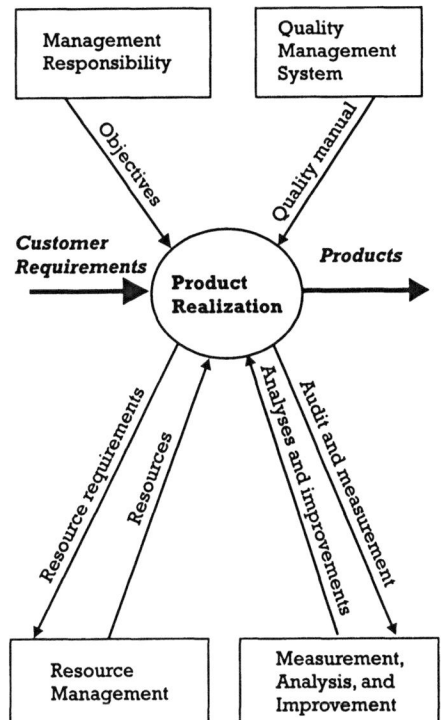

Figure 5.4 Product realization interactions.

Customer-related processes

The customer-related processes addressed in Section 7 of ISO 9001:2000 correspond to the CMMI® requirements definition, requirements review, and customer communication processes. The RD PA corresponds quite well to this ISO requirement. The first two RD specific goals, SG 1, *Develop Customer Requirements*, and SG 2, *Develop Product Requirements*, satisfy the requirements definition clauses. The third specific goal, SG 3, *Analyze and Validate Requirements*, supplements the ISO requirements of this section. It requires projects to analyze requirements based on operational concepts and functionality and then validate and balance those requirements. In addition, it requires an organization to address regulatory, safety, and organizational requirements. Specifically, it is sensitive to the difference between the requirements that are spelled out by an external customer versus those that are implied for organizations that deal with the general public marketplace, such as developers of shrink-wrapped software.

The REQM PA provides additional guidelines for managing requirements. Specifically, it addresses understanding requirements (SP 1.1), obtaining commitments to those requirements (SP 1.2), managing changes to the requirements (SP 1.3), and identifying inconsistencies between project work products and requirements (SP 1.5).

Requirements reviews are addressed in several instances in the CMMI®. Requirements for review of processes for handling requirements definition and management are covered by generic practices GP 2.7, *Identify and Involve Relevant Stakeholders*; GP 2.9, *Objectively Evaluate Adherence*; and GP 2.10, *Review Status with Higher Level Management*. In addition, specific practices of the PMC, PPQA, and VER PAs address both formal and informal reviews of the activities and products of the requirements definition and management process.

Customer communication is implemented by RD generic practice GP 2.7, *Identify and Involve Relevant Stakeholders*, and IPM specific goal SG 2, *Coordinate and Collaborate with Relevant Stakeholders*. The MA PA also provides several specific practices that enable effective communication with customers.

Design and development

The design and development section in ISO 9001 covers several related topics: planning, inputs and outputs, reviews, verification, validation, and control of changes.

Generic practices GP 2.2, 2.8, and 2.9 in the RD, REQM, TS, VER, and VAL PAs provide necessary planning, monitoring and control, and reviews required by ISO. The PP and PMC PAs amply cover design and development planning, and replanning, as required by ISO. In addition, specific practices SP 1.1, 1.2, 1.3, and 1.4 of the IPM PA are applicable to this ISO requirement, providing an additional benefit for organizations that desire conformity in their processes. ISO requirements for design and development are addressed in the TS and PI PAs. Most of the specific practices in these PAs apply.

The IPM specific goal SG 2, *Coordinate and Collaborate with Specific Stakeholders*, and GP 2.7 in the TS, PI, VER, and VAL PAs cover management of the interfaces between different groups. In addition, two goals associated with the IPPD domain, SG 3, *Use Project Shared Vision for IPPD*, and SG 4, *Organize Integrated Teams*, effectively address this issue.

The ISO requirements for determining, capturing, and reviewing product requirements were discussed earlier in the discussion of customer-related processes. Design and development reviews are covered in the PMC PA under specific practices SP 1.6 and SP 1.7.

ISO requirements for verification and validation are covered by the CMMI® in the VER and VAL PAs, respectively. By implementing generic practice GP 2.6, *Manage Configurations*, in the TS, PI, VER and VAL PAs and the CM PA, ISO requirements for controlling design and development changes are completely satisfied.

Purchasing

The SAM PA satisfies most ISO purchasing requirements regardless of the product category and includes outsourcing, acquisition of COTS products (including development tools), and subcontracting. This information is supplemented by specific practices SP 1.1, SP 1.2, SP 1.3, and SP 2.4 in the TS PA. These specific practices address the selection of alternative solutions that could include purchased components. Control and verification of the purchased product is also covered in the SAM PA. The CMMI® does not explicitly address verification at the supplier premises (except indirectly and in very general terms in SP 1.3, subpractice 3), but unlike ISO it discusses transitioning of the acquired products from the supplier to the project.

Production and service provision

Implementation of the CMMI® TI, PI, VAL, and CM PAs fulfills the spirit of the ISO requirements, although the CMMI® is weaker than the ISO standard in these areas. Replication, delivery, installation, and postdelivery activities are largely ignored in the CMMI®. Maintenance per se is not covered. In most cases, maintenance is addressed by following the typical development process and using specific interpretations such as trouble report versus requirement.

Identification and traceability are addressed by SP 1.4, *Maintain Bidirectional Traceability of Requirements*, in the REQM PA.

The CMMI® does not explicitly address ISO requirements for customer property. Although the CM PA supports the required activities, it is not sufficient to fully satisfy this requirement. Customer property may assume different aspects, such as hardware, development tools, intellectual property, or live data to be used for testing. In all of these cases, CM processes are invoked but implementation may be different. Similarly, the preservation of product, such as storing and maintaining product versions and protecting computer media required by ISO Section 7.5.5, have to be addressed. Therefore, we suggest that organizations specifically address those issues not explicitly covered by the CMMI®.

Control of monitoring and measuring devices

There is no CMMI® equivalent for the ISO requirements for calibration of measurement equipment and for assessing the impact of the malfunctioning equipment on the product. Although it is not clear that this ISO requirement has very much meaning for software development, the draft ISO 9000-3 standard [7] interprets it as the validation of development tools used for analysis development and testing, validation of data used for testing, and analysis of the impact of development tools on the product quality.

Organizations developing products that require calibration of measurement equipment will have to develop processes to satisfy these requirements.

5.5.2.5 Measurement, analysis, and improvement

The ISO measurement, analysis, and improvement section has a somewhat different purpose than the other sections. Measurement processes are required in every other ISO element to monitor performance. Based on the analysis of the results obtained, improvements will be identified. Although most measurement requirements are found in this section, other sections also address measurements, monitoring, and analysis.

What does this mean in terms of CMMI®? This ISO element corresponds, in general terms, to the MA PA. The CMMI® requires an organization to

- Develop measurement and analysis objectives;
- Align those objectives with its goals and objectives;
- Specify the measures, including their collection and storage, analysis techniques, and reporting mechanisms;
- Plan their implementation and use.

The distributed nature of the measurements and analysis that appears in the ISO standard is also found in the CMMI®. In addition to the MA PA, the PMC PA and GP 2.8, *Monitor and Control the Process*, satisfy this ISO requirement when applied to all PAs.

ISO requires organizations to plan and implement the collection and analysis of product and process measures needed to demonstrate conformity to applicable requirements and to continually improve the effectiveness of the QMS. Similarly, the CMMI® MA PA requires such planning and further requires definition of the measurements, analysis techniques, and data collection methods. Measurement of continual improvement is addressed in the OPF PA, while QPM SG 2, *Statistically Manage Subprocess Performance*, provides guidelines for selecting measurements, analysis techniques, implementation of statistical methods, and performance monitoring.

Customer satisfaction

Customer satisfaction, one of the most prominent new ISO requirements, is not strongly represented in the CMMI®. In the CMMI®, customers and end users are declared stakeholders. The CMMI® addresses stakeholders throughout the model and, in several instances, refers specifically to "customers," but it seems that measurement of customer satisfaction is not addressed. Customer satisfaction can be measured in several ways, such as customer satisfaction surveys (usually by a third party), measurement of *mean-time-to-repair* (MTTR), the number of help desk calls, or the number of requests for support. Therefore, organizations using the CMMI® will have to specify and implement customer satisfaction measurements and analyses to satisfy the ISO requirements.

Internal audit

The ISO requirement for internal audits is addressed in two ways in the CMMI®. One aspect of internal audits is the appraisal of the organization's processes addressed in the OPF PA. Those appraisals are intended to bring insight and understanding of the strengths and weaknesses of the OSSP. A second type of audit is addressed in the PPQA PA. Those audits focus on compliance to process and product standards. In addition, GP 2.9, *Objectively Evaluate Adherence,* is applicable to all PAs and addresses this ISO requirement.

The selection of auditors is not explicitly addressed in the CMMI® except in the definition of *objective evaluation*. The composition and qualification of process appraisal teams are addressed at length in the *Standard CMMI® Appraisal Method for Process Improvement*^{SM} (SCAMPI^{SM}). SCAMPI^{SM} satisfies the ISO requirements for objectivity and impartiality.

Monitoring and measurement of processes

Measurements are used to demonstrate that by following the QMS processes, the desired results will be achieved. Each PA identifies a number of measurements that can be used for analyzing and controlling processes. In general, those measurements cover product quality, product size, and development effort and cost. This ISO requirement is satisfied by GP 2.8, *Monitor and Control the Process,* and by specific practices in the MA, PMC, PPQA, and QPM PAs. The PPQA PA and PMC SG 2, *Manage Corrective Actions to Closure,* address corrective actions in terms of ensuring compliance.

Monitoring and measurement of product

Specific practices in the VER, VAL, and REQM PAs satisfy this ISO requirement. Acceptance criteria for purchased products are addressed in the SAM

PA. The CM PA addresses the release and integrity aspects of the developed products by requiring configuration control board approvals.

The CMMI® is silent on ensuring that all planned activities are satisfactorily completed prior to product release, but by performing configuration audits, the spirit of this ISO requirement is satisfied with the implementation of CM SP 3.2.

Control of nonconforming products

Nonconforming products should be isolated, segregated, and disposed of to avoid contamination of released products. The VER and VAL PAs ensure that products meet their specified requirements and are suitable for their intended use. The CM PA ensures that release of products is appropriately authorized and that the problem of nonconforming products is adequately addressed.

Analysis of data

Data analysis addresses information obtained, for example, from customer satisfaction surveys, process assessment and performance measurement, product quality measurement, and supplier performance. The CMMI® addresses this ISO requirement in the MA, VER, VAL, and OPF PAs. In addition, the RD PA addresses the analysis of the product requirements, and the SAM PA addresses analysis of the data obtained from monitoring suppliers. For more mature organizations, the OPP and QPM PAs address the use of the statistical process control and quantitative management techniques for data analysis and process control.

Continual improvement

Continual improvement is addressed in the OPF and MA PAs. For the organizations at higher capability and maturity levels, the OID PA provides an additional requirement for the collection and analysis of process and technology improvement proposals. OID is an advanced PA found at maturity level 5.

Corrective action

Corrective actions are addressed by the CMMI® in the OPF, PPQA, PMC, and CAR PAs. The OPF PA mostly addresses process improvement issues, while the other PAs address process and product corrective actions. CAR is an advanced PA found at maturity level 5.

Preventive action

Preventive action requirements are addressed in the OPF and CAR PAs, and, to some extent, in the PPQA PA. The CAR PA enables organizations to communicate identified problems across projects, thus helping them avoid reoccurrence of those problems. Causal analysis can be applied to defects as well as to other issues, such as cycle time. In the latter case, causal analysis may launch additional engineering analyses, simulations, or identify new business directives.

5.5.3 Relationship between ISO and the CMMI®

It is customary to develop mappings between models to help associate the more familiar model with a less familiar one. Some standards present their own mappings: ISO 9001:2000 includes an appendix showing the mapping between its clauses and ISO 9001:1994 clauses. Some standards, such as ISO 9000-3 [7], reference another standard to provide a more detailed description of a clause or requirement. Several organizations have published maps between various models; see, for example, [8, 9].

If mappings are developed at a high level, they may erroneously show more similarities or differences than they would have shown had they been developed at more detailed level. We developed our maps at the ISO requirement (*shall*) level and at the CMMI® practice level, thus providing sufficient granularity for understanding of both models. These ISO 9001:2000–CMMI® maps are presented in Chapter 9.

How should the mappings be used? Initially, the mappings highlight the similarities and differences between the two models using the more familiar model as a starting point. As understanding of a model increases, the mappings become less and less important—they serve as reminders of the issues that need to be addressed. In general, every map is a subjective interpretation of one model against another. Users of the mappings have to be aware that no map is a substitute for understanding the model's subtleties.

Many users will be motivated by the need to use more than one model, possibly driven by regulatory or contractual considerations. There is, therefore, a need to uncover those areas where additional work may be required to satisfy both models. Another use of the mappings is to assist in developing a process infrastructure based on multiple models and while considering model similarities and differences. This use is our primary objective.

Developing a map helps in the understanding of each model. One is forced to question what the model's authors intended. When developing a map, we are led to address those intentions in a much deeper sense than if we were to simply try to understand its literal meaning. In addition, when the maps are complete a different picture starts to emerge, leading to questions such as these:

- Are there aspects that were not covered by one model and are better addressed in another?
- Can we use one model to explain another?
- Are the models synergistic or contradictory?
- Can we use the synergy to help develop a more complete and extendable infrastructure?

We first mapped ISO 9001:2000 to the CMMI® and then used that map to develop the inverse map from the CMMI® to ISO. The inverse map showed that some practices we expected to be covered in ISO were not addressed. That prompted us to iterate the mappings several times to ensure that all possible associations were addressed. Several reviewers, facilitated by the SEI, provided valuable comments on our original maps. Most of their comments are reflected in the tables in Chapter 9. Through that process, we learned a lot about each model and their authors' intent.

So what are those maps telling us? The ISO-to-CMMI® map shows how each requirement in the ISO 9001:2000 standard relates to the CMMI® practices. We used that map in this chapter when discussing synergy and differences between the models. It helped us to understand where we need to interpret ISO statements in terms of the CMMI®. It also shows that there are ISO requirements that have weak or no correspondence in the CMMI®. Using the CMMI® when implementing ISO means additional effort is needed to specifically address those deficiencies.

Similarly, when using the CMMI®-to-ISO map we realized that several PAs are not explicitly addressed in ISO, such as the RSKM and DAR PAs. It became apparent that some ISO requirements map to a PA in such a manner that all specific practices are addressed. For example, ISO requirement 7.5.3 maps to the whole CM PA. However, some ISO requirements map to only one or two specific practices in a PA. For example, ISO requirements map quite well to the engineering PAs, whereas project management PAs are much weaker in the ISO standard. This does not mean that those PAs are not required. Rather, it means that there may be an efficient way to develop a process improvement infrastructure that will supplement ISO requirements with much more detailed CMMI® statements. It also means that one has to understand the CMMI® structure and intent to effectively use those maps.

One of the most interesting results of the mapping was that the PPQA specific practices map to only two ISO clauses, 8.2.2 and 8.2.4, which deal with internal audit and the monitoring and measurement processes. Our initial reaction was one of disbelief. After careful inspection of the ISO standard intent, we realized that the standard addresses quality management as noted earlier in this chapter. Quality assurance and quality control are defined as those parts of quality management focused on "providing confidence that quality requirements will be fulfilled" and "on fulfilling quality requirements," respectively [3]. Neither "quality assurance" nor "quality control" is used in the standard. Of course, this does not mean that quality assurance and control are not represented or are reduced to the internal audit functions. It simply means that the emphasis of the standard is on quality management—moving away from the misnomer of "quality assurance standard." The implementation of these functions is left to the organization. From the CMMI® point of view, this simply means that PPQA, which supports all PAs through the implementation of GP 2.9, *Objectively Evaluate Adherence*, is present throughout the model.

By studying the maps, we were able to develop a strategy for process improvement that is based on the synergy between ISO 9001:2000 and the CMMI®. The approach, described in the next chapters, capitalizes on the framework's similarities while minimizing the impact of their differences and ensuring that the CMMI® spirit is preserved. We will refer to those maps when we explain how those models may be used to develop such an infrastructure.

5.6 Summary of ISO requirements not covered by the CMMI®

This chapter discussed the ISO–CMMI® synergy and explained how the weaknesses of one model are supplemented by the strengths of another. We also indicated which ISO requirements are not covered in the CMMI®, as summarized here:

- Appointing a management representative;
- Internally communicating the effectiveness of the QMS;
- Requiring validation prior to delivery or implementation of the product;
- Verification of the suppliers on their premises;
- Handling of customer property;

- Control of monitoring and measuring devices;
- Defining a method for obtaining and using customer satisfaction information;
- Establishing internal audit criteria, scope, frequency, and methods;
- Ensuring independence of auditors;
- Determining the appropriateness of preventive actions to be commensurable with the effects of potential problems.

Development and implementation of additional processes and procedures will be necessary to address the ISO requirements that are not covered by the CMMI®. Some may have a significant impact on the emerging organizational process architecture. These activities must be considered during process improvement and will be addressed further in Chapter 7.

References

[1] Mutafelija, B., "Software Process Improvement: Synergy Between ISO 9001:2000 and CMMI®," paper presented at the SEPG Conference, New Orleans, LA, 2001.

[2] *Capability Maturity Model Integration® (CMMI®)*, Version 1.1, Pittsburgh, PA: Software Engineering Institute, December 2001.

[3] *Quality management systems—Fundamentals and vocabulary, ISO 9000:2000*, Geneva, Switzerland: ISO, December 2000.

[4] *Quality management—Guidelines for quality plans, ISO 10005*, Geneva, Switzerland: ISO, 1995.

[5] Carter, L., et al., "The Road to CMMI: Results of the First Technology Transition Workshop," CMU/SEI-2002-TR-007, Pittsburgh, PA: Software Engineering Institute, February 2002.

[6] Hoyle, D., *ISO 9001 Quality Systems Handbook*, 4th ed., Woburn, MA: Butterworth-Heinemann, 2001.

[7] *Software and Systems Engineering—Guidelines for the Application of ISO 9001:2000 to Software*, TC/SC SC7 WG18N61, ISO/IEC CD 9000-3, Version for FCD Ballot, Geneva, Switzerland: ISO, December 2001.

[8] Ibrahim, L., et al., *The Federal Aviation Administration Integrated Capability Maturity Model® (FAA-iCMM®)*, Version 2.0, Washington, D.C.: FAA, September 2001.

[9] *Mapping of the CMMI® v1.1 to SW-CMM® v1.1*, http://www.stsc.hill.af.mil/consulting/cmmi/cmmiseswippdv11.pdf, Hill AFB, Utah: Software Technology Support Center.

CHAPTER 6

Contents

6.1 Differences between the CMM® and CMMI®

6.2 Differences between ISO 9001:1994 and ISO 9001:2000

6.3 Transitioning from the CMM® to the CMMI®

6.4 Transitioning from ISO 9001:1994 to ISO 9001:2000

References

Transitioning from Legacy Standards

In Chapter 5 we introduced the concept of ISO–CMMI® synergy. In Chapter 7, we will address the use of this synergy for achieving ISO 9001 registration or reaching targeted CMMI® maturity or capability levels, but first we will discuss the steps that an organization can take to implement either standard.

We start this discussion by outlining the similarities and differences between the legacy standards and their current revisions. Then we outline the steps an organization may need to take to implement the new standards. This is the *transitioning* process.[1] Depending on process improvement status or process maturity, organizations will take different paths to achieve their goals. We will show a road map leading from the legacy versions to the current versions of ISO 9001 and the CMMI®. This road map takes the relative process maturity of the organization into account as it transitions from the initial state to more mature states. Figure 6.1 shows the structure of this chapter.

Sections 6.1 and 6.2 discuss similarities and differences between the revised standards and their legacy versions. Then, in Section 6.3.1, we develop a basic approach for organizations with no process improvement experience. Because of the versatility of the CMMI®, this approach has several variations: selecting the areas to emphasize first (such as institutionalization or

---

1. Transitioning is a process that typically follows a gap analysis or other benchmarking technique that an organization will undertake when moving from one well-established process model to another.

153

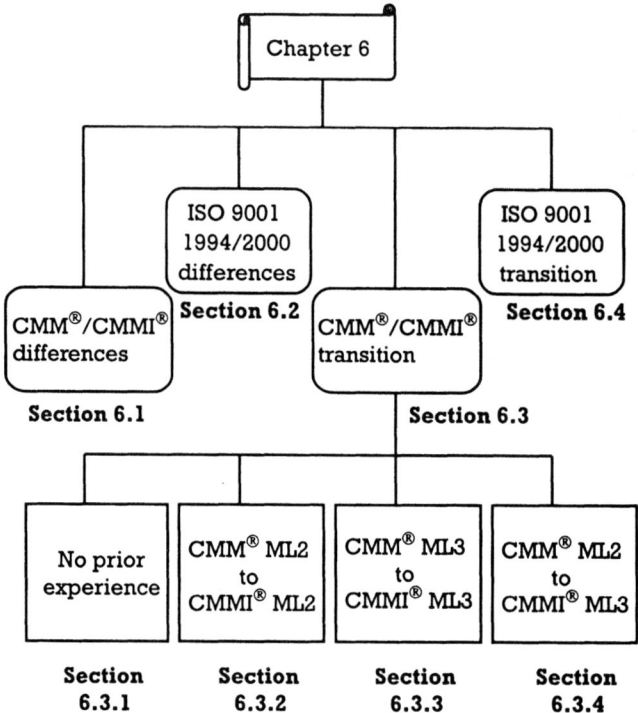

Figure 6.1 Chapter overview.

engineering) and choosing one of the CMMI® model representations (continuous or staged). For those organizations that have already achieved a CMM® maturity level, we show how they can transition to the CMMI® for these situations:

- CMM® maturity level 2 to CMMI® maturity level 2 in Section 6.3.2;
- CMM® maturity level 3 to CMMI® maturity level 3 in Section 6.3.3;
- CMM® maturity level 2 to CMMI® maturity level 3 in Section 6.3.4.

In Section 6.4, we show how an ISO 9001:1994 registered organization can transition to ISO 9001:2000. The ease of transition will greatly depend on the structure of the organization's QMS. Although transitioning from ISO 9001:1994 to ISO 9001:2000 is by no means easy, it is much more straightforward than the CMM® to CMMI® transition because there are no special cases. Due to ISO 9001's structure, an organization is either registered or not.

In Chapter 7, we extend these steps and show how the synergy between the standards can be used to efficiently achieve ISO registration, CMMI® maturity or capability levels, or both.

What does it take for an organization to achieve ISO registration or attain a CMMI® maturity level? First, a gap analysis is performed and process improvement is planned using the IDEAL℠ model discussed in Chapter 2. Then, in the establishing phase of the model, the actual transitioning steps are implemented. In the absence of a gap analysis reflecting specific organizational requirements, we will discuss such a transition in general terms.

6.1 Differences between the CMM® and CMMI®

To understand the transition steps and the impact of the transition itself, the similarities and differences between the CMM® and CMMI® should be understood. In Section 4.2.1 we listed the source models that were considered when the CMMI® was created. In this chapter, we limit our comparison to the CMM® v1.1 because it is the most widely used. In this section, we contrast the major features of the models. As noted earlier, one has to understand both models thoroughly to appreciate their similarities and differences. The similarities and differences are sometimes quite subtle, but are nevertheless important.

One often overlooked difference between the CMM® and CMMI® is the change in style. The CMM® uses the passive voice in the key practice descriptions, whereas the CMMI® uses active voice. To some, this may imply that the CMMI® is prescriptive, while the CMM® merely points to the best practices for managing and developing software. On the other hand, the CMMI® does not have the requirements for developing and using documented procedures that appear in the CMM®.

Let us address those differences starting with a discussion of the model architecture and continuing with the differences in the PAs. The descriptions in this chapter extend the Chapter 5 discussions.

6.1.1 Institutionalization

The structure of the PAs in the CMM® and CMMI® staged representation is somewhat different. In the CMM®, the *Commitment to Perform* (CO), *Ability to Perform* (AB), *Measurement and Analysis* (ME), and *Verifying Implementation* (VE) common features are used to institutionalize processes. They have an impact on the KPA goals through the links indicated in the appendix of [1]. In the CMMI®, each PA has generic goals that are used to group generic practices. These goals provide a stronger case and better visibility for institutionalization. The CMMI® contains common features similar to those in the CMM®, but has additional generic practices as shown in Figure 6.2.

The following discussion is based on the staged representation, showing how the common features of the CMM® have migrated to the CMMI®. The continuous representation contains the same generic goals and generic practices but does not segregate them into common features. There are no

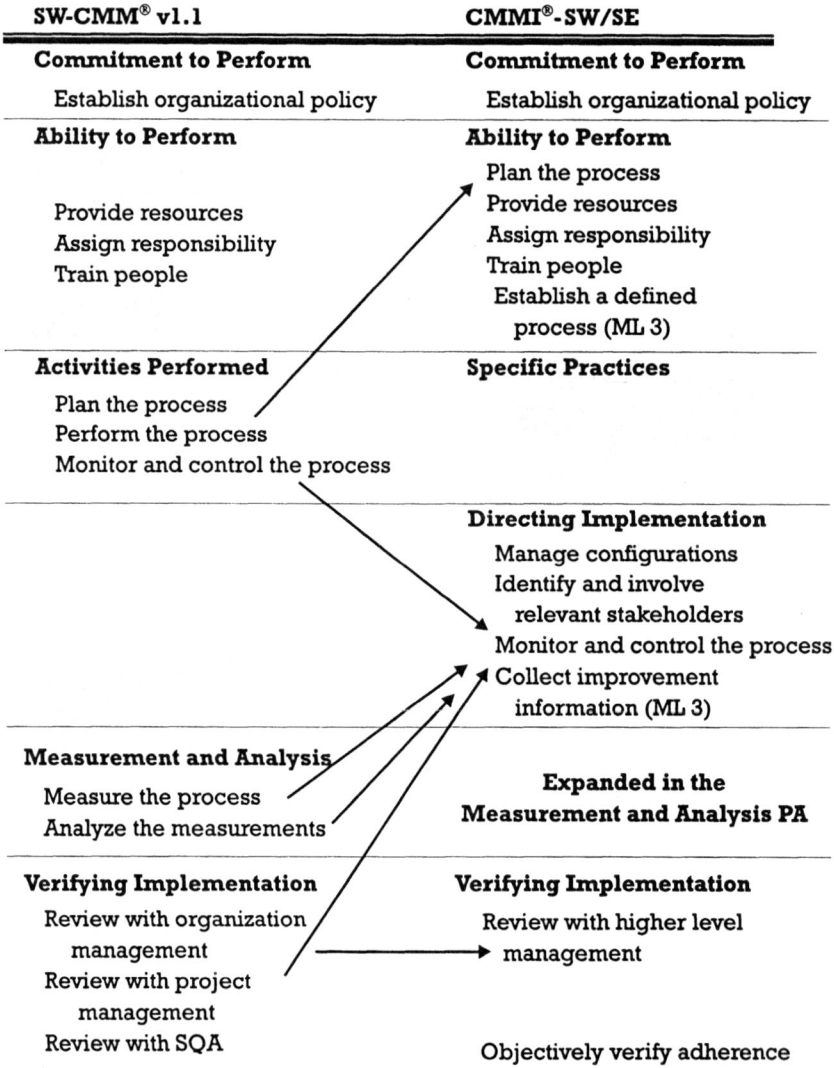

Figure 6.2 Relationship between the CMM® and CMMI® common features.

generic goals for maturity levels 4 and 5 in the staged model. In the continuous model, generic goals 4 and 5 indicate if the PA has reached capability levels 4 and 5, respectively.[2]

In the staged representation, GG 2 and GG 3 and their generic practices are listed separately in each PA. Satisfying GG 2 in addition to the specific goals of each PA enables an organization to attain maturity level 2. When an organization attempts to move to maturity level 3, it should satisfy both GG 2 and GG 3. It should revisit level 2 PAs, enhance them by implementing GG 3, and institutionalize the PAs as defined processes. As shown in Figure 6.2, at level 3 the GPs associated with GG 3 are split between the AB (*Establish a Defined Process*) and *directing implementation* (DI) (*Collect Improvement Information*) common features.

Commitment to Perform

In the CMMI®, the CO common feature has stayed the same as in the CMM® and requires an organization to establish and maintain the organizational policy. However, the wording of the generic practice associated with this common feature (GP 2.1, *Establish and Maintain an Organizational Policy for Planning and Performing the Process*) emphasizes that the policy is not only formulated, but is also documented and used throughout the organization [2].

Ability to Perform

Most KPAs in the CMM® have an activity for developing a plan to be used for implementing that KPA. In the CMMI®, these activities have migrated to GP 2.2, *Establish and Maintain the Plan for Performing the Process*, in the AB common feature. In addition, the "plans" required by the CMM® and the "plans" in CMMI® GP 2.2 are quite different. The plan in the GP 2.2 sense must include a process description for each PA that is documented and agreed to by relevant stakeholders. The implementation of this GP may differ from PA to PA because the sources of the process descriptions may vary. For example, a process description may be given in another PA such as CM or it may come from the organizational standard process.

If we list all of the level 2 GPs, we see that they are used for institutionalizing a managed process, as shown in Table 6.1. Discussions with process

---

2. If an organization is to achieve capability level 4 for a PA, capability levels 1 through 3 have to be satisfied. Similarly for CL 5, CL1 through 4 have to be satisfied.

Table 6.1 Managed Process

Activity	GP	Project Plan Content
Adhere to organizational policies.	GP 2.1	
Follow established plans and process descriptions.	GP 2.2	• Process description • Standards for the work products and services of the process • Requirements for the work products and services of the process • Specific objectives for the performance of the process (e.g., quality, time scale, cycle time, and resource usage) • Dependencies among the activities, work products, and services of the process
Provide adequate resources.	GP 2.3	• Resources (including funding, people, and tools)
Assign responsibility and authority for performing the process.	GP 2.4	• Assignment of responsibility and authority
Train the people performing and supporting the process.	GP 2.5	• Training needed for performing and supporting the process
Place designated work products under appropriate levels of CM.	GP 2.6	• Work products to be placed under configuration management • Level of configuration management for each item
Identify and involve relevant stakeholders.	GP 2.7	• Involvement of identified stakeholders
Monitor and control the performance of the process against the plans for performing the process and take corrective actions.	GP 2.8	• Measurement requirements for insight into the performance of the process, its work products, and its services • Activities for monitoring and controlling the process
Objectively evaluate the process, its work products, and its services for adherence to the process descriptions, standards, and procedures, and address noncompliance.	GP 2.9	• Objective evaluation activities of the process and work products
Review the activities, status, and results of the process with higher level management and resolve issues.	GP 2.10	• Management review of activities and work products

improvement practitioners show that considerable confusion surrounds the process improvement community about the implementation of GP 2.2. Table 6.1 identifies the topics that have to be covered in the project plan.

Depending on the maturity level of the organization, this common feature may also contain GP 3.1, *Establish a Defined Process,* for which no equivalent exists in the CMM®. This GP requires the institutionalization of an organizational standard process, which then must be tailored for a particular implementation. It also implies that the IPM PA should be implemented before other PAs can be implemented and institutionalized at maturity level 3. With the project's defined process in place, GP 2.2 must be revisited to reflect process tailoring. As we will see later, this means that GP 3.1 will enable maturity level 2 PAs to improve as an organization matures. This situation is more critical in the continuous representation because PAs can be implemented without a specific order, whereas GP 3.1 will follow level 3 maturity institutionalization in the staged representation.

Directing Implementation

The newly created DI common feature in the CMMI® includes the following CMM® key practices:

- Monitor and control the process.
- Measure the process.
- Analyze measurements.
- Review with project management.

DI also includes the new generic practices, GP 2.6, *Manage Configurations,* GP 2.7, *Identify and Involve Relevant Stakeholders,* and the maturity level 3 practice, GP 3.2, *Collect Improvement Information.*

Many of the CMM® activities performed practices contain a subpractice stating that the "[Software work products, as appropriate] are managed and controlled." This practice has become CMMI® GP 2.6.

A discussion similar to that regarding GP 3.1 applies to GP 3.2 shown in Table 6.2. It implies that implementation of the OPD PA is required before GP 3.2 can be successfully implemented, because this generic practice requires an organization to have already established a measurement repository (OPD SP 1.4) and a process asset library (OPD SP 1.5).

Some of the GPs with corresponding practices invoked elsewhere in the CMM® are spelled out in the CMMI® in one place and are required for

Table 6.2 Defined Process

Activity	Generic Practice
Follow a plan that incorporates a defined process (defined process clearly states the following: purpose, inputs, entry criteria, activities, roles, measures, verification steps, outputs, and exit criteria).	GP 3.1
Collect work products, measures, and improvement information for supporting the use and improvement of the organizational process assets.	GP 3.2

institutionalizing the process. One of the more prominent new GPs is GP 2.7, *Identify and Involve the Relevant Stakeholders as Planned*. The CMM® uses the wording *other groups*, which seldom specifically includes customers and end users. Relevant stakeholders are the providers of process inputs, the users of the process outputs, and the process performers. Once stakeholders are identified, their involvement in the process is planned. Most organizations will have to address this specific requirement when transitioning from the CMM® to the CMMI®.

GP 2.8, *Monitor and Control the Process*, is new in the CMMI®. It is broader than the ME common feature found in all CMM® KPAs. It combines measurements of actual performance against the plan, reviews of accomplishments and results of the process, reviews with the immediate level of management responsible for the process, identification of problems in the plan for performing the process, and taking corrective action.

Verifying Implementation

In the CMMI® the VE common feature was "trimmed" a little bit. The requirement for reviewing the PA activities with a project manager has been dropped. In addition, the requirement for *software quality assurance* (SQA) review of project activities is now reworded as "Objectively evaluate adherence of the process against its process description, standards, and procedures, and address noncompliances" (GP 2.9). There are no requirements for the separate reviews that were required in some CMM® KPAs, such as independent reviews in the SQA KPA.

In the continuous representation, the generic practices that institutionalize a managed and defined process are the same as in the staged representation. By following generic practices in each PA we have a clear picture of what is required to bring each of the PAs to the managed or defined capability level.

6.1 Differences between the CMM® and CMMI®

In the CMMI®, some relationships between GPs and PAs have to be considered when institutionalizing processes. These relationships, although present in the CMM®, are not forcefully or explicitly stated. For example, the CMM® has boxes with references, such as "Refer to Activity X of the < > KPA," or explanations of concepts, such as "Managed and controlled," but does not clearly tie the ideas together. The close relationship between the GPs and PAs is especially significant when using the continuous CMMI® representation. Those relationships will be discussed later in this chapter when we address the concept of threads in Section 6.1.5.

6.1.2 Maturity level 2 PAs

Let us now consider differences between the CMM® KPAs and the CMMI® PAs at maturity level 2,[3] as shown in Figure 6.3. Although most CMM® KPAs have migrated to CMMI® PAs, the differences, including the introduction of the MA PA, require careful evaluation.[4] As we will see later in this chapter, this is particularly important for organizations that will transition from maturity level 2 in the CMM® to maturity level 2 in the CMMI®.

For the sake of clarity, the comparison of specific practices in the CMMI® to key practices in the CMM® is limited to those at the same maturity level

Software CMM® v1.1	CMMI®
Level 2 - Repeatable	Level 2 - Managed
• Requirements Management	• Requirements Management
• Software Project Planning	• Project Planning
• Software Project Tracking and Oversight	• Project Monitoring and Control
• Software Subcontract Management	• Subcontract Agreement Management
• Software Quality Assurance	• Process and Product Quality Assurance
• Software Configuration Management	• Configuration Management
	• ***Measurement and Analysis***

Figure 6.3 CMM® to CMMI® comparison, level 2.

---

3. In the continuous model, these PAs are in the project management and support categories.
4. In general, where the CMMI® appears to be similar to the CMM® it is also more detailed.

wherever possible. If there is no equivalent specific practice at the same maturity level, we will consider key practices at the next higher level. When analyzing similarities and differences between the models, a mapping, such as that given in [3], may be useful. Because of the cumulative nature of KPAs and PAs, projects in high-maturity organizations will benefit from their higher maturity processes even when they implement lower level PAs. When comparing the models we may distinguish two cases: (1) organizations that are new to process improvement and are committed to using the CMMI® and (2) organizations that are transitioning from the CMM® to the CMMI®. Organizations in either of those cases will approach the CMMI® requirements differently. An organization transitioning from the CMM® to the CMMI® will have to perform a gap analysis to determine what it has to do to preserve its investment in the CMM® and still satisfy the CMMI® requirements. On the other hand, an organization new to process improvement will also perform a gap analysis, but will be free to select the implementation road map that best suits its business goals.

As Figure 6.3 shows, most KPAs have migrated from the CMM® to the CMMI®. They have been extended to include systems engineering concepts not present in the CMM® resulting, at least, in name changes. For example, *Software Configuration Management* (SCM) in the CMM® has become Configuration Management in the CMMI®. *Software Project Planning* (SPP) is now Project Planning. A new PA that is not in the CMM®, Measurement and Analysis, has been added.

Requirements Management (REQM)

Let us start with the REQM PA. The first specific practice, SP 1.1, *Obtain Understanding of the Requirements,* is new in the CMMI®. It merges activities from *Software Process Engineering* (SPE) and *Intergroup Coordination* (IC)[5] and extends them to include all system requirements, not just software requirements. SP 1.2, *Obtain Commitments to Requirements,* and SP 1.3, *Manage Requirements Changes,* closely match the CMM® RM activities 1 and 3, respectively.

In the CMM®, requirements traceability is buried in level 3 as a subpractice to SPE activity 10. The CMMI® elevates traceability to SP 1.4, *Maintain Bidirectional Traceability of Requirements.* This means that the source and the user of each requirement is known and that related information such as

---

5. SPE.AC.2: "The software requirements are developed, maintained, documented, and verified by systematically analyzing the allocated requirements according to the project's defined software process."
IC.AC.1: "The software engineering group and the other engineering groups participate with the customer and end users, as appropriate, to establish the system requirements."

project plans, systems designs, implementation, and user documentation associated with each requirement are also known. In the continuous representation, it is expected that the REQM PA will be implemented with the RD and TS PAs. Unfortunately, this is less obvious in the staged representation where the RD and TS PAs belong to maturity level 3 and REQM belongs to level 2. However, this should not preclude those organizations using the staged CMMI® representation from implementing these PAs even though they appear to be "out of sequence."

Project Planning (PP)

Most of the CMM® SPP activities are repackaged in the CMMI® as specific practices, resulting in more high-level practices than are in the CMM®. An explicit requirement for establishing the *work breakdown structure* (WBS) has been added in SP 1.1, *Estimate the Scope of the Project,* subpractice 1, *Develop a WBS based on the product architecture.* The WBS is used for defining work packages, estimation, and resource allocation.

The CMM® requires the management of important work products. This is extended in the CMMI® through SP 2.3, *Plan for Data Management.* It requires an organization to plan for the documentation required to support all project areas, such as engineering, administration, logistics, and quality. Project deliverables and nondeliverables are included.

The SP 2.4, *Plan for Project Resources,* addresses CMM® SPP activities 11 and 14. It also adds a requirement for determining process and staffing requirements based on the WBS, which is addressed in only general terms ("adequate resources") in the CMM® SPP AB 3.

SP 2.5, *Plan for Needed Knowledge and Skills,* is equivalent to activity 1 in the CMM® training program KPA but it now appears at maturity level 2.

SP 2.6, *Plan Stakeholder Involvement,* is stronger in the CMMI® than the CMM® requirement for keeping "all affected groups" informed. It suggests that for each major activity, a project should identify the affected stakeholders and those who have the expertise needed to conduct the activity. A two-dimensional matrix with stakeholders along one axis and project activities along the other axis is a convenient format for accomplishing this identification [2]. This specific practice provides a foundation for GP 2.7, *Identify and Involve Relevant Stakeholders,* in most other PAs.

One of the more prominent changes is the rigorous requirement for obtaining commitment to the plan, described in SG 3, *Obtain Commitment to the Plan.* This goal integrates the requirements of the CMM® SPP, *Software Project Tracking and Oversight* (SPTO), and IC KPAs. It requires review of all plans that affect the project, reconciling work and resource levels, and obtaining commitment from relevant stakeholders, both internal and external. It also distinguishes between an informal go-ahead and formal full commitment to the plan.

Project Monitoring and Control (PMC)

The PMC PA parallels the PP PA and does not add any major requirements to the CMM® SPTO KPA. It seems a little crisper than the CMM®—requirements are specified for monitoring commitments, monitoring stakeholder involvement (explicitly required in SG 1), and managing corrective actions to closure (SG 2). This second specific goal is significant because it requires that issues identified by verification and validation processes, reviews, deviations from project plans, or changes in risk status are gathered and analyzed. Corrective actions are then taken and managed. These requirements are scattered over many SPTO activities in the CMM® (such as activities 5 through 9). It is important to note that this PA supports GP 2.8, *Monitor and Control the Process*, in the other CMMI® PAs.

It is interesting that while the CMM® does not address planning of the project tracking process, except by inference in SPP activity 6 and later in OPD activity 2 and *Integrated Software Management* (ISM) activity 1, it is required by the CMMI® by virtue of GP 2.2.

Supplier Agreement Management (SAM)

The SAM PA replaces and expands the *Software Subcontract Management* (SSM) KPA of the CMM®. It extends subcontract management to include management of product acquisition from suppliers using formal agreements. In-house vendors and commercial vendors, including subcontractors, are distinguished and the PA can be extended to the acquisition of development tools and test environments. New processes to be addressed include determination of the type of acquisition, evaluation of COTS products to ensure they satisfy specified requirements, and transition of these products to the projects. Although most CMM® SSM key practices can be traced to the CMMI®, it appears that this PA is more encompassing and more detailed in its requirements. Two specific practices, SP 1.1, *Determine Acquisition Type*, and SP 1.2, *Select Suppliers*, are not covered in the CMM®. Similarly, several CMM® practices dealing with the subcontractor's project planning, QA, and CM activities are not addressed in the CMMI®.

Process and Product Quality Assurance (PPQA)

The PPQA PA may appear, at first, to be more demanding than the CMM® SQA KPA, but it has fewer practices and covers basically the same topics.

The focus of this PA is objective evaluation of processes, work products, and services. Objective evaluation is defined as "the review of activities and work products against criteria that minimize subjectivity and bias by the reviewer" [2]. This objective evaluation is critical to the success of the project.

The CMMI® is less specific than the CMM® about the reporting structure of the QA function. Actual implementation of QA activities may vary among organizations, depending on the organization's structure and culture. The fundamental requirement inherited from the CMM® is still valid: Those who perform QA activities must be trained and have an independent reporting channel to the appropriate level of management. The independent reporting channel allows noncompliance issues to be escalated when necessary. In general, PPQA specific practices are more detailed than the corresponding CMM® key practices. The CMMI® requirements specified in SP 2.1, *Communicate and Ensure Resolution of Noncompliance Issues*, and SP 2.2, *Establish Records*, that have their roots in the CMM® subpractices are now elevated to the specific practice level. It is important to note that this PA supports GP 2.9, *Objectively Evaluate Adherence*, in most of the other CMMI® PAs.

Two other CMMI® PAs, VER and VAL, should not be confused with PPQA. Although these PAs may address the same work products, the perspectives are different. VER and VAL ensure that requirements are satisfied, whereas PPQA ensures that processes and products were implemented as planned. Thus, PPQA also ensures that the VER and VAL processes are appropriately implemented.

Configuration Management (CM)

The CM PA is basically the same as in the SCM KPA in the CMM®. It follows a standard CM process including identification, establishment of baselines, control and management of changes, establishment of records, and performance of audits. The existence of the configuration control board is de-emphasized although the CMMI® refers to it when discussing creation and release of the baselines. The requirement for the standard CM reports (the CMM® SCM activity 9) is "downgraded" in the CMMI® to a subpractice (subpractice 6) in SP 1.2.

Measurement and Analysis (MA)

At CMMI® maturity level 2 (staged representation), there is a new PA to be considered: *Measurement and Analysis*.[6] Although this is in some respects

---

6. In the continuous representation, the MA PA is included in the support PAs.

an extension of the CMM® ME common feature, this PA has additional requirements not found in the CMM®. It requires an organization to identify information needs, specify measurements, and define the processes for collecting, storing, analyzing and communicating measurements. The CMM® simply required that measurements be collected and used in each PA to determine its status. In the CMMI®, measurement and analysis must be institutionalized as, at least, a managed process. This means the following:

- A measurement and analysis policy is in place.
- Resources are allocated.
- Responsibilities are assigned.
- Staff is trained.
- Specific work products are controlled.
- Stakeholders are kept informed.
- Activities are evaluated against the standard process.
- Senior management is kept aware of the status and progress of measurement and analysis activities.

This PA also supports GP 2.8, *Monitor and Control the Process,* and in turn supports all other PAs.

At the managed level, collected data need not be stored in an organizational repository. However, it is often advantageous to specify measurements and their collection and analysis methods across the organization and collect these data in one central place.

An organization that does not have a strong CMM® level 3 measurement program or does not understand the importance of the ME common feature may have difficulty when implementing this PA. Those organizations may find that the measurement program requirements are quite different from the CMM® requirements for the collection and use of basic project management, process, and quality metrics.

6.1.3 Maturity level 3 PAs

Now let us consider similarities and differences between the CMM® and CMMI® level 3 PAs as shown in Figure 6.4.

Organizational Process Focus (OPF)

The OPF and OPD PAs changed in subtle ways. Some activities are more rigorous in the CMMI®, such as SP 2.2, *Implement Process Action Plans,* and

6.1 Differences between the CMM® and CMMI®   167

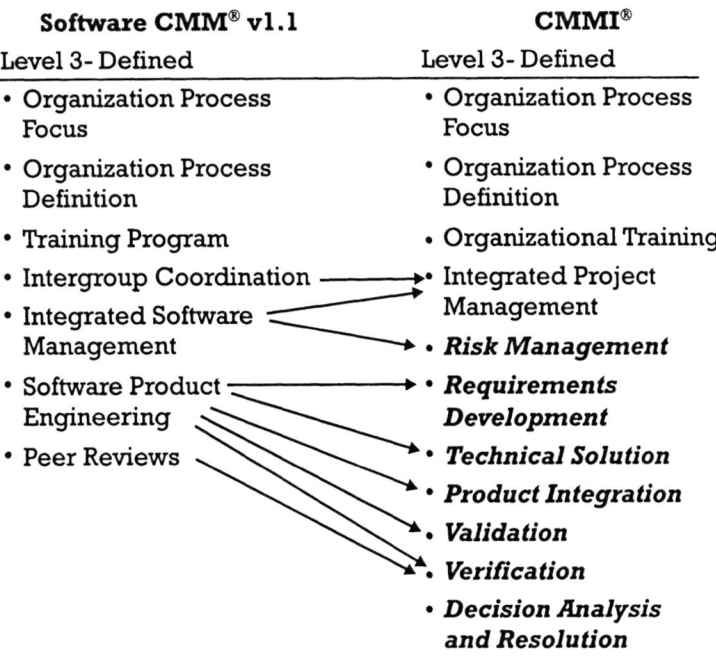

Figure 6.4 CMM® to CMMI® comparison, level 3.

SP 2.4, *Incorporate Process-Related Experience into the Organizational Process Assets.* An important addition is SP 1.1, *Establish Organizational Process Needs,* which did not exist in the CMM®. This SP requires an organization to explicitly identify its process improvement goals, objectives, and process needs. This important step precedes appraisal, so that needs can be compared to appraisal results and process improvement plans sensibly developed.

The CMM® OPD AB 1,[7] is more detailed than the CMMI® GP 2.4, *Assign Responsibility,* in specifying *Software Engineering Process Group* (SEPG) responsibilities. On the other hand, the CMMI® also identifies a management council or steering committee that is not present in the CMM®. Although most organizations using the CMM® establish and brief management councils, some delegate responsibility to lower levels. Implementation of this GP helps sustain management involvement.

Organizational Process Definition (OPD)

The OPD PA closely follows the spirit of its CMM® counterpart. The CMM® has sometimes been incorrectly perceived as requiring a single, monolithic

---

7. OPD.AB.1: "A group that is responsible for the organization's software process activities exists."

standard process. The CMMI® eliminates this concern by referring to a "set of standard processes." This set of standard processes can be designed in a hierarchical manner (for example, by enterprise, division, and site), or can cover processes need for different domains (for example, telecommunications, management information systems, or maintenance).

Through GP 2.7, *Identify and Involve Relevant Stakeholders*, the CMMI® requires an organization to identify and involve the organizational process definition stakeholders. Stakeholder involvement includes, for example, selection of life-cycle models, process tailoring, and measurement definition.

Organizational Training (OT)

The OT PA is similar to the CMM® Training Program KPA, but is more detailed and rigorous. In the CMM®, the need for an organization to identify its long-term training needs is subtle. The CMMI® more clearly distinguishes strategic and tactical training needs and plans. Organizational training needs are established through analysis of business needs and existing and required skills. The organizational tactical training plan addresses those organizational training needs and the means for training delivery and training record collection.

Evaluation of training effectiveness is not a strong point in the CMM®, although hints appear in the measurement and verification practices.[8] OT SP 2.3 focuses clearly on the *effectiveness* of the training program, verifying that the organizations needs are being met.

The CMM® requirements for training waivers are now "downgraded" to a note associated with SP 2.1.

Integrated Project Management (IPM)

The IPM PA incorporates requirements from the CMM® ISM and IC KPAs. As in the CMM®, IPM establishes a project's defined process based on a tailored version of the organizational standard process and requires that the project use this defined process. IPM SP 1.3 and SP 1.4 indicate explicitly that the project's plans (such as the QA plan and the CM plan) must be integrated. In the CMM®, this requirement is less forceful and is spread over a number of KPAs.

IPM SG 2, *Coordinate and Collaborate with Relevant Stakeholders*, incorporates most of the IC key practices. This specific goal requires stakeholders to be

---

8. TP.ME.2: "Measurements are made and used to determine the quality of the training program."
TP.VE.2: "The training program is independently evaluated on a periodic basis for consistency with, and relevance to, the organization's needs."

6.1 Differences between the CMM® and CMMI®

identified, their involvement and dependencies managed, and coordination issues resolved.

Although several CMM® key practices, such as managing effort and cost and critical computer resources, are not explicitly addressed in this PA, they are tied to the tasks of the project's defined process.

In the IPPD version of the CMMI® this PA has two additional goals, SG 3, *Use Project Shared Vision of IPPD*, and SG 4, *Organize Integrated Teams for IPPD*, associated with the IPPD discipline. These goals are important from the ISO point of view because they provide guidance for implementing ISO clause 7.3.1, as we will see in Chapter 7.

Three CMMI® PAs, RSKM, DAR, and, in the IPPD domain, IT, are not related to ISO requirements and therefore we do not discuss them in detail. Although the RSKM PA is an expansion of ISM activity 10, and DAR is a new addition to the CMMI®, organizations are urged to consider these PAs because they contribute greatly to successful and effective project management.

In Figure 6.4 we see that in addition to accommodating the systems engineering concepts, there are additional PAs that are mostly generated from the activities performed in the CMM® SPE KPA.

Requirements Development (RD)

As indicated in Chapter 4, the RD PA is new but has its origins in the SPE KPA.[9] This single CMM® key practice is now elevated to a complete PA with its own institutionalization aspects and thus is much more rigorous. This PA extends and combines systems and software engineering aspects of requirements elicitation, analysis, documentation and validation. It specifies requirements allocation; creation of interface requirements; requirements analysis, including evaluation of operational concepts and scenarios as a source of requirements; and functional analysis to develop a functional architecture.

In addition, comprehensive methods for requirements verification and validation are required starting very early in the project.

Technical Solution (TS)

The RD PA is implemented interactively with the TS PA: As alternative solutions to customer requirements are developed, detailed requirements, their allocation, and interfaces may be modified.

---

9. SPE.AC.2: "The software requirements are developed, maintained, documented, and verified by systematically analyzing the allocated requirements according to the project's defined software process."

The TS PA origins are in SPE activities 3, 4, and 5.[10] However, many of the specific practices found in this PA are new[11] and have their roots in systems engineering practices. These practices should be used early in a project's life cycle to develop alternative solutions, evolve operational concepts and scenarios, and select product-component solutions based on specific selection criteria. When the solution is selected, the design evolves from the top-level product architecture through the lower detailed levels. Design evolution includes reuse and make–buy decisions, development of technical data packages, design of interfaces, and product implementation. Because many specific and generic practices are new, they have to be evaluated in the context of the TS PA and the CMMI® as a whole, rather than by trying to identify the similarities and differences between the CMM® and CMMI®.

Product Integration (PI)

The CMMI® PI PA extends SPE activity 6.[12] Whereas the CMM® simply requires that product integration be conducted according to the project's defined process, the CMMI® is more detailed. Specific integration activities are required, such as these:

- Developing an optimal product integration strategy;
- Establishing the integration environment;
- Developing integration procedures and criteria;
- Reviewing and managing interfaces between products or their components;
- Assembling products from those components;
- Evaluating components;
- Packaging and delivering the products or product components.

---

10. SPE.AC.3: "The software design is developed, maintained, documented, and verified according to the project's defined software process, to accommodate the software requirements and to form the framework for coding."
    SPE.AC.4: "The software code is developed, maintained, documented, and verified according to the project's defined software process, to implement the software requirements and software design."
    SPE.AC.5: "Software testing is performed according to the project's defined software process."
11. The specific practices associated with SG 1, *Select Product-Component Solutions*, are not addressed in the CMM®.
12. SPE.AC.6: "Integration testing of the software is planned and performed according to the project's defined software process."

Similar to the TS PA, PI has to be evaluated in the context of the CMMI® as a whole.

Verification (VER) and Validation (VAL)

The VER and VAL PAs in the CMMI® are based on SPE activity 7,[13] and most of the peer review KPA. Although verification and validation are similar and are often confused, they address different aspects of the development process. Verification confirms that work products properly implement specified requirements, whereas validation confirms that the product will fulfill its intended use [2]. SG 2, *Perform Peer Reviews*, in the VER PA is directly related to the Peer Review KPA of the CMM®. Likewise, the specific practices associated with the other two goals, SG 1, *Prepare for Verification*, and SG 3, *Verify Selected Work Products*, are quite similar to key practices in SPE. As noted earlier for the TS and PI PAs, CMM® key practices rely on the project's defined process, whereas the CMMI® lists specific activities that are required for verifying products or components. The VAL PA is similar in structure to VER and also has roots in activity 7 of the SPE KPA. Organizations transitioning to CMMI® level 3 may find that they require more rigor than is required in the CMM® when implementing these two PAs.

6.1.4 Maturity level 4 PAs

Maturity level 4 contains two PAs: OPP and QPM. Those PAs address processes that are quantitatively managed, where quantitative objectives for product quality and process performance are established and used for managing the processes through the life cycle. These processes must be understood in statistical terms. Figure 6.5 shows a comparison of the CMM® and CMMI® maturity level 4 and 5 PAs.

Organizational Process Performance (OPP) This PA strengthens the CMM®'s notion of quantitative process management at the organizational level. In the CMM®, most of the key practices in the QPM KPA deal with a project's processes. In the CMMI®, the emphasis is on the organization's set of standard processes. The measurements collected from various projects are analyzed to establish a process performance baseline and the expected range of results. This baseline is then used when the individual project's process performance expectations, including quality objectives, are defined.

---

13. SPE.AC.7: "System and acceptance testing of the software is planned and performed to demonstrate that the software satisfies its requirements."

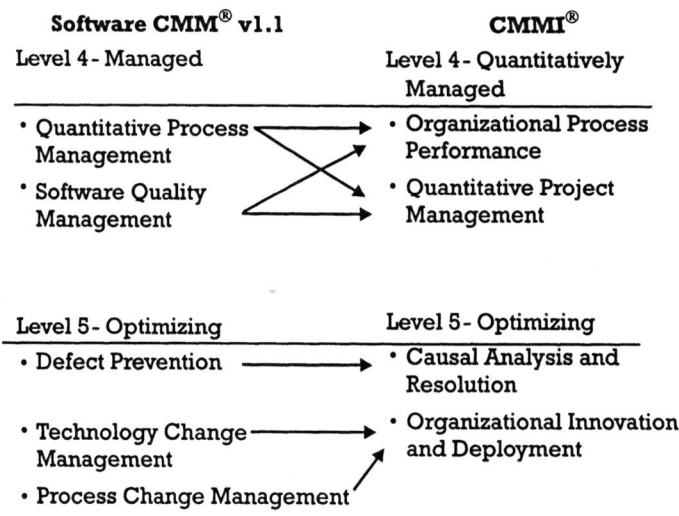

Figure 6.5 CMM® to CMMI® comparison, levels 4 and 5.

Quality Project Management (QPM) This PA combines the concepts of the CMM® QPM and *Software Quality Management* (SQM) KPAs, with an emphasis on the project's process performance. While the quality and process performance objectives, measures, and baselines are defined in the OPP PA, this PA requires the uses of statistical techniques for understanding process variation and achieving stable and predictable process performance.

6.1.5 Maturity level 5 PAs

Maturity level 5 contains two PAs: OID and CAR. These PAs address quantitatively managed processes that are changed to meet relevant current and projected business objectives. Process improvements are selected based on the identification of common causes of process variation and are evaluated based on their cost and impact to the organization.

Organizational Innovation and Deployment (OID) This PA combines the CMM® *Process Change Management* (PCM) and *Technology Change Management* (TCM) KPAs. It enhances an organization's ability to meet its quality and performance goals by selecting appropriate incremental and innovative improvements. This PA assumes that innovation and improvement recommendations are implemented in quantitatively managed processes.

Causal Analysis and Resolution (CAR) The CAR PA builds on the CMM® Defect Prevention KPA and is quite similar in spirit. Causal analysis implies activities that are performed at the project level to determine and eliminate causes of defects. Causal analysis, however, goes beyond examining defects. It can be applied to problems ranging from narrow project problems to business and engineering problems that require systematic analysis and resolution.

6.1.6 Continuous CMMI® representation: concept of threads

Maturity levels, used in CMM®-SW for many years, indicate a preferred order for process improvement. First, project management is stabilized. Process variations are then minimized through the introduction of the organizational standard process. Finally, processes are quantitatively controlled and optimized. This order is also sanctioned in the CMMI® and is shown in Table 6.3 [4].

Table 6.3 Activities Versus PAs—Staged Representation

Activity	Associated PA
	Level 2
Build a plan.	Project Planning
Track performance against the plan.	Project Monitoring and Control
Manage inputs to the plan.	Requirements Management
Make sure the plan is followed.	Process and Product Quality Assurance
Control the artifacts being created.	Configuration Management
Get basic measurements in place.	Measurement and Analysis
Manage your suppliers.	Supplier Agreement Management
	Level 3
Provide an atmosphere for acceptance of standard processes.	Organization Process Focus
Minimize unnecessary process variation.	Organization Process Definition
Standardize engineering processes because they are now protected by effective project management practices.	Organization Process Definition, Requirements Development, Technical Solution, Product Integration, Verification, Validation
Extend project management.	Integrated Project Management, Risk Management
Provide support for engineering and management decision making.	Decision Analysis and Resolution
Ensure knowledge of the organization's standard processes for current and future needs.	Organizational Training

With the introduction of the CMMI® continuous representation, process improvement has received the freedom to choose the order of PA implementation. Simply stated, there is no specific order for implementing PAs in the continuous representation of the CMMI®. Each PA can be at any capability level. Capability levels are, however, cumulative; they build on one another. As shown in Figure 6.6, higher capability levels include the attributes of the lower capability levels and, therefore, cannot be skipped.

Further inspection of the generic and specific practices within and among PAs shows that some GPs depend on the support of the associated PAs. For example:

- GP 2.6, *Manage Configurations*, depends on the implementation of the CM PA.

- GP 2.9, *Objectively Evaluate Adherence*, depends on the PPQA PA.

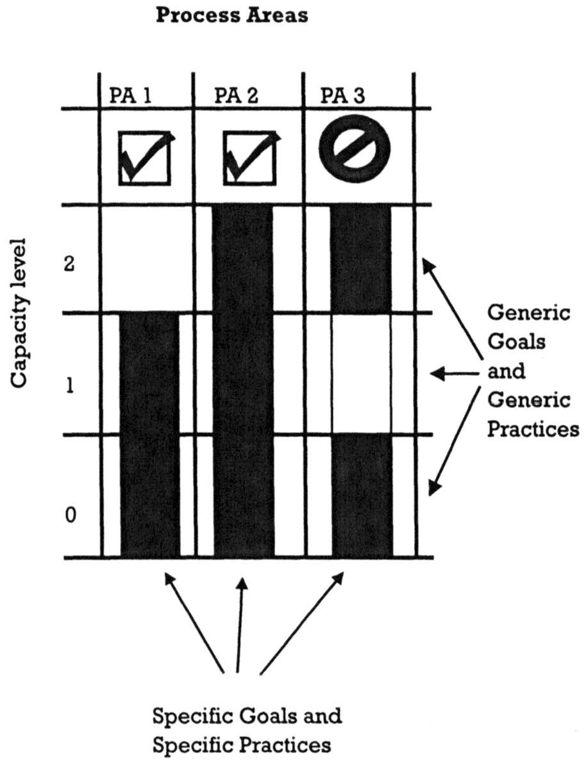

Figure 6.6 Capability levels are cumulative.

- GP 2.8, *Monitor and Control the Process*, relies on both the MA and PMC PAs.

Other GPs cannot be implemented without having certain PAs in place. For example, GP 3.1, *Establish a Defined Process*, requires that the OPD and IPM PAs be implemented.

Thus, there are certain threads to be considered when implementing generic practices and associated PAs. The CMMI® provides some help by indicating cross-references from one PA to another in italicized text in the PA descriptions. Although common features of the CMM® also depend on the implementation of some KPAs, this is not strongly emphasized.

Capability level 3 generic practices subsume part of the IPM PA [2]. This means that in order to implement GP 3.1 and 3.2, some portions of the IPM PA have to be implemented. On the other hand, even if all of the individual PAs up to capability level 3 are implemented, IPM may not be satisfied if the capability level 3 implementation is not integrated.

Although these relationships sound complicated, understanding them will lead to an effective process improvement strategy. Later, we will explore this in a little more detail, contrasting the required progression found in the staged representation of the CMMI® with the implementation freedom found in the continuous representation. We will also see that a hybrid approach, using a combination of the staged and continuous representations, is possible and may be effective for certain organizations [5].

6.2 Differences between ISO 9001:1994 and ISO 9001:2000

We now discuss the major similarities and differences between the 1994 and 2000 versions of ISO 9001. For a quick reference, Annex B to ISO 9001:2000 shows correspondence between the new standard and ISO 9001:1994 [6]. However, as pointed out in Chapter 5, the use of cross-reference tables may be inadequate when implementing this new standard. Very often the wording of the clauses may be the same but the requirements and explanations are quite different.

Because ISO 9001:2000 is based on eight quality management principles and a process and systems engineering approach, it is markedly different from the 1994 version. The new requirements encompass not only product development and implementation, but also emphasize continual improvement of those processes. A superficial translation of the requirements is no substitute for deep understanding. For a more detailed explanation of the differences and enhancements, refer to [7].

Because the ISO 9002 and 9003 documents were eliminated, ISO 9001:2000 allows organizations to exclude some requirements of clause 7 of the standard providing that those exclusions do not affect its ability to provide products that satisfy the customer's requirements. For example, design control may be omitted if the organization is not involved in design activities.

Whereas the 1994 version focused on the prevention of nonconformities, the focus of the 2000 version is on effective implementation of a system engineering approach and continual process improvement. The process engineering aspects of a QMS and, in turn, the quality manual are emphasized through requirements for definitions for the following:

- Processes needed for the QMS;
- Process sequence and interaction;
- Criteria and methods needed for effective execution of these processes;
- Resources needed for implementing the processes;
- Measurement and monitoring of the processes;
- Continual improvement.

Several clauses deal with customer focus and the responsibility of senior management to address customer focus in the form of policies, commitment to complying with the customer requirements, and continual improvement of the effectiveness of the QMS. The documentation requirements are also reduced: Only six procedures are now required as indicated in Tables 6.4 through 6.8.

The language in ISO 9001:2000 is now applicable to all types of organizations, unlike the language of the 1994 version, which many considered to be focused on manufacturing organizations. From the implementation point of view, one of the most significant differences is the shift from the procedural approach found in 1994 version to the process and systems engineering approach of the 2000 version. The famous 20 clauses of the 1994 version have been replaced by five elements. Although many clauses can be traced to the 1994 version, the focus of the 2000 version is quite different: All activities revolve around customer satisfaction and continual process improvement.

Several reports and books address the differences between these two standards [6, 8, 9]. Major differences, based on [6], are summarized in Tables 6.4 through 6.8.

Table 6.4 ISO 9001:2000 Section 4 Requirements

ISO 9001:2000 Clause	Description
4.1	The QMS is now required to describe a set of processes, their interactions, effectiveness, resources required for their successful implementation, and measurement and improvement activities.
4.2.1	There are fewer specific requirements for documented procedures (only six procedures are specifically required). Documents related to planning, operation, and control of processes must be included. The extent of those documents is based on the organization's size, type of its activities, complexity, and process interfaces.
4.2.2	Quality manual defines the scope of the quality management system, including the justification for any exclusions the organization has taken under clause 1.2. Requires the quality manual to describe the interactions among the processes that make up the system.
4.2.3	No change; requires a procedure for controlling documents
4.2.4	No change; records are required to remain legible, identifiable, and retrievable; requires a procedure for controlling documents.

6.3 Transitioning from the CMM® to the CMMI®

Organizations using the CMMI® for process improvement can chose between the continuous and staged representations. It seems natural that an organization that has already attained a CMM® maturity level or is familiar with CMM®-based process improvement would select the staged approach for transitioning to the CMMI®. However, during the IDEAL℠ initiating phase, all organizations should establish the goals and objectives that address the selection of CMMI® representation. To facilitate comparison between the staged representation maturity levels and continuous representation capability levels, the CMMI® outlines equivalent staging, as discussed in Chapter 4.

For organizations that are planning to transition from the CMM® to the CMMI®, several transition cases can be distinguished, as shown in Table 6.9. There are more transitioning cases, particularly those involving higher maturity levels, but these basic cases are sufficiently representative to cover most situations.

An organization without previous process improvement experience seeking higher CMMI® maturity or capability levels clearly has two options: selecting either the continuous or the staged representation. Each option has advantages and disadvantages, as will be discussed in the following chapters.

Table 6.5 ISO 9001:2000 Section 5 Requirements

ISO 9001:2000 Clause	Description
5.1	Top management commitment is required not only to develop the QMS and provide the necessary resources, but also to review those processes and ensure that they are continually improving their effectiveness. Management must also provide evidence of these activities. In addition, top management must communicate to the organization the importance of meeting customer and regulatory and statutory requirements.
5.2	Top management must ensure that customer requirements are determined, understood, and met.
5.3	The quality policy should be appropriate for the organization and must create a framework for setting and reviewing objectives. The policy must mandate a commitment to meet requirements and improve the QMS.
5.4.1	Quality objectives must be measurable and be linked to the quality policy.
5.4.2	Similar to 1994 version; top management must ensure that plans for developing and maintaining the QMS address all requirements including meeting quality objectives and improvement. It also requires the integrity of the QMS to be maintained when it is changed.
5.5.2	The management representative must now ensure that there is an awareness of customer requirements throughout the organization.
5.5.3	Requires internal communication about the effectiveness of the QMS.
5.6.2 and 5.6.3	Similar in spirit to 1994 version; specifies minimum review input items and output actions (wording is more prescriptive).

Table 6.6 ISO 9001:2000 Section 6 Requirements

ISO 9001:2000 Clause	Description
6.1	No major difference; resources needed to implement, maintain, and continually improve the effectiveness of the QMS must be determined and provided.
6.2.2	Determination of needed competencies is introduced; greater emphasis placed on taking actions to close competency gaps, and keeping employees aware of the importance of their work
6.3 and 6.4	Similar to 1994 version but without references to production, installation, and so on. The organization should determine and manage the infrastructure and work environment needed for achieving conformity to product requirements, such as buildings, workspace, or process equipment.

Table 6.7 ISO 9001:2000 Section 7 Requirements

ISO 9001:2000 Clause	Description
7.0	Most of the requirements from 9001:1994 are still included in this section but are more generic.
7.1	This clause provides the essence of the use of the process and system approaches: All processes are linked to result in delivery of products that satisfy customer requirements, create customer satisfaction, and foster continual improvement.
7.2.1	There is a new specific requirement to address product requirements that have not been specified by the customer but are necessary for the intended process, such as regulatory and statutory requirements.
7.2.3	There is a new requirement for determining and implementing customer communications.
7.5.2	There is a new requirement for defining process validation and the conditions and criteria for revalidation.

Table 6.8 ISO 9001:2000 Section 8 Requirements

ISO 9001:2000 Clause	Description
8.2.1	There is a new requirement for measuring and monitoring customer satisfaction.
8.2.2	Similar to 1994 version; it also requires that results of previous audits must be considered in planning new audits. Must define audit scope, frequency, and methodology. Auditors must be objective. The results of audits can be used to identify opportunities for improvement. A procedure for performing internal audits is required.
8.3	No change from 1994 version; requires a procedure for controlling nonconformances.
8.4	Requires data analysis in the preventive action process to eliminate potential causes of nonconformity, to determine the suitability and effectiveness of the QMS, and to identify improvements that can be made to QMS effectiveness.
8.5.1	This is a new requirement; it requires that continual improvement be planned and implemented.
8.5.2	No change from 1994 version; however, once action to correct the cause of the nonconformity has been determined it needs to be implemented. The corrective action process must also provide for recording the results of the corrective action taken; requires a procedure for corrective action.
8.5.3	Similar to above—the results of the preventive actions taken must be recorded; requires a procedure for preventive action.

Table 6.9 Possible Transition Cases

CMM®	CMMI®
No previous process improvement experience	Continuous representation or Staged: maturity level 2
Organization at maturity level 2	Staged: maturity level 2
Organization at maturity level 3	Staged: maturity level 3
Organization at maturity level 2	Staged: maturity level 3
Organization at any level	Continuous representation

For an organization that has already attained CMM® maturity level 2 or 3, the choices between the staged and continuous representations still exist, but most organizations will probably continue to use the representation with which they are familiar, namely, staged. Similarly, those organizations that are at CMM® maturity level 2 and want to advance to CMMI® maturity level 3 will probably continue to use the staged representation.

Because there are clear advantages to using the continuous representation regardless of previous process improvement experience, we will explain how an organization can capitalize on the benefits of the continuous representation and, by using equivalent staging, attain the desired CMMI® maturity level.

6.3.1 Basic approach—no previous process improvement experience

Usually, organizations analyze the gaps between their existing processes and the target model, in this case the CMMI®, to determine the transition effort and to prioritize process improvement activities. In the absence of an actual gap analysis, we assume that an organization has adopted goals similar to those that will be outlined in Section 7.2. Our explanation is based initially on the staged representation and then extended to the continuous representation. The two representations are quite often intertwined [5]. This can be further exploited when devising an ISO implementation strategy.

The relationships among the various approaches are shown in Figure 6.7.

The staged representation implies that an organization will follow the maturity level progression from the initial to more mature levels. It also implies that, for example, an organization at CMM® maturity level 2 will transition to CMMI® maturity level 2.

6.3 Transitioning from the CMM® to the CMMI®

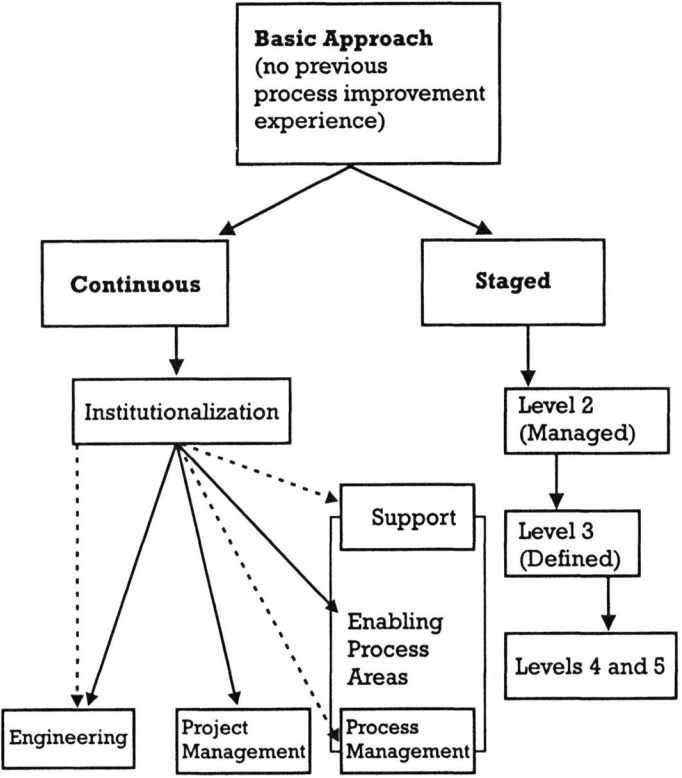

Figure 6.7 Process improvement approaches.

However, an organization at CMM® maturity level 3 has several possible ways to transition to CMMI® maturity level 3, as shown in Figure 6.8. Such an organization can attempt to extend those PAs with roots in the CMM®, such as RD or TS, and then implement those PAs that are not in the CMM®, such as DAR. Alternatively, it can transition to CMMI® maturity level 2, and then add maturity level 3 practices as shown in Figure 6.8(a). A hybrid approach can also be devised, in which an enhanced organizational standard process and associated tailoring criteria can be developed and implemented. Level 2 PAs can then be transitioned to the CMMI® using GP 3.1 and 3.2 generic practices, and finally all level 3 PAs including those that were added to the CMMI® can be implemented as shown in Figure 6.8(b).

The continuous representation provides even more options. An organization without previous process improvement experience may choose to first institutionalize all PAs by using threads. In this approach, the enabling PAs (explained in Chapter 5 and reinforced earlier in this chapter) are imple-

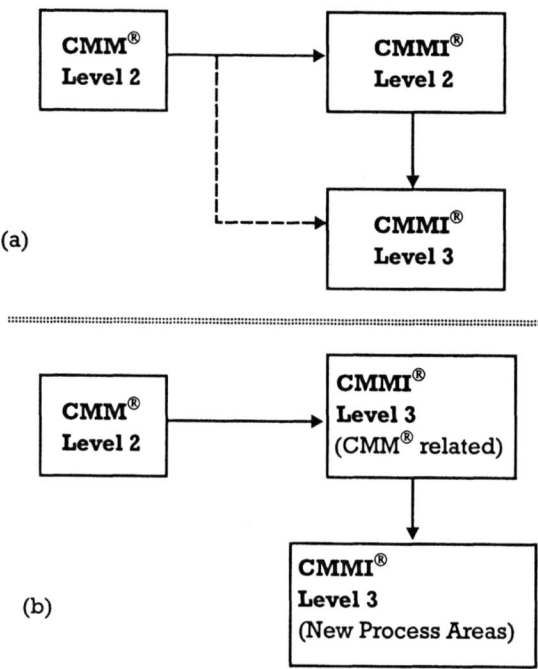

Figure 6.8 Alternative transitioning approaches: (a) progressive approach and (b) sequential approach.

mented and then appropriate specific practices are added. It can also choose to implement all base practices (all capability level 1 specific practices) first and then institutionalize all PAs in the most appropriate order. Similarly, an organization with a strong product development process may opt to transition the engineering PAs first and then add the support or project management PAs. From those examples, we can see that the continuous representation provides more diverse transition approaches than the staged representation even for organizations that have been using the CMM®. Again, we stress that the approach depends on the organizational goals and culture. We describe next selected approaches that specifically help organizations to achieve ISO registration using ISO–CMMI® synergy.

Institutionalization approach

Let us first consider the institutionalization approach. In this approach, we first implement the PAs that support selected GPs and thus enable institutionalization. For an organization without previous process improvement experience, this is quite a challenge. However, experience has shown that most

6.3 Transitioning from the CMM® to the CMMI®

organizations have *some* well-established PA—perhaps CM or REQM—that will enable an efficient start for process improvement. We are not going to address the impact of change management on process improvement but will concentrate on the technical challenges only.

Institutionalization approach—continuous representation

The institutionalization approach is most easily understood by using the continuous representation. Although one can implement individual PA goals or even selected practices, we encourage implementation of complete PAs. The transition steps are shown in Table 6.10.

Table 6.10 Institutionalization Case

Step	Activities
1	Implement the OPF process area (at least SG 1, but also SG 2)
2	Implement GP 2.1, Establish an Organizational Policy, for all relevant process areas
3	For the PP, PMC, CM, PPQA, and MA process areas:
a	Implement GP 2.2, Plan the Process
b	Implement GP 2.3, Provide Resources
c	Implement GP 2.4, Assign Responsibility
d	Implement GP 2.5, Train People
4	Implement specific practices of the PP process area
5	Implement specific practices of the CM process area
6	Implement specific practices of the PPQA process area
7	Implement specific practices of the MA process area
8	Implement specific practices of the PMC process area
9	For the PP, PMC, CM, PPQA, and MA process areas:
a	Implement GP 2.6, Manage Configurations
b	Implement GP 2.8, Monitor and Control the Process
c	Implement GP 2.9, Objectively Evaluate Adherence
d	Implement GP 2.7, Identify and Involve Relevant Stakeholders
e	Implement GP 2.10, Review Status with Senior Management
9	Implement SAM (satisfy GG 1 and GG 2), if applicable
10	Implement the basic Organizational PAs (OPF, OPD, OT) (satisfy GG 1 and GG 2)
11	Implement the IPM PA (satisfy GG 1 and GG 2)
12	For all process areas: Implement GG 3, Institutionalize a Defined Process
13	Implement the engineering process areas (GG 1, GG 2, and GG3): REQM, RD, TS, PI, VER, VAL

Institutionalization begins by establishing a management council and an engineering process group as the focal points for process improvement and transition as required by OPF.

With management commitment in place, the next step is development of organizational policies. A policy is a senior management vehicle used to communicate expectations, principles, and direction for performing and improving the processes. A policy typically establishes broad organizational direction. It should not simply restate PA requirements or specific practices, unless the organization feels that this is what has to be enforced and communicated. The policy should clearly state expectations at a fairly high level, leaving room for interpretation and implementation freedom when applied. We also recommend that organizations consider four "basic" GPs in order to provide a foundation for the forthcoming specific practices.

Next, two project management PAs (PP and PMC) and three support PAs (CM, PPQA, and MA) are implemented. Because this is the institutionalization approach, these PAs will enable the GPs described in previous sections and, in turn, will help the future stable and systematic implementation of all other PAs.

How long will it take an organization to implement and institutionalize these PAs?[14] Typically, this takes 8 to 12 months, but may take longer, depending on organizational priorities and commitment. If senior management is committed and the organization is ready for change, a shorter implementation time may be possible. In contrast, if priorities are constantly changing and process improvement forces are scattered, implementation will be slower.

After these PAs are implemented and institutionalized, the organization will be ready for additional process implementation and institutionalization. We recommend implementing and institutionalizing all remaining generic practices for the previously selected PAs (PP, PMC, CM, PPQA, and MA) thus achieving, but not necessarily appraising, capability level 2 for those areas.

If projects participating in process improvement have subcontractors, the SAM PA, up to capability level 2, should be implemented to help them select and manage their subcontractors.

Next, as shown in Table 6.10 and Figure 6.7, we may implement either all of the process management PAs and IPM or all engineering PAs. Implementing IPM is important when institutionalizing capability level 3 goals

---

14. Here, *implement* means that capability level 1 generic goals, GG 1, *Achieve Specific Goals*, in all relevant PAs are satisfied. *Institutionalize* means that generic goal GG 2 is satisfied in all relevant PAs.

because GG 3, *Institutionalize a Defined Process*, subsumes the IPM PA for its successful implementation.

Institutionalization approach—continuous representation: a variant

A variant of this approach is the one that capitalizes on implementation of organizational standard processes. A process at capability level 3, *Defined*, is tailored from the organizational set of standard processes, using tailoring guidelines, and is described in more detail than the managed process (capability level 2). This specifically helps organizations interested in minimizing variation in process performance across the projects and in efficiently implementing well-described processes on multiple projects.

By now we know that every PA has a generic goal, GG 3, *Institutionalize a Defined Process*, with two associated generic practices, GP 3.1, *Establish a Defined Process*, and GP 3.2, *Collect Improvement Information*. Theoretically, one can raise each PA to capability level 3 by implementing all GPs at levels 1, 2, and 3. This, however, is not the most efficient or optimal approach. Bringing PAs to capability level 3 may not yield an integrated, defined process. GP 3.1 requires implementation of some aspects of the OPD PA. OPD requires establishing organizational standard processes, including descriptions of the life-cycle models and tailoring guidelines. It also requires establishing a process asset library and database for storing various work products, measurements, lessons learned, and indications of improvements to the organizational process assets. By performing these activities, an organization will avoid revisiting and revising all PAs when attempting to achieve higher level capabilities. Effective process assets can be generated that will support the process elements needed to implement other PAs. In other words, the OPD PA enables the capability level 3 GPs.

The IPM PA also supports GP 3.1 and GP 3.2. IPM is based on the notion of the defined process, which is a tailored version of the organizational standard process. Through development of the defined process, IPM integrates the project management, engineering, and support PAs.

When an organization reaches capability level 3, it starts to realize the benefits of process improvements.

As noted previously, the OPF PA addresses activities crucial in establishing the process infrastructure, such as forming a management steering committee, forming the engineering process group, and selecting process owners to manage process deployment. OPF also requires organizations to define process needs, appraise processes and develop a process improvement plan—activities that are part of IDEAL^{SM} phases 1 and 2, as described in Chapter 2.

Some organizations ask if it is possible to start process improvement at maturity or capability level 3. The answer is yes, but ... this approach requires senior management's understanding of and commitment to process improvement. Later we describe the activities an organization can undertake if management has made the required commitment to process improvement.

With a management council established and the engineering process group staffed with process improvement professionals, the organization can solidify the process improvement infrastructure.

Next, the organizational policies, covering all relevant PAs, required by GP 2.1, *Establish an Organizational Policy*, must be documented and established. Because GPs 2.1 through 2.10 are all related to generic goal GG 2, *Institutionalize a Managed Process*, they are capability level 2 practices. GP 2.1 applies to all PAs, so one can apply it to all relevant PAs.

GP 2.2, *Plan the Process*, has to be addressed. As previously noted, this GP requires descriptions of each PA, including these:

- The process;

- Resulting work products;

- Work product standards;

- Specific objectives for the performance of the process;

- Dependencies among the process's activities;

- Resources needed for performing the process;

- Training required for process support;

- Measurements needed for process control;

- Reviews;

- Evaluation of process performance.

In addition, this GP requires an organization to develop a plan for performing the process and to identify the stakeholders that may be impacted by this process. This GP is most easily satisfied by organizations that have defined and described a set of organizational standard processes and have implemented tailoring guidelines, as required by the OPD and IPM PAs.

Depending on the standard process architecture, processes associated with each CMMI® PA can be easily identified. For example, the process architecture may contain configuration management and quality assurance process elements that will easily map to the CM and PPQA PAs of the CMMI®.

6.3 Transitioning from the CMM® to the CMMI®

This is not a requirement of the CMMI®, but it is an added convenience when defining the process architecture, appraising the processes, and determining potential improvements. Establishing a family of organizational standard processes is an efficient way of satisfying the requirements of each PA for defining activities and yielding optimal process descriptions and implementation.

GPs 2.3, 2.4, 2.5, 2.7, and 2.10 have to be implemented in all PAs regardless of CMMI® representation or approach. This will ensure that processes are implemented as described, resources are available, responsibilities are assigned, the staff is trained, stakeholders are identified, and status is reviewed by senior management.

GPs that are enabled by other PAs, such as GPs 2.6, 2.8, and 2.9, will obviously benefit from the higher maturity processes if organizational standard processes are already institutionalized and are implemented in the enabling PAs.

This means that an organization will do the following:

- Establish a management council and engineering process group.
- Publish its policies.
- Establish a set of organizational standard processes.
- Assign responsibilities and authority for performing the processes.
- Ensure that resources for performing the process are adequate.
- Train its staff in defining, tailoring, and performing the processes.

To further support the generic practices, CM, PPQA, and MA are the first PAs to implement.

Next, we can address institutionalization. By starting with the CM, PPQA, and MA PAs, GP 2.6, GP 2.8, and GP 2.9 will be enabled, as shown in Table 6.11. Implementing PP and PMC next will support GP 2.2, GP 2.4, GP 2.7, and GP 2.8.

Regardless of representation or approach, GP 2.3, GP 2.4, and GP 2.10 ensure that processes are implemented as planned, and that resources and responsibilities indicated in the process description are actually implemented.

What did we gain by using this approach? As an example, let us consider the CM PA. First of all, we have established an organizational policy for configuration management (GP 2.1). We have a process description in the organizational standard process that will support GP 2.2 in the CM PA. This process description, which will be tailored for use on a project, requires the organization to accomplish these tasks:

Table 6.11 Comparison of Generic Practices and Enabling Process Areas

	Generic Goal/Practice	Enabling Process Areas
GG 1	Achieve Specific Goals	The staged representation does not have GG 1.
GP 1.1	Perform Base Practices	The staged representation does not have GP 1.1.
GG 2	Institutionalize a Managed Process	
GP 2.1	Establish an Organizational Policy	N/A
GP 2.2	Plan the Process	None; in some instances, this can be adequately covered in PP. OPD can be used in more mature organizations.
GP 2.3	Provide Resources	N/A
GP 2.4	Assign Responsibility	N/A; the PP process area can be used.
GP 2.5	Train People	None; in more mature organizations OT can be used.
GP 2.6	Manage Configurations	CM
GP 2.7	Identify and Involve Relevant Stakeholders	PP
GP 2.8	Monitor and Control the Process	PMC and MA
GP 2.9	Objectively Evaluate Adherence	PPQA
GP 2.10	Review Status with Higher Level Management	N/A
GG 3	Institutionalize a Defined Process	
GP 3.1	Establish a Defined Process	OPD, IPM
GP 3.2	Collect Improvement Information	OPD
GG 4	Institutionalize a Quantitatively Managed Process	
GP 4.1	Establish Quantitative Objectives for the Process	QPM
GP 4.2	Stabilize Subprocess Performance	QPM
GG 5	Institutionalize an Optimizing Process	
GP 5.1	Ensure Continuous Process Improvement	N/A
GP 5.2	Correct Root Causes of Problems	CAR

- Provide resources.
- Assign responsibilities for implementing the process.
- Train the staff.

- Identify work products that will be under CM.
- Identify stakeholders that will participate in CM.
- Measure the configuration management process and determine its effectiveness.
- Evaluate adherence to the process by examining baselines and change control.
- Require senior management to periodically review process status and results

Because level 3 processes are described in more detail and are performed more rigorously than level 2 processes, they will support GPs 2.3 through 2.10. This ensures that these processes are evaluated and corrected if necessary. In other words, they are institutionalized. There are, however, some potential problems and issues. The IPM PA requires process plans to be integrated. For example, a project may have described the CM process in a CM plan while at level 2. To satisfy the IPM requirements, however, the CM process must be integrated with elements of other processes, such as management use of CM metrics or the use of peer reviews as part of change control.

Implementation of IPM may be too complicated for organizations without process improvement experience. To fully implement the IPM PA, an organization has to rely on both maturity level 2 (PP, PMC, and MA) and maturity level 3 (RSKM and VER) PAs. This also means that in order to implement IPM efficiently, we have to first implement the PP, PMC, and MA PAs, regardless of the capability level, and then the RSKM and VER PAs. Fortunately, RSKM and VER have smaller impacts on IPM than the other three PAs. In addition, RSKM is not required by ISO.

This section shows how one can use the continuous representation for CMMI® implementation and points to two possible routes for PA implementation. Most of the basic project management and support PAs can be implemented first. Alternatively, a somewhat tailored organizational standard process description can be used when describing those processes for individual project implementation. PP, PMC, and MA can be implemented when needed. In addition, the approach can be simplified by implementing only the first two specific practices of IPM (SP 1.1-1, *Establish the Project's Defined Process* and SP 1.2-1, *Use Organizational Process Assets for Planning Project Activities*), leaving the other practices for later inclusion.

Continuous representation—implementing engineering PAs

Although one can argue that implementing the engineering PAs is a maturity level 3 approach, what we describe next is markedly different. This approach is based on institutionalizing the engineering PAs first, as shown in Table 6.12.

Organizations develop products. Their processes may not be well described, managed, trained, or controlled, but they are still able to deliver their products. For organizations with strong engineering practices, it make a lot of sense to raise all engineering PAs to at least capability level 1 by implementing all of their base practices and satisfying GG 1, *Perform Base*

Table 6.12 Engineering Process Areas

Steps	Activities
1	Implement the OPF process area (at least SG 1, but also SG 2)
2	Implement GP 2.1, *Establish an Organizational Policy*
3	Implement base practices for the engineering PAs (GG 1): REQM, RD, TS, PI, VER, VAL
4	For OPF, PP, CM and each engineering process area:
a	Implement GP 2.2, *Plan the Process*
b	Implement GP 2.3, *Provide Resources*
c	Implement GP 2.4, *Assign Responsibility*
d	Implement GP 2.5, *Train People*
e	Implement GP 2.7, *Identify and Involve Relevant Stakeholders*
f	Implement GP 2.10, *Review Status with Senior Management*
5	Implement the PP process area
6	Implement the CM process area
7	For OPF, PP, CM, and each engineering process area: Implement GP 2.6, *Manage Configurations*
8	Implement the PMC and MA process areas
9	For each engineering, OPF, and basic project management process area: Implement GP 2.8, *Monitor and Control the Process*
10	Implement the PPQA process area
11	For each engineering, OPF, and basic project management process area: Implement GP 2.9, *Objectively Evaluate Adherence*
12	For each engineering process area: Implement capability level 2 practices (SP x.y-2)
13	Implement the SAM process area (satisfy GG 1 and GG 2)
14	Implement basic organizational PAs (OPD, OT) (satisfy GG 1 and GG 2)
15	Implement the IPM process area (satisfy GG 1 and GG 2)
16	For all process areas: Implement GG 3, *Institutionalize a Defined Process*

Practices. Please note that engineering PAs are the only CMMI® PAs that have base and advanced specific practices.

Again, we require OPF and GP 2.1 to be implemented first. Once the engineering base practices are implemented, the next step should include implementation of the PP PA. GPs 2.2, 2.3, 2.4, 2.5, 2.7, and 2.10 can then be implemented for those PAs. This is followed by implementing several PAs that enable implementation of GPs. The CM PA enables GP 2.6; the MA and PMC PAs enable GP 2.8; and the PPQA PA enables GP 2.9.

By implementing the organizational PAs and IPM, the organization is ready for capability level 3 implementation and institutionalization.

How is this approach different from the approach described in the previous section? It capitalizes on the implementation of those PAs that are the most important to the organization and with which the organization is most familiar. Once the organization becomes comfortable with improving those processes that are important to its business, and when some measurable process improvement results are achieved, it can address more complex PAs that may require additional training and deeper understanding.

Implementation of the OPF PA is vital for successful process improvement. Because it must be implemented regardless of the organization's selection of either basic approach, we started our process improvement approaches with OPF.

Staged representation

For the staged representation, a slightly different approach is required. Maturity level 1 is the default maturity level, at which some practices may not be performed. Obviously, in the staged representation one should consider implementing maturity level 2 first, as shown in Figure 6.7.

Even in the staged representation, we should select the order of PA implementation. Although it is a maturity level 3 PA, OPF is vital to successful process improvement implementation and should be implemented first.

The staged representation allows much less freedom than the continuous representation in selecting PAs. Typically, level 2 maturity is followed by level 3 maturity, and so on. Although there is no restriction on implementing certain higher maturity level PAs, it is expected that maturity level 2 PAs are satisfied first. However, even though OPF and OPD are level 3 PAs, they may be implemented before the level 2 PAs. For example, we would implement OPF and parts of the OPD before the level 2 PAs, such as SP 1.4, *Establish the Organization's Measurement Repository,* and SP 1.5, *Establish the Organization's Process Asset Library.* Then we would address all maturity level 2 PAs, and follow with the relevant maturity level 3 and higher PAs. Restrictions on the implementation sequence come when formally appraising the processes using one of the formal appraisal methods rather than from the CMMI® itself.

The staged representation does not encourage large variations in PA implementation. Let us look at the PA structure. At maturity level 3 the AB common feature GP 3.1, *Establish a Defined Process*, is followed by GP 2.2, *Plan the Process*. As was shown earlier, GP 3.1 requires the IPM PA to be implemented before it can be institutionalized. Although this is a natural sequence of GPs, an organization will benefit from raising all PAs to capability level 2 first, similar to CMMI® implementation using the continuous representation. In addition, all level 2 PAs contain the generic goal GG 3, *Institutionalize a Defined Process*. This means that as an organization climbs the maturity ladder it has to revisit the maturity level 2 PAs and elevate them to maturity level 3 by institutionalizing GG 3.

Again, there are several ways to address the level 3 PAs. Obviously, organizations should first implement and institutionalize the OPF, OPD, and IPM PAs and then tackle the other PAs. We recommend addressing the engineering PAs (in continuous representation terminology): REQM, RD, TS, PI, VER, and VAL, in parallel with, for example, RSKM and DAR, or OT.

Summary

The preceding discussion described how an organization without process improvement experience could advance its process capability or maturity level by judiciously implementing PAs and systematically improving its processes. Although either the continuous or the staged representation can be used, it appears that the continuous representation provides somewhat more freedom of implementation. However, careful inspection of the described steps shows that the majority of the PAs implemented in the initial steps of the continuous representation approach are identical to the staged representation level 2 PAs. This also points to the potential hybrid approach described in [5].

6.3.2 Transitioning from CMM® maturity level 2 to CMMI® maturity level 2

We have analyzed the similarities and differences between the CMM® and CMMI® PAs and their practices and explored the concept of threads in Section 6.1.5. Now let us see what a CMM® maturity level 2 organization has to do to transition to CMMI® maturity level 2. As mentioned earlier, such an

6.3 Transitioning from the CMM® to the CMMI®

organization will usually select the staged representation for this transition because of the familiar model structure. Table 6.13 indicates what a CMM® maturity level 2 organization has to do to satisfy CMMI® requirements.

Because a CMM® level 2 organization already has experience in process improvement, it should now concentrate on the similarities and differences between the models described in Section 6.1. To establish a stable framework for further implementation and institutionalization, we again start by implementing and institutionalizing the OPF PA, followed by the implementation of GP 2.1.[15]

It is important to note that some steps in Table 6.13 may be executed iteratively or in parallel with other steps. This is especially true for the PAs that support or enable generic practices.

Table 6.13 Level 2 Transitioning

Steps	Activities
1	Ensure that the process improvement infrastructure is still valid; include systems engineering (or software systems engineering) (OPF SG 1).
	For each level 2 process area:
2	Review and revise organizational policies; extend software engineering to include systems engineering (GP 2.1, *Establish an Organizational Policy*).
3	Review process descriptions and associated plans. Revise if necessary. (*Note:* if plans do not include process descriptions, they will have to be modified.) (GP 2.2, *Plan the Process*)
4	Train staff in new policies, processes, plans (GP 2.5, *Train People*).
5	Ensure that each process area has adequate resources and that responsibilities for performing the process are assigned (GP 2.3, *Provide Resources*; GP 2.4, *Assign Responsibility*).
6	Review stakeholder identification and involve stakeholders in process activities (GP 2.7, *Identify and Involve Relevant Stakeholders*).
7	Review implementation of the REQM, PP, PMC, SAM, PPQA, and CM process areas. Make sure that the CMMI® differences are accounted for.
8	Develop and execute a strategy for implementing the MA process area.
9	Ensure adequate implementation of GP 2.6, *Manage Configurations*; GP 2.8, *Monitor and Control the Process*; and GP 2.9, *Objectively Evaluate Adherence*.
10	Make sure that the MA contribution is taken into account for GP 2.8.
11	Periodically review this effort with senior management (GP 2.10, *Review Status with Senior Management*).

---

15. Note that in a practical application, a gap analysis would be performed to identify the gaps in the CMMI® implementation to be addressed.

Level 2 organizations need to revisit the already established PAs in light of newly added systems engineering aspects. A slightly different approach may be required after considering questions such as these:

- Is the organization developing software systems?
- Is the organization developing systems that contain hardware, such as satellite communications?
- Is the organization performing software maintenance?
- How large is the organization?
- How is the CMMI® going to be interpreted in each of these cases?

At maturity level 2, the inclusion of systems engineering in the model requires some clarification of certain specific practices. In the CMMI®, these clarifications are called *discipline amplifications*. For example, in the REQM PA, SG 1, *Manage Requirements,* has amplifications for both software engineering and for systems engineering. For software engineering, the CMMI® provides amplification by explaining that requirements may be a subset of overall product requirements (where there are other requirements, such as for hardware components) or that they may constitute the entire product requirements (for a purely software product).

Similarly, in the PP PA, SP 1.3, *Define Project Life Cycle*, has two amplifications. For software engineering, the CMMI® indicates that determination of project phases typically includes selecting and refining a software development model and addressing the interdependencies and interactions of its activities. For systems engineering, an organization should identify major product phases for the current state of the product and expected future phases, and the relationships and effects among those phases. In such cases, an organization should evaluate its approach. Several different approaches can be envisioned to support different applications and fields of implementation while maintaining the major core practices common to all applications. In all of these cases, the organization benefits from CMMI® implementation.

GP 2.5, *Train People,* also requires attention. The training curriculum of an organization transitioning to the CMMI® will have to address the differences between the newly added processes and the existing CMM®-based processes. For example, a data management process added to the PP PA or aspects of measurement and analysis that are also new at maturity level 2 will have to be addressed. In addition, SP 2.5, *Plan for Needed Knowledge and Skills*, in the PP PA represents a new requirement at level 2.

6.3 Transitioning from the CMM® to the CMMI®

Similarly, GP 2.7, *Identify and Involve Relevant Stakeholders*, will require reexamination of stakeholder identification and involvement for each PA. SP 2.6, *Plan Stakeholder Involvement*, in the PP PA helps to institutionalize this generic practice across all PAs.

The new MA PA will require special attention. Although level 2 organizations have some experience in specifying and collecting measurements, most of them will be deficient in several aspects with respect to this PA. They will need to complete these SPs:

- Establish measurement objectives (SP 1.1).
- Specify the measures (SP 1.2).
- Specify data collection and storage procedures (SP 1.3).
- Specify the analysis procedures (SP 1.4).

SP 1.1 implies that measures should be related to organizational needs and objectives. In the CMM®, this notion is not introduced until the QSM KPA at level 4. It is important to understand that there must be a reason for collecting and analyzing measurements. The data should answers questions about processes, products, and services. Responsibilities for data collection, validation, and analysis must be defined. In addition, this PA requires that the collected data be stored in the project-specific repository. As noted earlier in this section, organizations will benefit by establishing a process database for storing gathered information.

When implemented, the MA PA helps institutionalize GP 2.8, *Monitor and Control the Process*, across the PAs that also added some new requirements to the level 2 PAs.

For organizations that have achieved CMM® level 2 maturity and have established an independent software QA group, we suggest maintaining those groups, regardless of the CMMI's relaxed requirements. The SQA organization can be augmented with systems engineering skills, as required. Similarly, for those organizations that have established strong configuration management processes, we suggest maintaining those processes. With configuration control boards established, the stakeholders for that PA are clearly identified. The discipline amplification in this PA tells the reader that all software can be designated as one single configuration item, if software represents just a small portion of the overall product.

As indicated in Section 6.1.2, the SAM PA augments the CMM® SSM KPA. Transition will require attention in the areas of supplier selection, evaluation, developing agreements, transitioning purchased products into projects, as well as the inclusion of COTS products in this process.

6.3.3 Transitioning from CMM® maturity level 3 to CMMI® maturity level 3

An organization that has achieved CMM® maturity level 3 is well versed in process improvement and should not experience great difficulty when transitioning to CMMI® level 3. Typical steps for transitioning the CMM® maturity level 3 organization to the CMMI® level 3 are given in Table 6.14.

Similar to level 2 transitioning, some of the steps in Table 6.14 may be repeated and others may be executed iteratively or in parallel with the other steps. This is especially true for the PAs that were spawned from the SPE KPA in the CMM®.

In addition, all organizations transitioning from the CMM® to the CMMI® will have to develop, document, or revise their processes and will have to add new CMMI® activities to their existing process descriptions. If a well-architected process infrastructure is in place, it will have to be augmented but not significantly revised.

Obviously, level 3 organizations will also have to address transition from the CMM® level 2 KPAs. We expect that those organizations will first revisit the OPF and OPD PAs to make sure that all the required activities found in the CMMI® are addressed. For more details about the similarities and differences between the CMM® and CMMI® PAs, please refer to Sections 6.1.2 and 6.1.3.

First, organizational policies will have to be revisited and revised to reflect the new CMMI® requirements, particularly with respect to the newly added systems engineering activities. As required by the OPD PA, the additional processes, such as MA at level 2, and DAR at level 3, will have to be captured, documented, and included in the organization's standard process. OPD SP 1.2, *Establish Life-Cycle Model*, and SP 1.3, *Establish Tailoring Criteria and Guidelines*, will just require some fine-tuning. The CMMI® encourages organizations to generate a "family" of organizational standard processes, thus providing existing level 3 organizations with the means to elevate some of their defined processes to the level of organizational standard processes. Although this concept does exist in the CMM®, the CMMI® makes it more prominent.

Next, the organization has to revisit the IPM process and the generation of its defined processes. The CMMI® requires the project-defined process to consist of defined processes that form an integrated, coherent life cycle for a project. It also requires a project to integrate plans in an integrated project plan and to manage the project using those integrated plans. In addition, the CMMI® explicitly requires projects to contribute to the organizational

---

16. In this context *relevant* means PAs that are relevant to ISO 9001 implementation.

process awareness and their business goals. Our assumption for this discussion is that there is a senior management commitment to transition to the CMM® and a commitment to process improvement besides just attaining a maturity level.

An organization at CMM® level 2 that plans to transition to CMMI® maturity level 3 has several options from which to choose. The most fundamental choice is the selection of the representation: staged or continuous. We discuss both approaches next.

Within each representation, several strategic and tactical options can be selected. For example, if the organization chooses the staged representation as its transition option, its ultimate goal may be achieving staged maturity level 3. The same organization, by selecting a continuous option, may advance certain PAs to capability level 3 and then, by using equivalent staging, attain maturity level 3 after bringing all of the required PAs to the capability level 3.

Staged approach

An organization at CMM® maturity level 2 should start exploring the similarities and differences between the two models described in Section 6.1, with special emphasis on systems engineering activities. It should then address the approach described in Section 6.3.2 for transitioning to CMMI® maturity level 2 without actually attempting to attain level 2 maturity. The same strategy used for attaining CMM® maturity level 3 can then be followed using the CMMI®: institutionalizing the organizational PAs and then implementing the other level 3 maturity PAs. Detailed steps are shown in Table 6.15.

As we can see from Table 6.15, this approach is quite similar to the one described in Section 6.3.3, but with some subtle differences. Whereas the transition from CMM® level 3 to CMMI® level 3 requires augmenting the process infrastructure, transition from CMM® level 2 to CMMI® level 3 requires revising and rebuilding the infrastructure in terms of the CMMI®.

Undeniably, this approach is much more difficult than the one described earlier but it can also be more rewarding. The organization that undertakes this approach will have to establish organizational processes and then revisit the level 2 processes, add new process requirements, and institutionalize them as required by the newly developed organizational process definition. It will have to develop, for example, organizational training and an organizational process asset library and database. This approach requires both resources and an understanding of level 3 concepts similar to the steps outlined in Section 6.3.1. However, this approach may provide the organiza-

Table 6.15 Transition from CMM® Level 2 to CMMI® Level 3

Steps	Activities
1	Update the process improvement infrastructure; include systems engineering (or software systems engineering) processes (OPF).
	For each level 2 and relevant level 3 process area:
2	Review and revise organizational policies. Include systems engineering (GP 2.1, *Establish an Organizational Policy*).
3	Establish the organizational standard process, process library and database, and develop tailoring guidelines. Include additional processes as necessary and revise as appropriate.
4	Implement the IPM process area. Make sure that all new aspects of the IPM PA are addressed (e.g., SP 1.3 and SP 1.4).
5	Use new process descriptions and develop required plans. Revise existing plans, if necessary (GP 3.1, *Establish a Defined Process*; GP 2.2, *Plan the Process*). Manage projects using integrated plans.
6	Develop and execute a strategy for implementing the MA process area.
7	Review OT and make sure that the CMMI® differences are accounted for (OT SG 2).
8	Train staff in new policies, processes, and plans (GP 2.5, *Train People*).
9	Ensure that each process area has adequate resources and that responsibilities for performing the process are established (GP 2.3, *Provide Resources*; GP 2.4, *Assign Responsibility*).
10	Implement IPM SG 2.
11	Review stakeholder identification. Involve stakeholders in process activities (GP 2.7, *Identify and Involve Relevant Stakeholders*).
12	Review implementation of the REQM, PP, PMC, SAM, CM, and PPQA process areas from the level 3 point of view and make sure that the CMMI® differences are accounted for. Implement the remaining practices of OPD, OT.
13	Make sure that GP 2.6, *Manage Configurations*; GP 2.8, *Monitor and Control the Process*; and GP 2.9, *Objectively Evaluate Adherence*, are adequately implemented.
14	Develop and execute a strategy for implementing RD, TS, PI, VER, and VAL.
15	Implement GP 3.2.
16	Periodically review these efforts with senior management (GP 2.10, *Review Status with Senior Management*).

tion larger return on investment due to increased process efficiency and shorter process improvement implementation times.

Continuous approach

The continuous approach for moving an organization from CMM® level 2 to CMMI® level 3 may closely follow the variants described in Section 6.3.1.

In general, the objective is to establish the OPD and tailoring procedures and institutionalize the IPM processes. Then one would either institutionalize the engineering PAs or revisit the CMM® level 2 maturity levels to bring them to CMMI® level 3 maturity. Organizations aiming at attaining CMMI® maturity level 3 will have to address the new PAs such as RSKM and DAR, as well as the IPPD process aspects. By using equivalent staging, the CMMI® maturity level can subsequently be determined.

CMM® to CMMI® transitioning summary

After analyzing several potential transitioning approaches, we can see that there is no single optimal approach for successful process improvement implementation. Most approaches depend on the organization's process maturity (or lack thereof), gaps in the implemented processes, and process improvement objectives and goals. However, we can point to some of the more successful and more efficient approaches:

1. If an organization has no previous process improvement experience, the CMMI® continuous representation approach may be most effective.

2. For an organization that achieved a targeted CMM® maturity level, the CMMI® staged representation approach may be more effective.

3. In many instances, a "hybrid" approach may be the most advantageous.

6.4 Transitioning from ISO 9001:1994 to ISO 9001:2000

Differences between ISO 9001:1994 and 2000 were described in Section 6.1. Most transitioning approaches are based on those differences. Probably the most important difference is that ISO 9001:2000 now requires users to approach the QMS as a series of interconnected processes. For those organizations that simply used the 20 ISO 9001:1994 clauses, this change may involve significant and time-consuming rework. Although transitioning to the process-based approach may be difficult for some organizations and may require some additional work, they will not have to start from scratch—they should be able to reuse many of their procedures. However, to develop an efficient transitioning approach, they will have to understand the standard in depth. ISO has also issued transition planning guidance [7] that covers many of the items listed next.

As in the previous section, based on the initial IDEAL[SM] phases, a gap analysis should be performed. Based on this gap analysis and the organization's business and process improvement goals and objectives, a transition plan should then be developed.

Typical steps that an organization may take are shown in Table 6.16.

The first step is the most critical to the success of the transition effort; without management commitment, the effort will fail.

Next, staff will have to be trained on the new ISO requirements. Many commercially available training courses can be purchased. Alternatively, an organization can develop training courses tailored to its specific needs and culture. Many organizations have realized that it may not be sufficient to train their staff in the ISO requirements only. What they really needed was an understanding of the principles on which ISO 9001 was developed, particularly the customer-centered requirements and its process and system approach.

Similarly, internal ISO staff can evaluate the existing QMS and quality manual, or outside experts can be hired to help in quickly determining the problems. It may be more efficient to have outside experts evaluate the QMS because of their objectivity and knowledge of the applicable processes and

Table 6.16 Steps for Transitioning to ISO 9001:2000

Steps	Activities
1	Obtain management commitment: Get wide participation with representatives from all functional groups.
2	Familiarize staff with the changes from ISO 9001:1994 to ISO 9001:2000: Provide ISO 9001:2000 training.
3	Perform gap analysis: Review the existing QMS and quality manual. Does it conform to ISO 9001:2000?
4	Revise the QMS and quality manual to conform to ISO 9001:2000: Determine processes and their interactions.
5	Review existing procedures: Revise procedures and ensure that they conform to newly defined processes and ISO 9001:2000. Ensure that ISO 9001:2000 required procedures are included.
6	Train staff on: • QMS; • Quality manual; • Procedures.
7	Rerun gap analysis and identify problems and issues.
8	Correct problems.
9	Apply for certification/registration upgrade.

manuals. However, involving internal staff in the gap analysis has an advantage over hiring outside auditors, primarily due to the internal staff's process knowledge and interest in making necessary improvements to those processes.

Based on the gap analysis results, an organization should define processes that are comprised in its QMS [7]. This is by far the most difficult step. Procedures written to satisfy the ISO 9001:1994 requirements may still be applicable but will require an in-depth review to make sure that they fit the newly defined processes and can be efficiently applied. The processes may already exist but they may not be visible, that is, documented and maintained. ISO does not provide any help in deciding which processes should be considered. The scope should include not only those processes needed for product realization, which in most cases will be fairly well defined, but also those that are needed to manage, monitor, measure, and improve the production processes.

It is important that organizations determine the big picture first and then define their processes, process interactions and interfaces, resource needs, and measurements required to control the processes. Doing this process definition top down and bottom up is probably the most efficient way, resulting in larger process ownership. Going top down may appear to be the most systematic way but it may take too long to determine all the process, particularly those that are already being practiced. Going bottom up may enhance process ownership but it may be difficult to abstract processes from all of the detail.

In general, what the existing processes may lack are the measurement and control points that have to be determined for providing feedback needed for process management and control. Here again, the ISO requirements go beyond simple data collection and analysis. They imply a measurement process that interacts with the other processes, such as design, production, and purchasing.

An organization has to determine how it will provide the resources necessary for production, management, and measurement. Decisions must be made to address low-level details, such as determining which measurements are necessary for controlling production and determining customer satisfaction and deciding how they will be collected. Addressing customer satisfaction may be another challenge even for those organizations that are already monitoring it. The ISO standard requires that organizations enhance customer satisfaction, which implies not only reacting to the customer complaints but also proactively searching for ways to improve.

What is often neglected is the requirement for training the staff in the use of the new QMS. The processes embedded in the QMS will be quite different from the set of 20 quality procedures used in the earlier QMS. Therefore, the organization must ensure that the staff really understands this new process-oriented, customer-centered QMS. When the training is completed and sufficient measurements have been collected and analyzed, the organization will be ready to rerun the gap analysis and correct problems that may have surfaced.

Then they will be ready for the formal certification. This follow-up gap analysis may be skipped and the organization may attempt to go directly to certification because registrars may award certification with conditions and revisit the organization later.

As noted earlier, organizational objectives and goals define the course an organization may take. Is this organization truly interested in improving its processes or is its major objective to get certification and registration in the fastest possible way? Organizations that truly desire to improve their processes will have the largest return-on-investment when implementing the ISO standard.

References

[1] Paulk, M. C., et al., *Key Practices of the Capability Maturity Model® for Software, Version 1.1*, CMU/SEI-93-TR-25, DTIC Number ADA263432, Pittsburgh, PA: Software Engineering Institute, February 1993.

[2] CMMI® Product Team, *Capability Maturity Model Integration® (CMMI®)*, v1.1, Continuous or Staged Representation, CMU/SEI-2002-TR-003 or -004, Pittsburgh, PA: Software Engineering Institute, December 2001.

[3] *Mapping of the CMMI® to SW-CMM® v1.1*, http://www.stsc.hill.af.mil/consulting/cmmi/cmmiseswippdv11.pdf, Hill AFB, Utah, Software Technology Support Center.

[4] CMMI® Product Team, *Intermediate Concepts of the CMMI® Models, Overview Workshop, v1.0*, Pittsburgh, PA: Software Engineering Institute, June 2001.

[5] Savolou, A., and T. Kasse, "The 'Constagedeous' Approach to Process Improvement," *SEPG Conference*, New Orleans, LA, 2001.

[6] Cianfrani, C. A., J. J. Tsiakals, and J. E. West, *ISO 9001:2000 Explained*, 2nd ed., Milwaukee, WI: ASQ Quality Press, 2001.

[7] *Transition Planning Guidance for ISO 9001:2000*, ISO/TC 176/SC 2/N 474R2, Geneva, Switzerland: ISO, March 2001.

[8] Hoyle, D., *ISO 9000 Quality Systems Handbook*, 4th ed., Woburn, MA: Butterworth-Heinemann, 2001.

[9] Ketola, J., and K. Roberts, *ISO 9000:2000 in a Nutshell*, Chico, CA: Paton Press, 2000.

CHAPTER 7

Approaches Using ISO–CMMI® Synergy

Contents

7.1 Process improvement

7.2 First phase: Initiating

7.3 Second phase: Diagnosing

7.4 Third phase: Establishing

7.5 Fourth phase: Acting

7.6 Fifth phase: Learning

References

7.1 Process improvement

Chapter 2 discussed process improvement approaches and selected the IDEAL^{SM} model as the preferred approach. Chapters 3 and 4 described major frameworks for process improvement and concluded that we can efficiently and effectively create a framework based on the synergy between ISO 9001:2000 and the CMMI®.

Chapter 5 discussed that synergy. Because of their underlying engineering principles, we can even talk about their "equivalence." Thus, by satisfying one standard, we will be able to satisfy the other. This was shown for the CMM® and ISO 9001:1994 many years ago in an SEI report [1]. For organizations with CMM® experience, it is therefore sufficient to transition from the CMM® to the CMMI® and satisfy those additional ISO registration requirements not covered by the CMMI®. Similarly, organizations that were ISO 9001:1994 registered will have to identify gaps with reference to ISO 9001:2000 and then use the synergy to achieve both ISO registration and a CMMI® maturity level. Chapter 6 described the transition from legacy standards to the new versions.

In this chapter, it all comes together. Here we show how an organization can develop a process improvement strategy using the IDEAL^{SM} approach and ISO–CMMI® synergy.

As previously discussed, ISO 9001:2000 does not provide sufficient guidance for implementing improvements. Therefore, we will use the CMMI® to explain process improvement activities and then, by using the ISO–CMMI® synergy mapping, show how ISO requirements can be implemented.

We generally limit ourselves to discussions of capability and maturity levels up to level 3, although higher maturity levels will sometimes be addressed, particularly in cases where ISO 9001 may require processes consistent with capability or maturity levels 4 and 5. We will show that the IPPD version of the CMMI® may be beneficial when implementing ISO 9001.

7.2 First phase: Initiating

In the *Initiating* phase, the IDEAL^{SM} model requires an organization to set process improvement goals based on business objectives. Both ISO and the CMMI® also require (or at least urge) organizations to develop process improvement strategies based on their business objectives, mission, and vision.

When developing its objectives, an organization has to prioritize its goals and determine the consequences of weak or ineffective processes. The following typical business objectives may result from such analyses [2]:

- Reduce time to market.
- Reduce rework.
- Reduce the number of system errors that are discovered by customers.
- Improve delivery date predictability.
- Increase product quality.
- Increase market share.

Objectives and goals have to be measurable in order to determine progress and provide a stimulus for change. It is not unusual to find "Attain CMM® maturity level x" or "Achieve ISO 9001 registration" as business goals. During process improvement efforts, goals may evolve and need to be adjusted and changed. Such changes have to be communicated to the stakeholders.

Both ISO and the CMMI® stress management's responsibility to play an active role in sponsoring and establishing an infrastructure to support process improvement across the organization. As a reflection of these goals, organizations typically form management councils that oversee all process improvement initiatives, approve funding and staffing levels for process improvement, review progress toward goals, and adjust goals as required. In ISO terms, this responsibility is assigned to the management representative. In some organizations, a management representative is also known as the chief quality officer. Rightly or wrongly, such a person has historically been more interested in product quality than in process improvement. Hopefully, this will change with ISO 9001:2000, in which the management representative is required to report to senior management on the performance of the QMS, in addition to reporting on ISO compliance and customer satisfaction. The CMMI® requires an equivalent responsibility, which is typically assigned to senior management. In most cases, senior management forms a steering committee or an advisory group to address process improvement issues. This is achieved through implementation of the OPF KPA, as shown later in this chapter.

The CMMI® addresses the need to establish a lower level of management responsibility, which is typically vested in an *engineering process group* (EPG). The ISO standard does not specifically call for such a technical and implementation function, but instead vests this responsibility in management at both the senior and departmental levels. Having an EPG gives an organization clear advantages from many points of view. Most importantly, EPG members act as change agents, process engineers, process consultants, educators, and appraisers. Therefore, we urge organizations coming from an ISO background to form such groups. Several papers describe the organization and responsibility of the EPG. The original and oldest report [3] predates the publication of the CMM®.

In summary, in this first process improvement phase, a management council will be established to set process improvement goals and objectives, provide funding, and assign responsibility for process improvement to the EPG. By comparing ISO and CMMI® features, we see their synergy in action because both of them require similar management actions. We hope that organizations familiar with ISO and new to the CMMI® will be able to see the advantages of the EPG function, which strongly supports the spirit of the ISO 9000:2000 continual improvement principle.

7.3 Second phase: Diagnosing

With objectives defined and a process improvement focal point identified, an organization can start the *Diagnosing* phase. In this phase, existing processes are identified, captured, and documented and then compared to the models. This process is known as a *gap analysis* or *benchmarking*.

This analysis can be implemented in any of several ways. The most complete analysis uses a formal appraisal, such as the SCAMPI^{SM} method, which is described in some detail in Chapter 8. SCAMPI^{SM} has three approaches ranging from a complete detailed appraisal to a "quick look" appraisal. Similarly, for ISO 9001:1994 registered organizations, an ISO registrar may perform an initial gap analysis with respect to the new ISO requirements.

We recommend that organizations that do not have current gap analyses perform a formal appraisal based on ISO 9001, the CMMI®, or both. In the case of the CMMI®, an authorized lead appraiser familiar with both the model and the appraisal method leads this appraisal. With the help of the organization's appraisal sponsor, the lead appraiser assembles an appraisal team composed of several people familiar with the organization's processes and documentation. The size of the team depends on the maturity levels being explored and the number of projects being appraised. Typically, the appraisal team includes independent participants from outside the organization or from divisions or groups outside the appraised entity. Such outside members of the appraisal team add to its independence and objectivity. The team receives training on the model and the appraisal method. For ISO 9001, a registrar will typically perform a gap analysis, which will be then used for developing the organization's process improvement plan.

Why do we recommend a formal appraisal? The SCAMPI^{SM} appraisal method includes a well-defined set of documentation reviews, interviews, feedback sessions, and presentations to corroborate findings. The appraisal method rigorously determines an organization's process strengths and weaknesses and provides management with the data needed to develop a process improvement strategy. Because of the wide exposure the findings receive as part of the SCAMPI^{SM} method, it is expected that they will generate management and staff buy-in. Although the ISO gap analysis may be implemented less rigorously than SCAMPI^{SM}, it is also effective because it provides a detailed view of the gaps found in the documentation.

For organizations with some previous process improvement experience, a less expensive quick look, or SCAMPI^{SM} type C appraisal, may be more appropriate. While it lacks the rigor of a formal appraisal, it enables an experienced organization to address the areas with the greatest weaknesses and provides a road map for selecting an improvement strategy. For more details regarding SCAMPI^{SM} appraisals and the ISO registration process, refer to Chapter 8.

Appraisal results are delivered in the form of strengths and weaknesses, or in the case of ISO, as gaps. Typically, organizations concentrate on identified weaknesses or gaps, using their strengths as an indication that processes are already implemented and are being institutionalized.

The appraisal results may be provided as viewgraph presentations, reports written after the appraisal, or in simple spreadsheets that show how each model practice was satisfied. Typical output for a SCAMPI^{SM} appraisal is shown in Figure 7.1. In this figure, one can see at a glance which CMMI® goals and associated practices are satisfied. Practices are characterized as *not implemented* (NI), *partially implemented* (PI), *largely implemented* (LI), and *fully implemented* (FI), providing clear indications where process improvement efforts should be concentrated. ISO gap analyses provide textual information following the ISO requirements format. With both ISO and CMMI® gap analyses, an organization will be able to determine its process improvement approach, using the ISO–CMMI® synergy. Because many different gap analysis results are possible, we will limit ourselves to a few basic cases, which can then be generalized.

7.4 Third phase: Establishing

In this phase, an organization armed with the identified gaps, or weaknesses, develops its process improvement approach and starts to plan process improvements. Because process improvement may be spread over several years and consume sizable amounts of resources, it is important to treat process improvement as a project and include steps to define requirements, select an approach, develop a plan, track the plan, and report progress. In this spirit, as part of the *Establishing* phase, the organization develops a process improvement plan. This plan links identified weaknesses (or process gaps) to the process improvement goals and objectives that flow from business goals and objectives. The plan, described in Section 7.4.3, outlines an approach for achieving these goals and objectives. The following sections address the strategy portion of the plan and describe several approaches.

7.4.1 Process improvement approaches

Determining the process improvement approach is a major activity in this phase. Both the ISO technical committee and the SEI assert that the latest document revisions will not require major changes to existing documentation or process improvement approaches and that organizations using those models will be able to preserve their earlier investments. In practice, however, organizations that used earlier versions of the standards have realized that they must adjust their process improvement approaches and revise some of their governing policies, procedures, and processes.

In the past, many organizations started their process improvement efforts by first implementing the ISO standard and then adding the CMM®, or they started with the CMM® and then added ISO. Few organizations addressed both standards at the same time and capitalized on their synergy. An informal

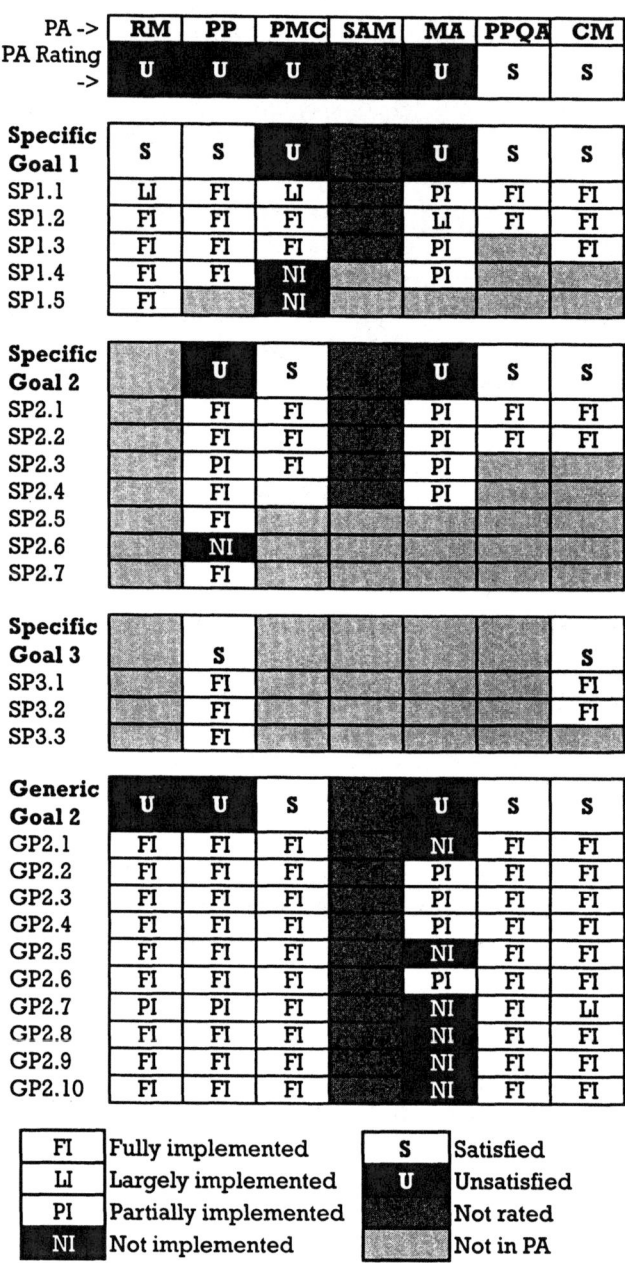

Figure 7.1 Typical output of the SCAMPI[SM] appraisal.

poll of process improvement practitioners shows that most would rather implement both standards at the same time if given the option. Concurrent implementation is more efficient because both models have similar concepts and have based their requirements for developing and managing product development on the best industry practices.

To prepare ourselves to use the ISO–CMMI® synergy, we first have to understand the major similarities and differences between the CMM® and the CMMI®, as described in Chapter 5, and consider the steps required to transition from one to the other, as shown in Chapter 6.

7.4.2 Potential transition cases

Chapter 6 discussed the transition from the CMM® to the CMMI® and from ISO 9001:1994 to ISO 9001:2000. This chapter explores using the ISO–CMMI® synergy not only to transition but also to create more robust processes, while attaining ISO registration, a CMMI® rating, or both.

We described several frameworks in Chapters 3 and 4 that can be used for process improvement. Here we consider how process improvement experience can be advantageous when using the ISO–CMMI® synergy. Table 7.1 indicates some possible cases for organizations that have decided to register with ISO 9001:2000 and attain a specific CMMI® maturity level. Transition approaches for these cases are described in detail in the following sections.

To preserve their certification, most ISO 9001:1994 registered organizations will have to transition to the new ISO standard. Similarly, many organizations have reached some CMM® maturity level and wish to transition to the CMMI®. Many organizations are both ISO 9001:1994 registered and have attained some CMM® maturity level. Because the sunset for both standards is at the end of 2003, those organizations will have to address the changes in both standards and develop transition strategies.

Table 7.1 Cases for Transition to ISO 9001:2000 and the CMMI®

Experience with ISO 9001:1994	Experience with CMM® v1.1 Level 2	Experience with CMM® v1.1 Level 3	Case Number
No	No	No	Case 1
No	Yes	No	Case 2(a)
No	Yes	Yes	Case 2(b)
Yes	No	No	Case 3
Yes	Yes	No	Case 4(a)
Yes	Yes	Yes	Case 4(b)

Since this book is primarily for organizations that would like to capitalize on the synergy between ISO 9001:2000 and the CMMI®, we do not address those cases in which the synergy between ISO and the CMMI® cannot be explored. For example, a number of organizations have attained some EIA 731 maturity level and will have to transition to the CMMI®. In addition, we do not address the cases in which an organization without previous process improvement experience plans to implement just the CMMI® or ISO 9001:2000. Although such cases are very important, they are beyond the scope of this book. Many basic transitioning steps found in Chapter 6 can be used for that purpose.

7.4.2.1 Case 1: transitioning to ISO 9001:2000 and the CMMI® without previous process improvement experience

Any organization embarking on the road to process improvement must understand the state of its processes, define the objectives to be achieved, and meticulously plan the process improvement effort. For organizations that have never previously implemented process improvements, this poses quite a challenge, especially when addressing management of change (Figure 7.2).

To describe potential process improvement cases, we assume that the organization is committed to process improvement and has established a set of process improvement goals and objectives. Without management commitment, as indicated by policies, funding, and resources, process improvement will falter. We also assume that the organization has executed the first two phases of the IDEAL^{SM} model.

Now the organization is ready to develop an approach based on the synergy between ISO and the CMMI®. The staff developing such an approach will have to be intimately familiar with and understand both standards. Even with the help of mapping tables, such as those presented in Chapter 9, a

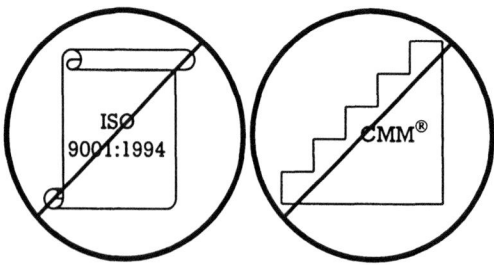

Figure 7.2 Case 1.

7.4 Third phase: Establishing

detailed understanding of the standards is required. Our discussion will often rely on the reverse mapping table shown in Chapter 9 relating CMMI® specific practices to ISO 9001:2000. Because this table presents the similarities in the CMMI® sense, it may be more useful in defining the direction of ISO implementation than the forward ISO–CMMI® table.

Consider the explanation of synergy given in Chapter 5. For the sake of clarity, we described the ISO requirements in light of the CMMI®—but we could have done it the other way around.[1] In that chapter, we showed how the CMMI® can be used to implement and satisfy the ISO requirements.

Implementing and institutionalizing the CMMI® will largely satisfy the ISO requirements. Of course, ISO requirements that are not addressed in the CMMI® will have to be added in order to be ready for ISO registration. However, organizations still have to determine the order of CMMI® implementation. The desired approach gradually satisfies both the ISO and CMMI® requirements, provides visible process improvement along the way, and achieves some intermediate organizational goals.

In general, the granularity of CMMI® implementation is at the PA level except when implementing the whole area would pose extraordinary difficulties for the organization. In some cases, implementing the whole PA will introduce processes that are not required for a particular ISO requirement but may be needed later when implementing another ISO requirement or a different CMMI® PA.

In practice, when a process required by the CMMI® is implemented it may not be immediately executed. Sometimes, those initial steps are quite time consuming and require long lead times. In the PP PA, for example, an organization estimates and plans a project, but it may take time before it starts to execute this plan and collect pertinent data. Similarly, the VER and VAL processes are established early, but are executed toward the end of the life cycle.

By examining the CMMI® architecture, one can see that most PAs have some specific goals that can be characterized as *establishing*. They are used once or infrequently during process implementation for creating the process infrastructure. The other goals, which can be characterized as *invoking*, implement and execute the process. They are used repetitively during process execution. This means that even where a PA is addressed in the early establishing steps, it will not be fully operational until an organization is ready to execute the invocation steps. Sometimes, the time lapse between establish-

---

1. The maps in Chapter 9 are many-to-many format. It is therefore difficult to explain the correspondence between these documents without the proper context.

ing and implementing may be quite long, particularly on the long-term projects.

Similarly, generic practices can be divided into those that support or enable the establishing activities and those that support the invoking activities, as shown in Table 7.2.

CMMI®-specific practices are shown in Table 7.3 as establishing or invoking practices. For example, in the CM PA, SG 1, *Establish Baselines*, contain practices that a project will execute when identifying configuration items, establishing a CM system, and creating or releasing baselines. In contrast, SG 2, *Track and Control Changes*, contains specific practices that are executed periodically during CM implementation, such as tracking changes, and controlling the configuration items. SG 1 is executed once or very seldom, while SG 2 is invoked periodically.

The separation of goals and practices into establishing and invoking can be efficiently used when implementing PAs. Table 7.4 shows that many goals and practices will be implemented infrequently, whereas others will be executed periodically. Therefore, one can group the establishing practices based on their technical relationships and execute the other practices periodically based on the selected life-cycle model.

Table 7.4 presents a generic approach to the use of ISO–CMMI® synergy. This approach can be used in organizations with little or no process improvement experience. Later, the approach is extended to address cases where organizations already have ISO or CMM® experience.

The table shows the ISO sections (or subsections) and the corresponding CMMI® PAs (and in some instance the CMMI® specific and generic practices). ISO-specific requirements that are not addressed in the CMMI® are shown in boldface. The table segregates the initial (establishing) steps from the

Table 7.2 Generic Practices: Establishing Versus Invoking

Establishing	Invoking
GP 2.1, Establish an Organizational Policy	GP 2.5, Train People (ongoing)
GP 2.2, Plan the Process	GP 2.6, Manage Configurations
GP 2.3, Provide Resources (may need to be revisited during implementation)	GP 2.7, Identify and Involve Relevant Stakeholders
GP 2.4, Assign Responsibility	GP 2.8, Monitor and Control the Process
GP 2.7, Identify and Involve Relevant Stakeholders	GP 2.9, Objectively Evaluate Adherence
GP 3.1, Establish a Defined Process	GP 2.10, Review Status with Higher Level Management
	GP 3.2, Collect Improvement Information

7.4 Third phase: Establishing

Table 7.3 PAs: Establishing and Invoking Practices

	SG 1							SG 2							SG 3					SG 4		
SP	1	2	3	4	5	6	7	1	2	3	4	5	6	7	1	2	3	4	5	1	2	3
Level 2																						
REQM	Inv	Inv	Inv	Inv	Inv																	
PP	Est	Est	Est	Est				Est	Est	Est	Est	Est	Est	Est	Inv	Inv	Inv	Inv (infrequent)				
PMC	Inv	Inv	Inv	Inv	Inv	Inv	Inv	Inv	Inv	Inv												
SAM	Est	Inv	Inv					Inv	Inv	Inv	Inv											
MA	Est	Est	Est	Est				Inv	Inv	Inv	Inv											
PPQA	Inv	Inv						Inv	Inv													
CM	Est	Est	Est					Inv														
Level 3																						
RD	Inv	Inv						Inv	Inv	Inv	Inv				Inv	Inv	Inv	Inv	Inv			
TS	Inv	Inv	Inv					Inv	Inv	Inv	Inv				Inv	Inv	Inv					
PI	Inv	Inv	Inv					Inv	Inv	Inv					Inv	Inv	Inv	Inv				
VER	Est	Est	Est					Inv	Inv	Inv					Inv	Inv						
VAL	Est	Est						Inv	Inv													
OPF	Inv	Inv	Inv	(infrequent)				Inv	Inv	Inv	Inv	Inv (infrequent)										
OPD	Est	Est	Est	Est	Est			Inv														
OT	Est	Est	Est	Est																		
IPM	Est	Est	Est	Inv	Inv			Inv	Inv	Inv					Est	Est					Est	Est
RSKM	Inv	Inv	Inv					Inv	Inv						Inv	Inv						
IT	Est	Est						Est	Est	Est	Est											
DAR	Inv	Inv	Inv	Inv	Inv	Inv	(as needed)	Est	Est	Est	Est	Inv										
OEI	Est	Est						Est	Est	Est	(infrequent)											
Level 4																						
OPP	Est	Est	Est	Est	Est			Est	Inv	Inv	Inv											
QPM	Est	Est	Est	Inv																Est	Est	Est
Level 5																						
OID	Inv	Inv	Inv	Inv				Est	Inv	Inv												
CAR	Inv	Inv						Inv	Inv													

Table 7.4 Process Improvement Steps Based on ISO–CMMI® Synergy

Step	ISO 9001:2000	CMMI®
1	Establish management responsibility, authority and communication (5.1, 5.5.1, 5.5.2, 8.2.2, 8.5.1).	Implement OPF. Implement GP 2.4, *Assign Responsibility*, and GP 2.7, *Identify and Involve Relevant Stakeholders*, in all organizational process areas. **Name management representative** (ISO 5.5.2).
2	Establish quality policy (5.3) and specify quality objectives (5.4.1); communicate the policy (5.5.3).	Implement GP 2.1, *Establish an Organizational Policy*, in all relevant process areas. Consider OPP SP 1.3, *Establish Quality and Process Performance Objectives*, and QPM SG 1, *Quantitatively Manage the Project*, to establish quality and process performance objectives. Communicate the policy (included in GP 2.1). Ensure that channels of communication are established.
3	Define and plan QMS (4.1, 4.2.1, 4.2.2, 5.4.2).	Establish OPD. Implement GP 2.2, *Plan the Process*. Implement GP 3.1, *Establish a Defined Process* (may need to revisit level 2 process areas in the staged representation).
4	Provide resources (6.0).	Implement GP 2.3, *Provide Resources*, in all relevant process areas. Implement GP 2.5, *Train People*, in all relevant process areas. Establish OT. May need to establish OEI SP 1.2, *Establish an Integrated Work Environment*, for ISO 6.3 and 6.4.
5	Establish configuration management (4.2.3, 4.2.4, 7.3.7 and 7.5.3).	Establish the CM process area. Specifically, establish SG 1. Need ISO **required procedures for defining the control of records** (ISO 4.2.3) and **for controlling identification, storage, protection of records** (ISO 4.2.4).
6	Establish quality assurance (8.2.2).	Implement PPQA generic practices. Establish VER and VAL process areas. Specifically, establish SG 1 for each PA. Revisit OPF (which was already implemented). Need ISO **required procedures for responsibilities and requirements for planning and conducting audits and process for selecting auditors** (ISO 8.2.2).

7.4 Third phase: Establishing 217

Table 7.4 Process Improvement Steps Based on ISO–CMMI® Synergy *(continued)*

Step	ISO 9001:2000	CMMI®
7	Establish measurement and analysis function (8.1, 8.2.1, 8.2.3, 8.2.4, 8.4).	Establish the MA process area. Specifically, establish SG 1. May also need to establish QPM SG 2, *Statistically Manage Subprocess Performance*, and CAR SG 1, *Determine Causes of Defects*. Need to address how the **customer satisfaction** will be obtained and used (ISO 8.2.1).
8	Plan product realization (7.1).	Establish the PP process area (SG 3 may not yet be required). Establish the SAM process area. Specifically, establish SP 1.1. Establish IPM process area (IPPD SG 3 and 4 may not be required, and SG 2 is not needed until step 12). Implement GP 3.1, *Establish a Defined Process*, if not already implemented. Revisit OPD (which was already established).
9	Perform product realization (5.2, 7.2.1, 7.2.2, 7.2.3, 7.3.1, 7.3.2, 7.3.3).	Implement RD, REQM, TS, and PI process areas. Ensure that **customers are informed** about product development, contractual matters, and their **feedback is addressed** (ISO 7.2.3).
10	Perform verification and validation (7.3.5, 7.3.6, 7.5.2).	Invoke VER and VAL process areas. Specifically, VER SG 2 and 3 and VAL SG 2.
11	Implement purchasing (7.4).	Invoke SAM process area. Specifically, invoke SG 2; SG 1 may have to be periodically revisited.
12	Perform measurement, tracking, reviewing, and auditing (5.6, 7.3.4, 8.2.1, 8.2.3, 8.5.2, 8.5.3).	Invoke PMC process area. Invoke PPQA specific practices. Invoke CM and MA SG 2. Implement CAR process area, as needed. Revisit OPF and IPM (which were already established). Perform GP 2.6, *Manage Configurations*; GP 2.8, *Monitor and Control the Process*; GP 2.9, *Objectively Evaluate Adherence*; and GP 2.10, *Review Status with Higher Level Management*; in all relevant process areas. Perform GP 3.2, *Collect Improvement Information*, in all relevant process areas. Need ISO **required procedures for the corrective and preventive actions** (ISO 8.5.2 and 8.5.3).

Table 7.4 Process Improvement Steps Based on ISO–CMMI® Synergy (continued)

Step	ISO 9001:2000	CMMI®
13	Other.	Need to address **control of production and service provision** (ISO 7.5.1). Need to address **handling of customer property** (ISO 7.5.4). Need to address **preservation of the product during internal processing** (ISO 7.5.5). Need to address **control of monitoring and measuring devices** (ISO 7.6.1). Need **procedure for handling of nonconforming products** (ISO 8.3).

execution (invoking) steps. The establishing steps, steps 1 through 8, address the CMMI® practices that are performed once, or seldom, during process improvement implementation. They are required for establishing effective processes and are a mixture of generic and specific practices. Steps 9 through 13 are the execution steps.

Note that the separation of the ISO requirements into steps is subjective and only indicates a systematic process improvement and implementation approach—in practice, those steps will be executed sequentially, in parallel, and iteratively. Similarly, when we indicate that a PA is implemented in a step, in most cases it will exceed requirements of that particular step and will contribute processes to several downstream steps.

It is natural for an organization to first establish the process infrastructure and then start executing those processes and collecting data. For those PAs, such as REQM, OPF, DAR, which have only periodically invoked practices, we will talk about their implementation when appropriate, and about their invocation when these practices are specifically called for.

Note that many PAs that are needed to satisfy the ISO requirements are at maturity level 3 in the CMMI® staged representation. Consequently, some organizations may find them difficult to implement because process and organizational changes may have to be introduced before those PAs can be successfully used. Thus, the continuous representation of the CMMI® may be a better choice for driving ISO implementation. In the continuous representation an organization can gradually increase the capability level of a PA and thus progressively satisfy ISO requirements. Even when using the continuous representation, an organization must decide when it is going to bring all PAs to some capability level to satisfy specific ISO requirements.

7.4 Third phase: Establishing

Let us now address each step in the table. To understand some of these steps, the reader may need to refer to Chapters 5 and 6.

Step 1: By implementing the OPF PA first, the organization will not only satisfy ISO Section 5 and some of its subsections, but will also satisfy certain ISO Section 4 and 8 requirements. Specifically, OPF will satisfy those requirements pertaining to internal audit (8.2.2) and to continual improvement (8.5.1), which are, of course, closely related. Section 4 requirements are addressed in step 3. Keeping the *diagnosing* phase of the IDEAL^{SM} approach in mind, we see how assessments and process improvement planning are related and how the synergy between ISO and the CMMI® is being used.

Implementing GP 2.4, *Assign Responsibility,* and GP 2.7, *Identify and Involve Relevant Stakeholders,* enables organizations to systematically address organizational responsibility and accountability and select and involve stakeholders, including customers and end users. Organizations should name the management representative as required by ISO. This responsibility may be vested in the management steering committee, or even better, in its chairperson.

Step 2: After responsibilities are assigned, the organization is ready to establish and communicate the quality policy and quality objectives. Organizational policies are established and communicated by implementing GP 2.1 in all relevant PAs. Practical experience has shown that publishing policies for all PAs at once is more efficient than publishing one policy at a time, particularly from the approval point of view. Although some PAs may not be required when implementing ISO requirements, organizations would be well advised to create policies for all maturity level 2 and 3 PAs. Because quality objectives are not addressed in the CMMI® until maturity level 4, OPP SP 1.3 and QPM SG 1 and its specific practices may have to be considered. However, addressing this SP or SG outside the quantitative process and project management context may be difficult, particularly considering the references to process performance objectives.[2] Many subpractices in those specific practices describe activities that an organization has to take when defining its quality objectives. Those practices and subpractices can be used for guidance only without fully addressing the process performance details. It is also necessary to ensure that the effectiveness of the QMS described by the organization's standard processes is communicated throughout the organization, as required by ISO Section 5.5.3.

Step 3: To define its QMS, an organization has to establish the OPD PA and implement its organizational standard process. OPD SP 1.4 and SP 1.5 require the establishment of the organizational process database and process

---

2. *Process performance* was defined in Chapter 4 in the QPM discussion.

asset library. Although these are not required by ISO, it is important for an organization to have a central repository where collected information can be stored. The database required by this PA is also needed later in the MA, OPP, and QPM PAs.

By implementing GP 2.2, all PAs will be planned. This can be done by establishing the organizational standard process and implementing it for each PA using GP 3.1. In contrast, using GP 2.2 alone to establish the QMS will require an organization to revisit each level 2 PAs when level 3 maturity is addressed and GP 3.1 is invoked. As noted in Chapter 5, implementing GP 2.2 repeatedly is not equivalent to establishing a QMS.

Step 4: Management's responsibility to provide resources is distributed across PAs through GP 2.3. Resources will have been needed to execute the previous steps, but this step ensures that resources are available to implement the plans.

GP 2.5 addresses the basic staff training requirements, but comprehensive training to ensure staff competence is established by implementing the OT PA. Implementation of the OT PA is the recommended approach. OT specific practices may have to be periodically invoked to implement a training program across the organization.

To address the infrastructure and the environment, the IPPD version of the CMMI® may have to be considered. In particular, SP 1.2, *Establish an Integrated Work Environment,* in the OEI PA addresses those concerns. Similar to the QPM and OPP PAs, OEI SP 1.2 can be used as a guideline for establishing an integrated work environment without actually implementing all of the IPPD concepts. However, it may be advantageous for an organization to institutionalize the whole OEI PA to help establish the IPPD infrastructure. This will allow the staff to be trained to exploit a collaborative environment in a workplace that maximizes productivity, and promotes and rewards team and individual excellence.[3]

Step 5: By establishing the CM PA, most related ISO requirements will be satisfied. ISO requires organizations to control design and development changes (7.3.7), perform identification and traceability of the products (7.5.3), and monitor and measure the product (8.2.4). The requirements in ISO Sections 7.3.7 and 8.2.4 will also be periodically executed in step 12.

The CM infrastructure is established in this step. Implementation of the CM PA will strengthen maintenance of product integrity through configuration identification, change control, status accounting, and audits. Although the ISO requirements will be exceeded by implementing this PA, it is defi-

---

3. Many organizations espouse concurrent engineering, which can be considered equivalent to IPPD.

7.4 Third phase: Establishing

nitely advantageous to implement CM in its entirety as soon as practical. Many configuration management tools are currently available to support implementation. CM SG 2 is invoked in step 12.

This step addresses two of the six documented procedures required by the ISO standard, although they are not necessarily required by the CMMI®. These are a procedure for controlling records (4.2.3) and a procedure for controlling storage, protection, retrieval, retention time, and disposition of records (4.2.4).

Although the spirit of those procedures may be adequately covered in the corresponding process descriptions and plans, organizations that aspire to ISO registration may be advised to explicitly write those procedures. This will satisfy the letter of the ISO standard and avoid potential misunderstandings.

Step 6: Although ISO does not explicitly require a QA function, we recommend establishing such a function by implementing the PPQA PA generic practices. PPQA specific practices will be implemented and executed in step 12. The CMMI® PPQA PA encompasses not only the audits required by ISO 8.2.2, but also provides visibility into, and feedback on, processes and products throughout the life of the project. Here again, ISO requires organizations to define a procedure addressing responsibilities and requirements for planning and conducting audits, and for reporting results and maintaining records (8.2.2). If such a procedure is not developed during PPQA implementation, it will have to be specifically written to satisfy this ISO requirement. Some of the ISO 8.2.2 requirements, such as internal process audits, were already addressed when implementing OPF. In this step, the organization may also establish the verification and validation environment and evaluation criteria.

Step 7: Next, an organization has to establish a measurement and analysis function by implementing the MA PA to support all of its management information needs. By implementing this PA, the organization will satisfy a majority of the ISO Section 8 requirements. [Control of nonconforming product (8.3) and improvement (8.5) are addressed in steps 6 and 1, respectively.] SG 2 of this PA will be invoked in step 12.

To address the statistical techniques indicated by ISO (8.1), an organization may establish some aspects of QPM. However, the QPM PA is more demanding than many organizations are able to sustain. Therefore, we suggest using QPM for guidance only (as opposed to fully implementing its specific and generic practices). Similarly, to analyze results to prevent problems from recurring, some aspects of the CAR PA may be implemented. Because CAR is a maturity level 5 PA (in the staged representation), it too should be used as a guideline only.

The CMMI® is not very explicit when addressing customer satisfaction and its measurement. For that purpose, organizations will have to specifically address customer perception of requirements satisfaction (8.2.1) by developing methods for collecting such data.

Step 8: To plan product realization, an organization has to implement either the PP PA, the IPM PA, or both. In CMMI® maturity level 2 terms, planning is achieved by implementing GP 2.2 in all relevant PAs, whereas in maturity level 3 terms, the organization's standard process is tailored and the project's defined process is established in this step. The project's defined process will be used when developing the product. Implementation of OPD, already addressed in step 3, is a prerequisite for this step.

IPM builds on PP processes so PP practices must be established first. Among other things, PP practices support definition and documentation of project scope, estimation of cost, effort, and schedule, planning for obtaining project resources and training, and stakeholder involvement.

The PP PA is sufficient to satisfy ISO requirements, but implementation of IPM will bring greater efficiencies. Organizations will be able to capitalize on their standard processes and use the more advanced project management concepts found in IPM.

For organizations with suppliers, SAM SG 1 is established in this step. Here again we are confronted with two IPPD-related goals that are not required by ISO. However, as indicated in step 4, the IPPD concepts may be beneficial and should be considered.

Step 9: This and the following steps address the process execution. The first process execution step deals with product realization. Product realization is well covered by the engineering PAs: RD, REQM, TS, and PI.

It is interesting to note that the specific practices in the RD PA that address requirements analysis and validation support the ISO requirement found in Section 8.4, *Analysis of data,* which specifically singles out conformance to product requirements. Depending on the selected life cycle, portions of this step may be invoked iteratively. In addition, this step and the following steps will constantly interact, meaning that the later steps use the work products produced here.

Step 10: Verification and validation are performed throughout the life cycle. The VER and VAL PAs satisfy and exceed the ISO requirements.

Step 11: Organizations that purchase products or parts of the products should consider the practices found in the SAM PA, particularly in light of ISO Section 7.4. This step may be invoked immediately after step 8, which also contains SP 1.1 of SAM.

Step 12: By implementing the PMC PA and relying on already established PAs (such as OPF, IPM, CM, and MA), the organization creates a measurement, tracking, reviewing, and auditing infrastructure that can support execution of all specific practices in those PAs.

In this step, PPQA specific practices are executed to provide an objective view into process and product implementation. This contrasts with the VER and VAL practices, which ensure that the product requirements are satisfied. In addition, PPQA also enables GP 2.8. GPs 2.6, 2.8, 2.9, and 2.10 further institutionalize the selected processes.

Implementation of the PMC PA satisfies many ISO measurement requirements. The ISO standard does not specify the measurements to be collected but does require that processes be measured to the extent necessary for them to produce quality outputs. In PMC SG 1, *Monitor Project Against Plan*, the CMMI® lists project performance measurements (such as monitoring planning parameters, project commitments, project risks, and data management) and provides additional guidelines in each PA by invoking GP 2.8. In the MA PA, the CMMI® provides guidelines for specifying measures such as earned value, reliability, and quality measures. Grouping all measurement and review processes together avoids duplication of certain practices defined across the CMMI®.

CM SG 2, *Track and Control Changes*, and SG 3, *Establish Integrity*, are invoked in this step. To address prevention activities, SG 1, *Determine Causes of Defects*, in the CAR PA may have to be invoked.

Two more ISO-required procedures, for corrective and preventive actions (ISO 8.5.2 and 8.5.3), are not found in the CMMI® and will have to be written.

Step 13: This step addresses those ISO requirements not covered in the CMMI® but needed for ISO registration. Although the handling of the customer property (7.5.4) can be accomplished by implementing the CM PA, special care should be taken when addressing intellectual property, customer supplied data needed for testing, and customer sensitive or secret data.

Two additional procedures for preserving the product during internal processing (7.5.5) and for handling of nonconforming product (8.3) have to be addressed.

Two CMMI® PAs were not invoked in the steps above, namely, RSKM and DAR. Similarly, some PA goals were also lightly represented, such as SG 3 in PP and SG 1 in PMC. An organization executing all of the listed steps would most probably attain level 2 maturity. To achieve level 3 maturity, it would also have to implement the RSKM and DAR PAs. Specifically, RSKM would be established in step 8 and then periodically invoked in step 12. DAR can also be established in step 8 and then invoked whenever a decision is required, for example, when selecting a supplier.

A major feature of process improvement efforts that are based on the SEI models, the CMM® and CMMI®, is the emphasis on institutionalization. The SEI's pioneering work on institutionalization since the late 1980s must be recognized. As noted in Chapter 4, the CMMI® further strengthened this concept by adding an institutionalization goal in each PA.

ISO 9001, through requirements for documented processes and procedures, enforces the notion of institutionalization, but has nothing that explicitly describes or encourages the concept. It is primarily concerned with the efficient and effective implementation of activities and their improvement. By using the CMMI® as a tool for implementing ISO requirements, an organization gains a lot more than just ISO registration. It gains enduring, stable processes that can be continually improved.

It is difficult to generalize this IDEAL^SM phase because gaps in process implementation depend on each organization's process maturity or PA capability. However, most organizations with no process improvement experience will exhibit similar problems. This is why the SEI developed the concept of maturity or capability levels to guide process improvement. The introduction of the continuous representation of the CMMI® provides an additional tool to address this difficult problem.

7.4.2.2 Case 2: transitioning to ISO 9001:2000 and the CMMI® without ISO experience but with CMM® experience

To address this case, it is sufficient to consider the transition from CMM® v1.1 to the CMMI® described in Section 6.3 and then, using the mappings between the ISO and the CMMI® given in Chapter 9, adding specific ISO 9001:2000 requirements.

This case postulates that an organization already has an active process improvement initiative based on the CMM® and has decided to transition to the CMMI®. At this point, we assume that the organization is at least at maturity level 2. If the organization is not rated, case 1, just described, can be used. As indicated earlier, to obtain ISO 9001:2000 registration, an organization must be at least at CMM® maturity level 2 and must implement many maturity level 3 PAs (or portions of thereof). Therefore, two instances can be distinguished: case 2(a), in which the organization operates at CMM® maturity level 2, and case 2(b), in which the organization operates at CMM® maturity level 3.

In case 2(a), in addition to transitioning to the CMMI®, an organization will have to add the required CMMI® maturity level 3 PAs and specific ISO requirements needed to achieve ISO certification. In case 2(b) the organiza-

7.4 Third phase: Establishing

tion will have to transition to the CMMI® and only add the specific ISO requirements needed to achieve certification.

In either case a CMMI® representation (staged or continuous) must be selected. For an organization familiar with the CMM®, it would seem natural to transition to the CMMI® using the staged representation and that is the approach taken here. Later, we address using the continuous representation advantageously in transition planning.

Approach for organizations at CMM® maturity level 2 An organization that has attained CMM® maturity level 2 has most project management and support processes already established and operational (Figure 7.3). However, the CMMI® has an additional PA, MA, which will have to be addressed. Also, institutionalization goals have been added to each PA and will have to be considered.

The steps a CMM® maturity level 2 organization must take to satisfy ISO requirements using the ISO–CMMI® synergy are shown in Table 7.5. The sequence of steps is the same as that shown in Table 7.4 for organizations without process improvement experience, but their interpretation changes due to organizational maturity.

To explain this case we use the staged representation approach based on the transitioning description in Section 6.3.2. Although the steps are the same, most of the organization's effort will be concentrated on reviewing the implementation of the CMM® KPAs to ensure that they are compatible with the CMMI® and then adding the CMMI® level 3 PAs. Implementation of the transition process from CMM® level 2 to CMMI® level 3 is described in Section 6.3.4.

Approach for organizations at CMM® maturity level 3 Organizations can benefit by implementing PAs that belong to higher maturity levels or by

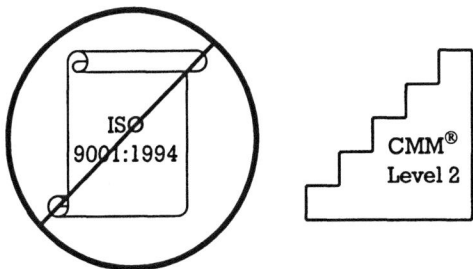

Figure 7.3 Case 2(a).

Table 7.5 Process Improvement Steps Based on ISO–CMMI® Synergy for Organizations at CMM® Maturity Level 2

Step	ISO	CMMI®
1	Establish management responsibility, authority and communication (5.1, 5.5.1, 5.5.2, 8.2.2, 8.5.1).	Implement OPF. Implement GP 2.4 (AB 4), *Assign Responsibility*, and GP 2.7 (DI 2), *Identify and Involve Relevant Stakeholders*, in all organizational PAs. **Name management representative** (ISO 5.5.2).
2	Establish quality policy (5.3) and specify quality objectives (5.4.1); communicate the policy (5.5.3).	Review Policies for maturity level 2 and 3 PA to ensure compatibility with the CMMI®. Revise as necessary using GP 2.1 (CO 1), *Establish an Organizational Policy*, for all level 2 and 3 PAs. Consider OPP SP 1.3, *Establish Quality and Process Performance Objectives*, and QPM SG 1, *Quantitatively Manage the Project*, to establish quality and process performance objectives. Communicate the revised policy (included in GP 2.1). Ensure that channels of communication are established.
3	Define and plan QMS (4.1, 4.2.1, 4.2.2, 5.4.2).	Establish OPD. Review existing CMM® level 2 plans and process definitions to ensure that they are compatible with the CMMI®. Revise as necessary using GP 2.2 (AB 2), *Plan the Process*. Implement GP 3.1 (AB 1), *Establish a Defined Process* (revisit level 2 PAs).
4	Provide resources (6.0).	Review level 2 PAs to ensure that required resources are adequate in CMMI® terms. Revise as needed using GP 2.3 (AB 3), *Provide Resources*. Implement GP 2.3 (AB 3) for all level 3 PAs. Review and update training for revised level 2 and newly required/revised level 3 processes. Implement GP 2.5 (AB 5), *Train People*, for all level 2 and 3 PAs. Establish the OT PA. May need to establish OEI SP 1.2, *Establish an Integrated Work Environment*, for ISO 6.3 and 6.4.
5	Establish configuration management (4.2.3, 4.2.4, 7.3.7, 7.5.3).	Review the implementation of the CMM® SCM KPA for adequacy in CMMI® terms. Revise if necessary to establish the CM PA. Need ISO **required procedures for defining the control of records** (ISO 4.2.3) and **for controlling identification, storage, protection of records** (ISO 4.2.4).

7.4 Third phase: Establishing

Table 7.5 Process Improvement Steps Based on ISO–CMMI® Synergy for Organizations at CMM® Maturity Level 2 *(continued)*

Step	ISO	CMMI®
6	Establish quality assurance (8.2.2).	Review implementation of the CMM® SQA KPA for adequacy in CMMI® terms. Revise if necessary to establish the PPQA PA. Establish VER and VAL PAs. Specifically, establish SG 1 in each PA. Revisit OPF, which was already implemented. Need ISO **required procedures for responsibilities and requirements for planning and conducting audits and process for selecting auditors** (ISO 8.2.2).
7	Establish measurement and analysis function (8.1, 8.2.1, 8.2.3, 8.2.4, 8.4).	Establish the MA PA. Specifically, establish SG 1. May also need to establish QPM SG 2, *Statistically Manage Subprocess Performance*, and CAR SG 1, *Determine Causes of Defects*. Need to address how the **customer satisfaction** will be obtained and used (ISO 8.2.1).
8	Plan product realization (7.1).	Review implementation of the CMM® SPP KPA for adequacy in CMMI® terms. Revise as necessary to implement the PP PA and the IPM PA. PP SG 3 may not be required. IPM (IPPD) SG 3 and 4 may not be required and SG 2 is not needed until step 10. Review assigned responsibilities (GP 2.4/AB 4) for all level 2 PAs. Implement GP 2.4 (AB 4), *Assign Responsibility*, in all level 3 PAs and GP 2.7 (DI 2), *Identify and Involve Relevant Stakeholders*, in all level 2 and 3 PAs. Implement GP 3.1 (AB 1), *Establish a Defined Process*, if not already implemented. Revisit OPD, which was already established.
9	Perform product realization (5.2, 7.2.1, 7.2.2, 7.2.3, 7.3.1, 7.3.2, 7.3.3).	Implement RD, REQM, TS, and PI PAs. Ensure that **customers are informed** about product development, contractual matters, and their **feedback is addressed** (ISO 7.2.3).
10	Perform verification and validation (7.3.5, 7.3.6, 7.5.2).	Invoke VER and VAL PAs. Specifically, invoke VER SG 2 and 3, and VAL SG 2.
11	Implement purchasing (7.4).	Review implementation of the CMM® SSM KPA and revise to make it compatible with the SAM PA. SG 1 may have to be periodically revisited.

Table 7.5 Process Improvement Steps Based on ISO–CMMI® Synergy for Organizations at CMM® Maturity Level 2 *(continued)*

Step	ISO	CMMI®
12	Perform measurement, tracking, reviewing, and auditing (5.6, 7.3.4, 8.2.1, 8.2.3, 8.5.2, 8.5.3).	Review implementation of the CMM® SPTO KPA for adequacy in terms of the CMMI®. Revise if necessary to implement PMC. Invoke PPQA specific practices. Invoke CM and MA SG 2. Implement CAR PA. Revisit OPF and IPM, which were already established. Perform GP 2.6 (DI 1), *Manage Configurations*; GP 2.8 (DI 3), *Monitor and Control the Process*; GP 2.9 (VE 1), *Objectively Evaluate Adherence*; and GP 2.10 (VE 2), *Review Status with Higher Level Management*; in all relevant PAs. Perform GP 3.2 (DI 4), *Collect Improvement Information*, in all relevant PAs. Need ISO **required procedures for the corrective and preventive actions** (ISO 8.5.2, and 8.5.3).
13	Other	Need to **address control of production and service provision** (ISO 7.5.1). Need to address **handling of customer property** (ISO 7.5.4). Need to **address preservation of the product** during internal processing (ISO 7.5.5). Need to **address control of monitoring and measuring devices** (ISO 7.6.1). Need **procedure for handling of nonconforming products** (ISO 8.3).

implementing PAs at higher capability levels (Figure 7.4). Most benefits are reflected in the scope of process implementation and in institutionalization, stability, repeatability, and ease of improvement. At maturity or capability levels 3 and higher, the scope of implementation is organization wide instead of project specific, thus enabling economies of scale.

Even for those organizations using the staged representation, implementing selected maturity level 3 PAs should not be a problem. Most process improvement professionals using CMM® v1.1 understand that establishing a software EPG (which is part of the OPF KPA) or implementing the Peer Reviews KPA bring benefits to the organization.

The steps for implementing process improvement based on ISO–CMMI® synergy for organizations at CMM® level 3 maturity are shown in Table 7.6.

7.4 Third phase: Establishing 229

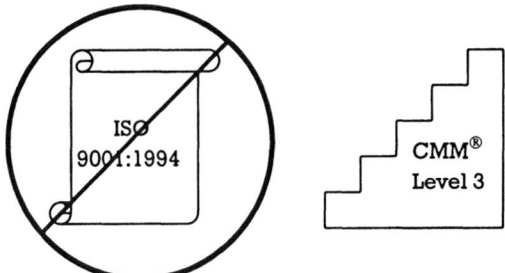

Figure 7.4 Case 2(b).

As before, the staged representation is used to explain the steps although it begins to look more like the continuous representation because we are only using selected PAs.

7.4.2.3 Case 3: transitioning to ISO 9001:2000 and the CMMI® with ISO 9001:1994 experience but without CMM® experience

More than 400,000 organizations are ISO 9001:1994 registered and most of them will have to transition to ISO 9001:2000 (Figure 7.5). Significant portions of those organizations develop software and will need guidance in applying the ISO 9001:2000 requirements to software. ISO 9000-3:1997 provided guidelines for applying ISO 9001:1994 to software. ISO initially considered the revised standard sufficiently generic to be used in most applications, and revision of ISO 9000-3 was transferred to a different committee. As of this writing, ISO 9000-3:2000 has not yet been released as an ISO standard.[4]

ISO 9001:1994 registered organizations (Figure 7.5) should review the transition steps described in Section 6.4 to familiarize themselves with the new ISO requirements. Because they develop systems with large software content, they may consider using the CMMI® to interpret those requirements in terms of systems and software engineering and to establish the process improvement activities required by ISO 9004:2000. For those organizations, the most appropriate approach is to follow steps in case 1 described earlier.

If the organization's quality manual was developed by following the 20 ISO 9001:1994 clauses, their first priority will be to determine how much of the manual can be preserved and how much will have to be revised.

---

4. From [4] one can see that it follows the structure of ISO 9000-3:1997.

Table 7.6 Process Improvement Steps Based on ISO–CMMI® Synergy for Organizations at CMM® Maturity Level 3

Step	ISO	CMMI®
1	Establish management responsibility, authority, and communication (5.1, 5.5.1, 5.5.2, 8.2.2, 8.5.1).	Review implementation of the CMM® OPF KPA for adequacy and revise to make it compatible with the CMMI® OPF PA, if necessary. Implement GP 2.4 (AB 4), *Assign Responsibility,* and GP 2.7 (DI 2), *Identify and Involve Relevant Stakeholders,* in all organizational PAs. **Name management representative** (ISO 5.5.2).
2	Establish quality policy (5.3) and specify quality objectives (5.4.1); communicate the policy (5.5.3).	Review policies for all relevant PAs to ensure compatibility with the CMMI®. Revise as needed using GP 2.1 (CO 1), *Establish an Organizational Policy.* Consider OPP SP 1.3, *Establish Quality and Process Performance Objectives,* and QPM SG 1, *Quantitatively Manage the Project,* to establish quality and process performance objectives. Communicate the policy (included in GP 2.1). Ensure that channels of communication are established.
3	Define and plan QMS (4.1, 4.2.1, 4.2.2, 5.4.2).	Review implementation of the CMM® OPD KPA for adequacy and revise to make it compatible with the CMMI® OPD PA, if necessary. Review existing plans and process definitions for all relevant PAs to ensure that CMMI® requirements are satisfied. Revise as needed to satisfy GP 2.2 (AB 2), *Plan the Process.* Revisit all relevant PAs to ensure that GP 3.1 (AB 1), *Establish a Defined Process,* is addressed.
4	Provide resources (6.0).	Review GP 2.3 (AB 3), *Provide Resources,* in all relevant PAs to ensure that required resources are adequate in the CMMI® terms. Review the CMM® TP KPA for adequacy. Revise, if necessary, to establish the CMMI® OT PA. Review GP 2.5 (AB 5), *Train People,* for all relevant PAs. May need to establish OEI SP 1.2, *Establish an Integrated Work Environment,* for ISO 6.3 and 6.4.

7.4 Third phase: Establishing

Table 7.6 Process Improvement Steps Based on ISO–CMMI® Synergy for Organizations at CMM® Maturity Level 3 *(continued)*

Step	ISO	CMMI®
5	Establish configuration management (4.2.3, 4.2.4, 7.3.7, 7.5.3).	Review implementation of the CMM® SCM KPA for adequacy, especially in light of GP 3.1. Compare to the CMMI® CM PA and revise, if necessary. Need ISO **required procedures for defining the control of records** (ISO 4.2.3) and **for controlling identification, storage, protection of records** (ISO 4.2.4).
6	Establish quality assurance (8.2.2).	Review implementation of the CMM® SQA KPA for adequacy, especially in light of GP 3.1. Compare to PPQA and revise, if necessary. Concentrate on the GPs. SPs will implemented in step 12. Establish VER and VAL PAs. Specifically establish SG 1 in each PA. Revisit OPF, which was already implemented. Need ISO **required procedures for responsibilities and requirements for planning and conducting audits and process for selecting auditors** (ISO 8.2.2).
7	Establish measurement and analysis function (8.1, 8.2.1, 8.2.3, 8.2.4, 8.4).	Establish the MA PA. Specifically, establish SG 1. May also need to establish QPM SG 2, *Statistically Manage Subprocess Performance*, and CAR SG 1, *Determine Causes of Defects*. Need to address how **customer satisfaction** will be obtained and used (ISO 8.2.1).
8	Plan product realization (7.1).	Review implementation of the CMM® SPP & ISM KPAs. Compare to the CMMI® PP and IPM PAs (especially in light of GP 3.1) and revise, if necessary. PP SG 3 may not be required. IPM (IPPD) SG 3 and 4 may not be required and SG 2 is not needed until step 10. Revisit GP 3.1 (AB 1), *Establish a Defined Process*, for all PAs. Revisit OPD, which was already established.
9	Perform product realization (5.2, 7.2.1, 7.2.2, 7.2.3, 7.3.1, 7.3.2, 7.3.3).	Implement RD, REQM, TS, and PI PAs. Ensure that **customers are informed** about product development, contractual matters, and their **feedback is addressed** (ISO 7.2.3).

Table 7.6 Process Improvement Steps Based on ISO–CMMI® Synergy for Organizations at CMM® Maturity Level 3 *(continued)*

Step	ISO	CMMI®
10	Perform verification and validation (7.3.5, 7.3.6, 7.5.2).	Invoke VER and VAL PAs; specifically invoke VER SG 2 and 3, and VAL SG 2.
11	Implement purchasing (7.4).	Review implementation of the CMM® SSM KPA and revise to make it compatible with the CMMI® SAM PA. SG 1 may have to be periodically revisited.
12	Perform measurement, tracking, reviewing, and auditing (5.6, 7.3.4, 8.2.1, 8.2.3, 8.5.2, 8.5.3).	Review implementation of the CMM® SPTO KPA for adequacy (especially in light of GP 3.1) in terms of the CMMI®. Revise if necessary to implement the PMC PA. Invoke PPQA specific practices. Invoke CM and MA SG 2. Implement CAR PA. Revisit OPF and IPM, which were already established. Perform GP 2.6 (DI 1), *Manage Configurations*; GP 2.8 (DI 3), *Monitor and Control the Process*; GP 2.9 (VE 1), *Objectively Evaluate Adherence*; and GP 2.10 (VE 2), *Review Status with Higher Level Management*; in all relevant PAs. Perform GP 3.2 (DI 4), *Collect Improvement Information*, in all relevant PAs. Need ISO **required procedures for the corrective and preventive actions** (ISO 8.5.2, and 8.5.3).
13	Other	Need to **address control of production and service provision** (ISO 7.5.1). Need to address **handling of customer property** (ISO 7.5.4). Need to **address preservation of the product** during internal processing (ISO 7.5.5). Need to **address control of monitoring and measuring devices** (ISO 7.6.1). Need **procedure for handling of nonconforming products** (ISO 8.3).

Annex B in the ISO standard can be used for evaluating the differences between the revisions. The ISO–CMMI® synergy described in Chapter 5 will also help. Armed with this knowledge, they will be able to further tailor the steps described for case 1 and capitalize on the reuse of existing processes and procedures.

7.4 Third phase: Establishing   233

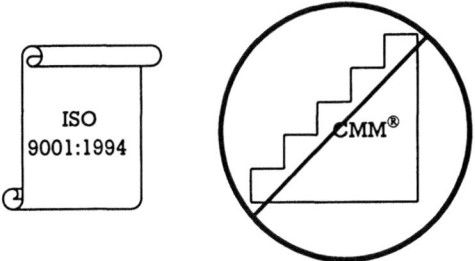

Figure 7.5 Case 3.

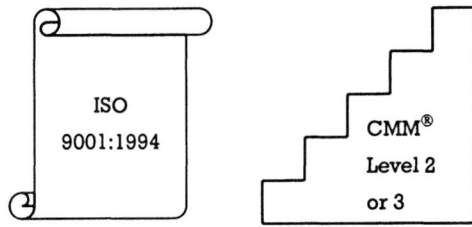

Figure 7.6 Case 4.

7.4.2.4 Case 4: transitioning to ISO 9001:2000 and the CMMI® with ISO 9001:1994 and CMM® experience

This case applies to the most advanced organizations—those who are both ISO certified/registered and have reached some CMM® maturity level (Figure 7.6). Depending on their CMM® maturity level, such an organization can use one of the cases described earlier. In general, those organizations have management councils and EPGs actively acting as catalysts for change. The EPG will, under management council guidance, develop the transition strategy.

The biggest challenge for those organizations will be restructuring their quality manual to reflect the new ISO requirements. Depending on the architecture of the quality manual, different activities will be required. Typically, organizations that are ISO 9001:1994 registered and have active software process improvement initiatives based on the CMM® used the ISO architecture to develop their quality manuals, either directly from ISO 9001:1994 or through ISO 9000-3. Most of them are familiar with the ISO–CMM® mapping described in [1], which may have helped them to understand the similarities and differences between those documents. They then added the software process requirements in the CMM® and eventually harmonized those requirements with the ISO requirements.

As in an earlier section, we distinguish two instances: In case 4(a), the organization is ISO 9001:1994 registered and operates at CMM® maturity level 2, and in case 4(b), the organization is ISO 9001:1994 registered and operates at CMM® maturity level 3.

ISO 9001:1994 registered organization that operates at CMM® level 2   Organizations that are ISO 9001:1994 registered and operate at CMM® maturity level 2 will have to transition to ISO 9001:2000 and the CMMI® by using Table 6.12 in Section 6.4 and the steps outlined earlier in this chapter for case 2(a).

ISO 9001:1994 registered organization that operates at CMM® level 3   Organizations that are ISO 9001:1994 registered and operate at CMM® maturity level 3 will have to transition to ISO 9001:2000 and the CMMI® by using Table 6.12 in Section 6.4 and the steps outlined earlier in this chapter for case 2(b).

7.4.3 Process improvement planning

After selecting a process improvement approach using the ISO–CMMI® synergy, the organization is able to start process improvement planning. Some organizations will distinguish strategic and tactical process improvement plans. Strategic plans address top-level organizational issues, whereas tactical plans address specific, mostly project-level, process improvement implementation issues. The plan(s) prioritize the issues to be addressed, describe the process improvement strategy, and estimate the resources required to implement the plan. The plan also addresses responsibilities, schedule, milestones, risks, and the measurements that will be used to track process improvement progress. A typical table of contents for a process improvement plan is shown in Table 7.7.

Organizations already familiar with process improvement under the CMM® will update their process improvement plans to reflect the new ISO and CMMI® requirements. In any case, resources and schedules for implementing the plan must be determined.

An effective approach to implementing process improvement is the use of PATs. Typically, a PAT is formed to address some process problem, such as one of these:

- Defining a requirements development process;
- Investigating estimation techniques;
- Developing a decision and analysis process.

Table 7.7 Typical Table of Contents for a Process Improvement Plan

1	**Introduction**
1.1	Purpose of this PIP
1.2	Corporate Goals
1.3	Scope
2	**Goals**
2.1	Process Improvement Objectives
2.2	Success Criteria
2.3	Constraints
2.4	Risks
3	**Process Improvement Participants**
3.1	Management
3.2	Engineering Process Group
3.3	Projects
4	**Process Improvement Implementation**
4.1	PI Tasks
4.2	PI Management
4.2.1	Tracking
4.2.2	Measurement
4.2.3	Risk Management
4.2.4	Configuration Management
4.2.5	Quality Methods
4.2.6	Training
4.3	Schedule
4.4	Resources

The PAT has a leader, who usually is an EPG member or subject matter expert interested in process improvement. Members of the PAT are also subject matter experts who bring project process implementation know-how to the PAT. In that way, the PAT ensures process buy-in and avoids the "not invented here" syndrome. The PAT determines deliverables, schedules, and interim milestones so that its progress can be measured. On completion of its assignment, which should not exceed a few months, the PAT disbands.

It is important to remember that process improvement efforts should be run as projects. Therefore, a process improvement plan should be accepted and approved by the major stakeholders in that plan—senior management, process improvement professionals, and practitioners. As is the case with project plans, this plan has to be realistic, with sufficient funding and resources, measurable goals, and milestones.

7.5 Fourth phase: Acting

By completing the *Establishing* phase, the organization has determined process deficiencies relative to both ISO and the CMMI® and has developed methods to improve those processes and, in turn, process work products. The *Acting* phase is very sensitive. It provides the bridge between process improvement activities and project production activities.

A large organization will often select a project or a group of projects to pilot newly developed processes, measure their effectiveness, and collect lessons learned. After analysis of the results, the processes will be propagated throughout the organization. Smaller organizations with more limited resources may not be able to afford the pilot approach and will tend to gradually implement those new processes and measure their effectiveness as they move toward selected goals.

Normally, PATs remain active during pilot efforts to collect process measurements and lessons learned and feed them back into process descriptions. The PATs disband on pilot or process implementation completion. Continuing support and improvement become the responsibility of the EPG and project change agents. Although the use of pilot projects is an effective technique, many ISO requirements will be satisfied when the process infrastructure is established and institutionalization has begun.

As organizations start implementing identified process improvements based on their process improvement plans, they will be able to determine if the CMMI® and ISO requirements have been satisfied and if their goals and objectives have been satisfied. The effectiveness of the introduced changes will be measured, resulting in feedback and corrective actions, if necessary.

7.6 Fifth phase: Learning

The *Learning* phase enables process practitioners using the IDEAL^{SM} model to continue process improvement by repeating the *Diagnosing* and subsequent phases without going back to the *Initiating* phase. The EPG should analyze the whole cycle and ensure that most procedural problems are resolved in the following cycle. In most cases, the EPG will address issues stemming from the selected approach and make corrections to that approach. It will review high-level process improvement goals, remove those that were satisfied, and add new high-level goals resulting from the new needs of the organization.

After lessons learned are analyzed and new goals are established, new process improvement proposals may be developed. These will result in requests to the management council for approval, funding, and resources.

The *Learning* phase may further fine-tune the synergy implementation, for example, by adding or modifying transitioning steps, changing process descriptions to better satisfy both standards, or by selecting measurements that are more appropriate for enabling rapid improvements.

In addition, it may be necessary to review how the process improvement program was managed and introduce changes.

References

[1] Paulk, M. C., *A Comparison of ISO 9001 and the Capability Maturity Model® for Software*, CMU/SEI-94-TR-12, Pittsburgh, PA: Software Engineering Institute, August 1994.

[2] CMMI® Product Team, *Capability Maturity Model Integration® (CMMI®), v1.1, Continuous Representation*, CMU/SEI-2002-TR-003, Pittsburgh, PA: Software Engineering Institute, December 2001.

[3] Fowler, P., and S. Rifkin, *Software Engineering Process Group Guide*, CMU/SEI-90-TR-24, Pittsburgh, PA: Software Engineering Institute, September 1990.

[4] *Guidelines for the Application of ISO/IEC 9001 to the Development, Supply, and Maintenance of Software*, TC/SC SC7 WG18N61, ISO/IEC CD 9000-3, Version for FCD Ballot, Geneva, Switzerland: ISO, December 2001.

CHAPTER 8

Appraisal/Registration

Contents

8.1 SCAMPI^{SM}

8.2 ISO 9001:2000 registration process

8.3 TickIT

8.4 Using SCAMPI^{SM} to prepare for ISO 9001:2000 registration

8.5 Summary

References

In this chapter, we briefly describe two processes—one for appraising the compliance of organizational processes to the CMMI® and the other for registering the organization with ISO. Then, based on the synergy between the CMMI® and ISO 9001:2000, we describe how the SCAMPI^{SM} method can be used to prepare an organization for ISO registration.

The primary purpose of appraisals should be for process improvement rather than for achieving a maturity or capability level or obtaining ISO certification. Any appraisal should be linked to organizational business goals and objectives. A major benefit that comes from understanding the appraisal method is that the organization gains an understanding of the process outcomes that have to be in place to ensure that those processes are properly implemented and will endure. The appraisal delivers a statement of organizational strengths and weaknesses that will then lead toward improving process performance.

Several questions must be answered when choosing an appraisal method:

- What is expected from an appraisal method?
- What are the characteristics of an efficient and effective appraisal method?
- What will be done with the appraisal results?

The appraisal method should provide insight into the organization's process capabilities by identifying its strengths and weaknesses relative to the chosen model, such as ISO 9001,

239

CMM®, CMMI®, or EIA 731. By knowing its weaknesses, the organization can prioritize improvement plans. A second appraisal objective is benchmarking—knowledge of the relative standing of organizational process capability as compared to the rest of the industry or field. A third objective is formal certification that can be used as a mark of excellence recognized by both users and competitors.

Obviously, all organizations want to minimize the time spent preparing for and executing the appraisal while still producing high-quality results. Unfortunately, as the models become larger and more complex, more time is needed to analyze organizational processes for compliance. Despite these difficulties, the selected method must provide consistent and repeatable results without depending on the appraisal leader or the appraisal team but instead relying solely on the examination of objective evidence.

8.1 SCAMPI^SM

The SCAMPI^SM method was developed over several years in parallel with the CMMI®. It is part of the CMMI® product suite, which includes models, appraisal materials, and training materials.

8.1.1 Some history

Several process assessment methodologies were developed in the late 1980s to determine how well an organization's processes complied with a selected model. Some of those methodologies were developed for specific models or purposes, most notably ISO registration or the Malcolm Baldrige National Quality Award. In addition, many professional societies developed benchmarking techniques to determine how well organizations comply with their own specific requirements.

For software, the *software process assessment* (SPA) method was developed by the SEI in the 1980s. This was the precursor to several current assessment methodologies. The SPA method provided good results in a short time—typically, 1 week of documentation reviews and interviews with the organizational personnel. However, it had some problems with accuracy and repeatability. There was a need for an appraisal method that had greater consistency and implementation rigor so the results could be used not only for process improvement but also for source selection and project monitoring.

The current SCAMPI^SM method, version 1.1 [1], released in December 2001, has evolved from earlier appraisal methods. It satisfies the *Appraisal Requirements for CMMI®* (ARC) [2]. ARC, in turn, has its roots in the *CMM®*

Appraisal Framework (CAF) [3]. Both of these documents were developed to capture a set of requirements for appraisal methods, thereby enabling the design of appraisal methods for the respective models. Because the CMMI® contains an expanded set of models in two representations, its appraisal method had to accommodate those special aspects.

Additional influences on the ARC requirements came from the EIA/IS 731.2 appraisal method [4], and the need to be compatible with the emerging international standard ISO/IEC 15504 (known as SPICE during its development and trial use) [5]. SCAMPI^{SM} itself is quite similar to the CBA IPI [6], a CAF-compliant method currently in wide use for assessing software process improvement.

The CMM® has an additional appraisal method—the Software Capability Evaluation^{SM} (SCE^{SM}), version 3.0 [7], which is used mainly as an aid in source selection and project monitoring. However, many organizations use the SCE^{SM} method instead of the CBA IPI method for evaluation of their process improvement initiatives. The SCAMPI^{SM} method is designed for both assessment and evaluation: *Appraisal* encompasses both assessment and evaluation. With publication of the CMMI®, SCAMPI^{SM} will replace both the CBA IPI and SCE^{SM} methods.

Because of the size of the model and different purposes for which the method can be used, the SEI postulated three classes of methods that exhibit various degrees of compliance with the ARC requirements. The factors to consider when selecting one of the classes are [2] as follows:

- The desired degree of confidence in the appraisal outcomes;
- The need to generate ratings;
- Appraisal cost and duration.

Class A appraisals must satisfy all ARC requirements, whereas class B appraisals satisfy a subset of those requirements, and class C appraisals satisfy a subset of class B requirements. Most of the differences are in the rigor of reviewing, validating, and corroborating the objective evidence, and in generating ratings. Only class A methods produce ratings. Class B methods are effective for initial assessments where the purpose of the investigation is the determination of major weaknesses and initiation of process improvements. Class C methods are known as "quick look" or gap analysis methods and are usually implemented before a formal appraisal. Many organizations periodically use such quick look methods to get an indication of the progress of their process improvement effort.

8.1.2 SCAMPI(SM) overview

The SCAMPI(SM) method is divided into three phases as shown in Figure 8.1. Each phase is further divided into the processes shown in Table 8.1.

A characteristic of the SCAMPI(SM) method—more pronounced than in its predecessors—is the definition of the *appraisal scope,* the determination of the sample of the organization's projects that will be subject to the appraisal. Organizations typically determine which units and projects within those units will participate in the appraisal. The consequence of this selection is that the rating given at the end of the appraisal may only reflect the organizational unit appraised and not the whole organization (unless the scope of the appraisal was the whole organization).

Another aspect of method tailoring is the selection of the model scope. Based on the organization's business and appraisal objectives, the organization may select either the staged or continuous model representation. Then,

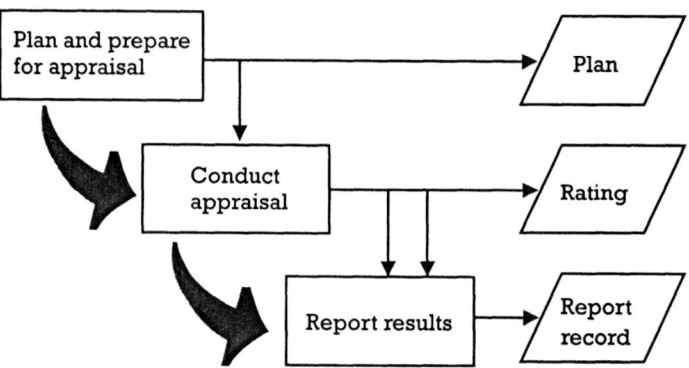

Figure 8.1 The three SCAMPI(SM) phases.

Table 8.1 SCAMPI(SM) Phases and Processes

Phase	Process
1 Plan and prepare for appraisal.	1.1 Analyze requirements. 1.2 Develop appraisal plan. 1.3 Select and prepare team. 1.4 Obtain and analyze initial objective evidence.
2 Conduct appraisal.	2.1 Examine objective evidence. 2.2 Verify and validate objective evidence. 2.3 Document objective evidence. 2.4 Generate appraisal results.
3 Report results.	3.1 Deliver appraisal results. 3.2 Package and archive appraisal results.

within the selected representation, the organization may select PAs to be considered in the appraisal. Although there is considerable freedom in selecting the model scope, certain constraints cannot be violated if the results are be valid. All tailoring decisions have to be documented in the appraisal plan and agreed to by the appraisal sponsor and the authorized lead appraiser.

To be consistent, repeatable, and accurate, the SCAMPI^{SM} method requires collection and analysis of objective evidence from various sources, such as questionnaires, presentations, documents, and interviews. Typically, a team of trained professionals, led by an authorized lead appraiser, examines this objective evidence, ensures its validity, and makes observations about its compliance with the CMMI®. The observations are then transformed into statements of strengths and weaknesses, and finally into findings that are presented to the appraisal sponsor. The ratings resulting from the validated observations and findings indicate how well the enacted processes reflect the CMMI® model requirements.

A major difference between this method and its predecessors is in the extent and timing of review of objective evidence. Documentation is objective evidence of institutionalization and implementation. The SCAMPI^{SM} method requires document review and emphasizes verification and validation of evidence. This differs from the discovery of evidence in the CBA IPI method. Because so many practices have to be examined for each project that has been selected to participate in the appraisal, it is absolutely essential that the appraised organization be well prepared. This means that evidence should be gathered and be readily available for the appraisal team to examine before the actual appraisal starts. It is in the organization's interest to know if the evidence is available and to determine if the time is right for conducting the appraisal.

In the CMMI® models, specific and generic goals are required model components, whereas specific and generic practices are expected model components. This means that the goals are used for rating purposes, while practices are used as a guide to evaluating their satisfaction. Because of the goal–practice relationship, goals can be satisfied only if the associated practices are implemented. Therefore, the extent of practice implementation is investigated to determine if the goals and, in turn, the PAs are satisfied. The objective evidence collected, examined, and analyzed is the basis for judgment of component satisfaction. Although the objective evidence associated with each individual practice is examined, the entire model and its intent are needed to reach decisions about the extent to which those practices are or are not implemented. The appraisal team keeps notes, develops observations, and characterizes the evidence as indicating strengths or weaknesses.

The concept of organizational scope was introduced earlier in this chapter. The importance of organizational scope is in determining the breadth of implementation of the CMMI® practices. Practices are implemented at the project level,[1] and the extent to which they are implemented in the organizational unit can be determined only by aggregating the extent to which those practices are implemented in the projects. Therefore, objective evidence must be collected for each practice at the project level. The evidence must have several sources: (1) artifacts resulting from the practice implementation and (2) face-to-face interviews. For example, if four projects are selected for the appraisal, objective evidence of each practice's implementation in each of the four projects must be collected, examined, and analyzed, and then aggregated to the organizational unit level.

To support that evaluation, the SCAMPI[SM] method has introduced the *practice implementation indicator* (PII). The PII is an objective attribute or characteristic used to verify the conduct of an activity or implementation of a CMMI® practice [1]. There are three types of PIIs:

1. *Direct artifacts* are outputs resulting from implementation of the process.

2. *Indirect artifacts* arise as consequences of performing a practice or substantiate its implementation.

3. *Affirmations* are oral or written statements confirming or supporting implementation of a practice.

Items listed as "typical work products" in the CMMI® documents are representative of direct and indirect artifacts. Meeting minutes, review results, and status reports are also indirect artifacts. Affirmations are obtained from interviews or through questionnaire responses. Each type of objective evidence must be collected for every practice in order to corroborate the practice implementation.

PIIs are verified throughout the appraisal process until there is sufficient objective evidence to characterize the implementation of a practice. For practice implementation evidence to be declared sufficient, it has to contain direct artifacts corroborated by either indirect artifacts or affirmations. This concept is shown in Figure 8.2.

---

1. The SCAMPI[SM] method refers to the "instantiation of the process" rather than to project implementation, because OPF, OPD, and OT practices are implemented at the organizational level and have no meaning at the project level. By using the term *instantiation,* the concept of practice implementation is generalized.

8.1 SCAMPI^{SM}

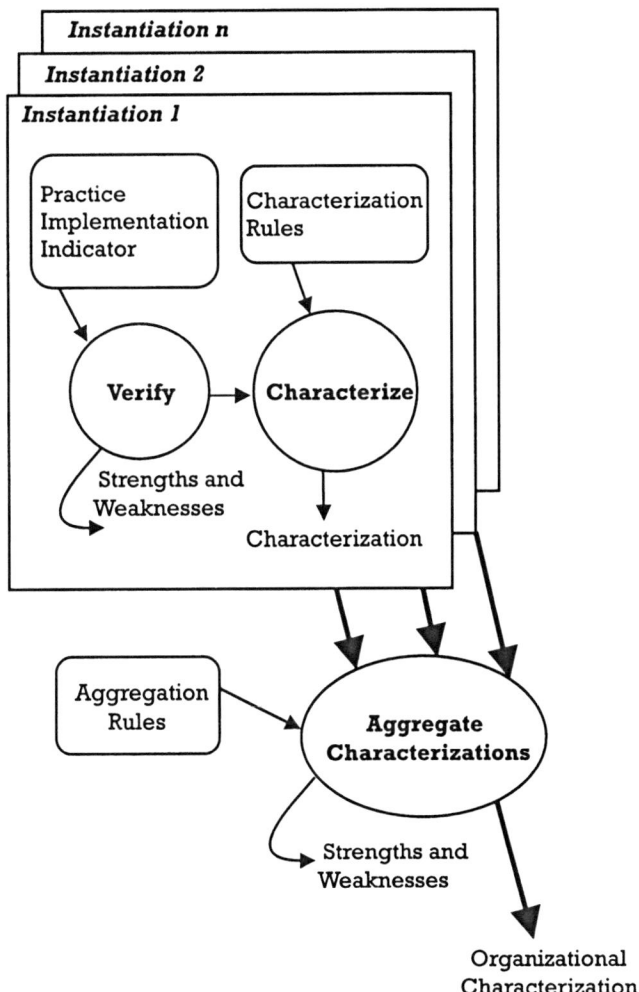

Figure 8.2 Characterization concept.

The consensus of the appraisal team, or the part of the team that specifically investigated that PA, has to be obtained to determine sufficiency. This enables the team to characterize practice implementation at a given instantiation level (such as the project level) as FI, LI, PI, or NI, as described in Chapter 7. An instantiation is characterized as FI if direct artifacts are present and are appropriate, at least one indirect artifact or affirmation is noted, and no substantial weaknesses are noted. In contrast, LI characterization allows for one or more weaknesses to be noted. A PI characterization means that the direct artifact is absent or inadequate, that practice may not be fully implemented, and that there are documented weaknesses. NI is self-explanatory.

After practices are characterized at this level, the appraisal team is ready to determine the organizational-level implementation of each practice for the set of selected projects by applying a set of well-defined rules. For example, if any instantiation is characterized LI or PI, the organizational-level implementation is characterized as LI. However, if any instantiation is characterized as NI, team judgment is required to choose either NI, LI, or PI.

The consensus of the full appraisal team is required to characterize practice implementation at the organizational unit level. Strengths and weaknesses are also aggregated at the same time.

Ratings are based on validated appraisal data and are generated for each PA's specific and generic goals. Ratings may also be generated for PAs, capability levels, or maturity levels[2] as shown in Figure 8.3.

The appraisal outputs are the findings, statements of strengths and weaknesses identified, and an appraisal disclosure statement that precisely identifies the following:

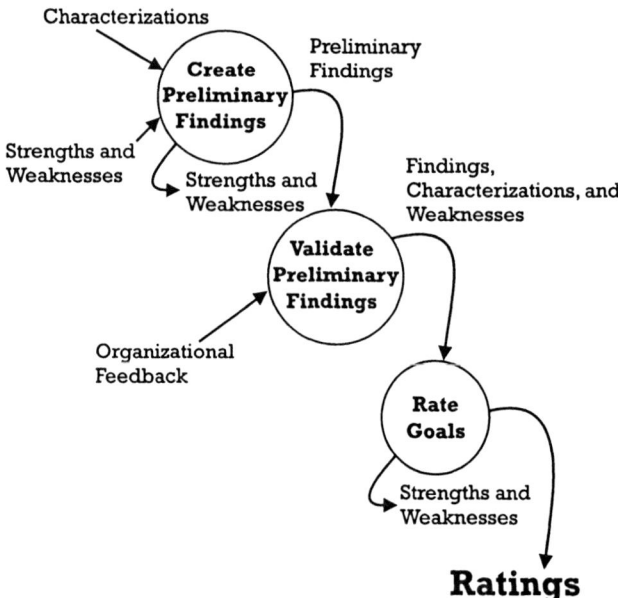

Figure 8.3 Goal rating process.

---

2. Capability or maturity level ratings are optional outputs of the SCAMPI[SM] appraisal method.

- Organizational unit;
- Model selected;
- PAs appraised;
- Specific and generic goal ratings;
- Maturity or capability levels ratings.

We now briefly describe each phase. For more details about tailoring guidelines, descriptions of parameters and limits, required and optional practices, and implementation guidance, refer to [1].

8.1.2.1 Plan and prepare for appraisal

The SCAMPI[SM] method requires the appraisal scope and objectives to be determined and documented by the lead appraiser and approved by the appraisal sponsor. The sponsor typically represents the organization that has commissioned the appraisal. This person works with the lead appraiser in defining the goals and objectives of the appraisal based on the organization's business goals and objectives. The sponsor is responsible for defining the scope of the organization and the scope of the CMMI® to be appraised. The sponsor's knowledge and desires are a blend of the understanding of the organizational business goals and the need and desire for process improvement. In many cases, the lead appraiser will have to explain the requirements, constraints, and needs of the SCAMPI[SM] method to the sponsor so the scope of the appraisal may be jointly defined. When the goals and objectives, scope, and constraints of the appraisal are known they are documented in the appraisal plan.

The purpose of the plan is to ensure mutual understanding of the goals, scope, activities, and constraints of the appraisal. The SCAMPI[SM] method contains many constraints but still offers a wide variety of choices that allow the appraisal team leader and sponsor to select the appraisal features that best address business objectives. The appraisal team leader is responsible for following the method's tailoring rules and documenting the sponsor's agreement in the appraisal plan. A typical table of contents for an appraisal plan is shown in Table 8.2.

A major activity in this phase is appraisal team selection and preparation. In the SCAMPI[SM] method, stringent requirements are laid out for appraisal team selection including certain minimum levels of engineering and management experience. While the CBA IPI method allows the lead assessor to provide CMM® training, the SCAMPI[SM] method requires CMMI® training to

Table 8.2 Sample Table of Contents for an Appraisal Plan

1	Introduction	
	Summarizes the appraisal purpose and the appraisal plan.	
2	Appraisal Purpose	
	Explains why the appraisal is being conducted. For example, the appraisal may be conducted to determine initial gaps, improvement progress, or for acquisition evaluation.	
3	Key Appraisal Participant Information	
	Identifies appraisal team members and appraisal participants.	
4	Appraisal Scope Specification	
	Defines the organizational scope (the specific projects representing the organizational unit) and the model scope (CMMI® representation, process areas that will be appraised, and model components that will be rated).	
5	Process Context Information	
	Describes the factors that influence the judgment and comparability of appraisal ratings, such as the size of the organizational unit to be appraised or the application domain of the products or services.	
6	Key Appraisal Parameters	
	Specifies the values of SCAMPI^{SM} parameters for this appraisal.	
7	Planned Tailoring	
	Tailoring includes selection of choices (if any) within the required practices, setting allowable appraisal parameters, and inclusion of optional practices.	
8	Appraisal Outputs	
	Expected outputs, such as final findings, maturity or capability levels, project-level findings and ratings.	
9	Appraisal Constraints	
	For example, availability of interviewees, time or schedule limitations, or control of resulting information.	
10	Activities, Resources, and Schedule	
	Documents estimates of the duration of key events in the schedule, the effort required for the people participating in the appraisal, and other associated costs (such as equipment and travel).	
11	Risk Management	
	Identifies appraisal risks and mitigation plans.	
12	Appraisal Logistics	
	Identifies dependencies, communication channels for providing status, and responsibilities for tracking logistical issues.	

be provided only by SEI-authorized instructors. This limitation is enacted because of the complexity of the model and the need for the team to be well trained before it can efficiently perform the appraisal. Lead appraisers are empowered to train their teams in the SCAMPI^{SM} method. The training is usually used as a team building effort and includes the documentation review period.

In the spirit of the CMMI®, appraisal team members are considered relevant stakeholders of the plan and should be aware of its content. Other relevant stakeholders must also be acquainted with the plan. These stakeholders include the appraisal participants, such as interviewees, staff members who will provide the objective evidence, management, and staff.

The preparation phase includes an extremely important activity: that of obtaining and analyzing initial objective evidence. The appraisal team must have objective evidence prior to the actual appraisal so it can understand the processes in use in the organizational unit. Because of the size of the model and the amount and type of objective evidence collected for each specific and generic practice for each project in the scope of the appraisal, collection of evidence is typically managed using the PIIs described earlier.

The appraised organization provides cross-references to objective evidence for the direct and indirect artifacts. Affirmations are collected via face-to-face interviews. Prior to the start of the appraisal, the inventory of objective evidence is reviewed and a decision is made as to proceeding with the appraisal or suspending the appraisal while additional evidence is collected.

8.1.2.2 Conduct appraisal

This phase is usually called the *on-site period*. A detailed view of this phase is shown in Table 8.3. When the appraisal team gathers for the appraisal, the objective evidence is again reviewed to determine if it is adequate. The team then decides if additional evidence is needed and creates questions to be asked during face-to-face interviews. Interviews are a necessary and required component of the SCAMPI^{SM} appraisal.

The SCAMPI^{SM} method includes criteria to determine the minimum acceptable number of face-to-face interviews. There are several types of interviews. Most managers of the projects participating in the appraisal are interviewed individually, while practitioners (known as functional area representatives in the SCAMPI^{SM} method), are interviewed in group sessions. The interview groups are selected by subject, such as requirements and design, integration and testing, quality assurance, and configuration management.

The team collects observations from documentation reviews and interviews and relates them to the model practices through a process called *tagging*. This effort verifies that the implementation of each model practice is supported by direct artifacts and corroborated by indirect artifacts or affirmations. Data collection and consolidation continue until sufficient evidence is obtained to enable characterization of individual practices.

When objective evidence for all practices and for all projects in the scope of the appraisal has been examined, the practices are characterized as FI, LI, PI, or NI. Figure 8.2 shows that after the practice characterization is com-

Table 8.3 Steps in the Conducting Appraisals Phase

Examine Objective Evidence
Examine objective evidence from PIIs and organization presentations. Create questions for project leads. Perform project lead interviews. Annotate PIIs with affirmations. Review and revise the data collection plan.
Verify and Validate Objective Evidence
Verify objective evidence (direct, indirect, and affirmation). Characterize practices. Review the data collection plan and determine information needs. Create questions for functional area representatives. Perform interviews. Annotate PIIs with affirmations. Review the data collection plan. Verify objective evidence. Characterize practices. Aggregate characterizations to the organizational unit. Generate preliminary findings. Present preliminary findings to appraisal participants. Review comments and revise findings if necessary.
Generate Appraisal Results
Rate goals. Determine maturity level. Develop final findings. Present final findings.

pleted, the project-level characterization is performed to derive the organizational-level characterization, as explained earlier.

In comparison to the predecessor methods, the SCAMPI[SM] method makes the appraisal team's decision-making process more repeatable by using well-defined characterizations of the implementation of practices on individual projects and in the organizational unit.

Next, the preliminary findings, which summarize the organizational unit's gaps in practice implementation, are created. An important SCAMPI[SM] requirement states: "Every model practice characterized as either Not Implemented or Partially Implemented, at the organizational unit level, must have at least one preliminary finding associated with it" [1]. This requirement forces the appraisal team to think through their observations and formulate findings that will help the organization to develop process improvement actions. The preliminary findings are normally presented to the organizational unit and their comments are solicited in order to obtain their buy-in. This step is an important milestone in the appraisal process. It marks the time in the appraisal process when the findings ownership migrates from the appraisal team to the organizational unit that will use them to develop process improvement plans.

After the appraisal findings are verified and validated, the goals are rated, PA satisfaction is determined, and maturity or capability levels are assigned. The rule for determining the goal satisfaction is rather simple. The PA goal is satisfied if all associated practices are characterized at the organizational unit level as either LI or FI, and the aggregation of weaknesses associated with the goal does not have a significant negative impact on goal achievement. If the goal is ruled to be "unsatisfied," the team must describe how the weakness(es) led to this rating.

PA satisfaction is a direct function of goal satisfaction. A PA is rated as satisfied if every goal in the PA is rated satisfied.

The maturity level is determined as the highest level at which all PAs contained within that maturity level and all lower maturity levels are rated as satisfied or not applicable. For example, for a maturity level 3 rating, all maturity levels 2 and 3 PAs must be rated satisfied. In the continuous representation, each PA in the scope of the assessment may be rated separately. As indicated in Chapter 4, the engineering PAs contain basic and advanced specific practices that have to be rated separately.

All decisions by the appraisal team are reached via consensus and not by a majority vote. This further strengthens the organizational ownership of the results.

8.1.2.3 Report results

The last phase of the appraisal deals with developing and presenting the final findings, developing the final report, and planning the next steps. The final findings must include a summary of the appraisal process and the findings that summarize strengths and weaknesses. The appraisal team must reach consensus on the wording of the final findings, while ensuring that the confidentiality and nonattribution principles are followed. For every model component that is reported as unsatisfied, the weakness(es) that prompted this rating must be reported. Final findings are presented in a face-to-face forum to the sponsor, senior management, and appraisal participants.

The results are also submitted to the *CMMI® steward*—the SEI. While the organization uses the appraisal results for generating process improvement plans, the steward collects appraisal data for statistical purposes. The SEI currently publishes a semiannual *Maturity Profile* report that contains cumulative results of appraisals since 1987. It relies on appraisal feedback and is accessible from the SEI Web site.

It is important to note that the SEI does not "certify" appraisal ratings. Although it keeps a database of all assessments and appraisals, it does not provide information about the scope or results of any organization's appraisal to the public. On the other hand, an appraised organization is free to use and publicize the appraisal results as it sees fit.

8.2 ISO 9001:2000 registration process

In this section we briefly describe the ISO assessment flow and the objective evidence needed for an ISO certification audit. Because the standard has been updated, there are at least two ways to approach an ISO 9001:2000 audit. One is for organizations that have upgraded their QMS from the 1994 version, and another is for those being audited for the first time using the 2000 version. We will concentrate on the later because it will, in general, encompass the former. The upgrade audit typically concentrates on the review of the requirements imposed by the ISO 9001:2000 standard, evidence that internal audits and management reviews focusing on process changes have been conducted, and personnel training in the new QMS.

Most organizations will perform a *preassessment* to determine if the QMS is satisfactory for the formal audit. ISO limits performance of the preassessment to only one instance. The flow of a typical registration process is shown in Figure 8.4.

It is expected that the organization has already selected the registrar and has the necessary information about ISO audit requirements. During the preparation phase, the auditor and the organization's representative develop an audit plan, which identifies the organizational unit to be assessed and the scope of the assessment. In addition, the optional preassessment will be arranged. Note that registrars are not allowed to provide consultation services because the standards require that they maintain their independence from the organizations that they will audit.

During preparation, the auditor will inform the organization about the documentation they will be required to provide and the support that will be needed during the assessment. The goal of the audit is to review as much of the organizational documentation and its implementation as possible in the time allotted, typically a week. Although an audit of a large organization will be different from an audit of a small organization, the processes practiced in those organizations must be reviewed in both cases.

A portion of a typical assessment plan is shown in Table 8.4. The plan indicates the areas of investigation and relates them to the responsible or cognizant organizational elements. Assessors develop questions at the level

8.2 ISO 9001:2000 registration process

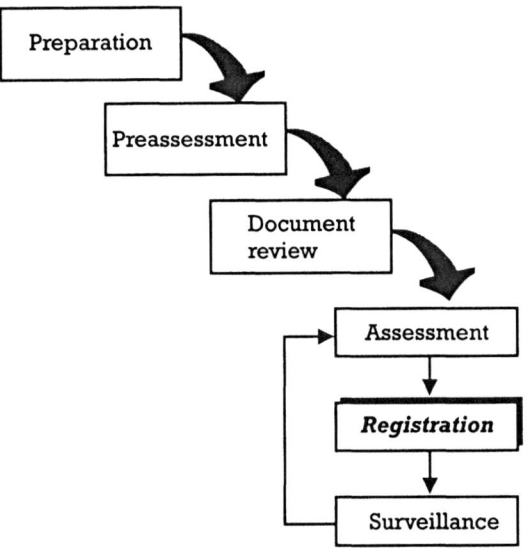

Figure 8.4 ISO registration process flow.

Table 8.4 Plan for ISO Assessment

		Executive	Engineering	Production	Quality	HR	Customer Service
6	Resource management						
	6.1 Provision of resources	X					
	6.2 Human resources					X	X
	6.3 Infrastructure			X			X
	6.4 Work environment			X			X

necessary for detailed investigation of those areas indicated with an X. Typically, investigation is at the *shall* level of the standard. By investigating several sources of information, assessors obtain a fairly thorough understanding of how the QMS is implemented in the organization. However, due to time limitations, only the most obvious noncompliances will be determined. Some assessors also review an organization's internal audit process in depth because, when implemented correctly, internal audits will discover most noncompliances before the formal audit is conducted.

The preassessment consists of a preliminary review of documentation, procedures, and processes as well as interviews to determine organizational readiness for a formal audit. The preassessment reviews the quality manual, procedures, and implementation of those procedures. Gaps in documentation are noted and the date for the formal audit is determined based on the severity and magnitude of the detected gaps.

During the documentation review, the assessor reviews the organization's quality manual and the procedures required by the standard. Findings are documented and reported. The documents to be reviewed fall into three categories: organizational (typically plans), implementation (such as procedures, work instructions, and process descriptions), and control (such as measurements, reports, and checklists). Documentation deficiencies have to be corrected before the organization can be recommended for registration. If documentation was initially reviewed during the preassessment, the auditor may choose to review only revised documentation during the assessment to ensure that recommended changes were implemented correctly. An example of the review form is shown in Table 8.5.

On the first day of the assessment, the auditor typically presents an overview of the assessment process. The assessment follows the ISO 19011:2002 standard [8] and, in some instances, additional procedures that were developed by the registrars themselves. The auditor then conducts in-depth reviews of the organization's procedures and evaluates their implementation for conformance with the ISO 9001:2000 standard.

In addition to the documentation review, the assessment will include interviews and observations to determine the extent of the implementation of the standard. Interview questions are typically derived from the requirements of the ISO 9001 standard. If there is more than one auditor, specific areas of activity may be examined in parallel. Through reviews, interviews, and observations, the auditors examine objective evidence of process conformance to the organizational documentation and conformance with the standard. Most assessors develop tools to facilitate data collection and analysis. For example, Tables 8.4 and 8.5 can be combined into one spreadsheet that will indicate the documentation collected, documentation reviewed, the staff to be interviewed, and the interview responses.

Table 8.5 Example of Typical Assessment Records

Clause	Description	Typical Evidence	Reference	Comments
6.2.2	Competency, awareness, and training	• Records of course/ seminar completion • Course attendance lists • Mentoring/OJT records • Résumés/waivers		

8.2 ISO 9001:2000 registration process

Several excellent references provide guidelines for auditing [9–11]. A very interesting approach to auditing is described in [12]. The author provides a detailed framework for auditing that emphasizes a business perspective rather than following the ISO requirements structure. The framework consists of five "audit trails" each covering a path through the complete ISO standard using threads that are designed to examine related ISO requirements. It outlines what to audit and the evidence required for showing that the ISO requirements were satisfied. These five audit trails are defined next:

A—*Business planning and management review:* Addresses the relationships between customer requirements, quality objectives, quality policy, quality planning, provision of resources, management reviews, customer satisfaction, and internal audits

B—*Process monitoring and improvement:* Addresses the relationships between general requirements for process improvement, monitoring and measurement of processes, analysis of data, improvement, and the need for corrective and preventive actions.

C—*New product development:* Addresses the customer-related processes, such as requirement definition and review, planning of the product realization, design and development including their reviews, verification and validation, and general measurement, analysis and improvement activities.

D—*Provision:* Addresses the control of production and service provision, purchasing, identification and traceability, control of nonconforming product, analysis of data, and improvement.

E—*Administration and resources:* Addresses a set of tasks that support activities in all other trails, such as responsibility, authority and communication, management representative, internal communication, documentation requirements, human resources, infrastructure, and work environment.

Those five audit trails are shown in Table 8.6. For example, the New Product Development audit trail (Trail C) covers the requirements of these ISO 9001 sections:

7.1 Planning of product realization;

7.2 Customer-related processes;

7.3 Design and development;

8.1 General (measurement, analysis, and improvement).

Table 8.6 Proposed Audit Trails

	A	B	C	D	E
4					
4.1		X			
4.2					X
5					
5.1	X				
5.2	X				
5.3	X				
5.4	X				
5.5					X
5.6	X				
6					
6.1	X				
6.2					X
6.3					X
6.4					X
7					
7.1			X		
7.2			X		
7.3			X		
7.4				X	
7.5				X	
7.6				X	
8					
8.1		X	X		
8.2	X				
8.3				X	
8.4		X			
8.5		X			

This means that the audit will address processes for identifying product requirements specified by the customer, requirements necessary for the product's intended use, and requirements specifically imposed by the organization itself. The auditor will verify that requirements were reviewed before commitments were made. The auditor will also examine the arrangements for customer communications.

When satisfied that the customer-related processes have been followed, the auditor will check planning of product realization. Planning involves definition of quality objectives, identification of technical activities and associated work products, and determination of responsibilities, resources, constraints, dependencies, and activities. In addition, the auditor will verify that criteria for product acceptance have been specified and that plans are documented.

Next, the auditor will concentrate on the design and development process. Typical questions asked includes these:

- Were design and development activities planned?
- Were design objectives specified?
- Was a life cycle with predetermined stages identified?
- Was the design reviewed, verified, and validated?
- Who was responsible for reviewing design and development?

In addition, the auditor will verify that the organization has implemented the QMS direction for review of design inputs, their relationships to the requirements, outputs, and their adequacy for performing subsequent processes such as production, coding, or purchasing. The auditor will verify that design changes were documented and were implemented only when approved.

Throughout the audit, the auditor verifies that measurement and monitoring activities were performed and that data were collected and analyzed.

In each instance of the process audit, the auditor will determine the effectiveness of those processes in practice. Because the audit trails are interactive, the auditor will be able to make sure that the processes implemented in an organization indeed form an interconnected system.

At the conclusion of the assessment, the assessor presents the identified noncompliances (classified as major or minor) to the client and makes the recommendation for certification or rejection. Shortly after the assessment, a written report is created and delivered to the organization's management and to the Committee on ISO Registration, which reviews the report and decides if certification will be granted. Any major noncompliance will require corrective action and may require a corrective action assessment to be conducted before certification is granted. The corrective action usually must be implemented within 90 days.

After registration, surveillance audits are conducted on a yearly basis to review compliance with selected elements of the standard. After 3 years, a reassessment must be conducted to maintain registration. The reassessment reviews all applicable ISO 9001 elements.

If the organization's QMS changes significantly, and those changes affect ISO compliance, the organization should inform the registrar. The registrar may then decide to perform a special assessment to address those changes, perform a new assessment, or take no action. Similarly, if the organization increases or decreases the scope of the registration, reassessment may be required or the changes in scope may be addressed in the next surveillance assessment.

8.3 TickIT

In the early 1990s, many software organizations realized that registration to ISO 9001 would require detailed guidance for implementing ISO requirements and ISO registrars who understood software. As described in Chapter 7, ISO 9000-3 [13] was developed to help interpret the ISO 9001:1994 standard for software applications. The TickIT program [14] was created by the British Standards Institution (BSI) to provide a method for registering software development systems based on the ISO 9000-3 standard. TickIT does not add any new requirements to ISO 9001:2000—it simply interprets those requirements. ISO 9000-3 is not used for registration but with TickIT, BSI made it possible to use ISO 9000-3 for certification purposes. Although this certification is not equivalent to ISO registration; a successful audit by a TickIT-accredited auditor results in the award of a certificate of compliance to ISO 9001:2000, endorsed with a TickIT logo. Certification is conducted by independent external QA agencies, using qualified TickIT auditors who have been specially trained and subjected to rigorous professional vetting. The International Register of Certified Auditors, with the support of the British Computer Society, administers this process.

TickIT has a very wide scope of application and can be used, for example, for the following products:

- Software as the delivered product;
- Embedded software, including the development of programmable hardware devices;
- Shrink-wrapped software;
- In-house software development when software affects the quality of the delivered product or service, including internal applications such as payroll;
- Computer operations services;
- Subcontracting.

An important aspect of TickIT development was in stimulating interest in software quality and providing a framework for managing software development and process improvement. The TickIT guide underwent several revisions to accommodate revisions of the ISO 9001 standard. The structure of the current version, Issue 5, shown in Figure 8.5, relates directly to the requirements set forth in ISO 9001:2000. Part E provides clause-by-clause guidelines for software development. Because a new revision of ISO 9000-3

8.3 TickIT

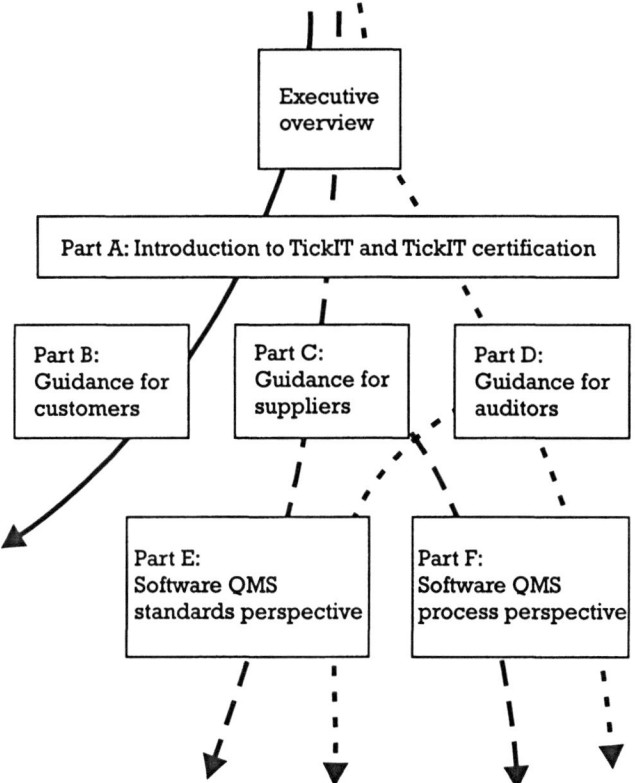

Figure 8.5 TickIT structure.

was not available at the time of the release of Issue 5, the guidelines in Part E are based on Issue 4 with additional suggestions and improvements. When the new revision of ISO 9000-3 becomes available, it will be reflected in a revised Part E. The guide also contains an extensive cross-reference to ISO/IEC 12207, resulting in a set of recommended practices related to ISO 9001:2000 on a process-by-process basis.

Figure 8.5 shows how clients and auditors use TickIT. Specifically, it shows the role of TickIT's six parts:

- Part A provides general information about TickIT and its application to process improvement.
- Part B describes the issues relating to certification.
- Part C describes guidance for the QMSs of software organizations using TickIT procedures and a process for assessing and improving their quality management systems.

- Part D describes the conduct of assessment using TickIT procedures.
- Part E interprets and provides guidance for implementing ISO 9001:2000 for software.
- Part F provides good practices for effective and continuous control of a software quality management system.

Because it is in alignment with ISO 9001:2000 and that standard's requirements for continuous process improvement, TickIT emphasizes process improvement but does not prescribe the approach to be used. Four TickIT appendices address the most prominent process improvement methods, such as ISO/IEC TR 15504 (SPICE) and the CMM®. Issue 4 of the TickIT guide, which predated ISO 9001:2000, introduced the concept of basing the QMS on software development processes. This concept has now been expanded and described in Part F, as a description of the new measurement process required by ISO 9001:2000.

Reference [15] shows how one U.S. organization used TickIT certification[3] to further stimulate process improvement after already achieving a CMM®-SW level 4 rating. The use of TickIT specifically led that organization to further address contractual and hardware process aspects, place greater emphasis on customer satisfaction, and implement corrective and preventive actions. They also credited recurring semiannual recertifications for maintaining their process improvement momentum and for preparing them for the CMMI® implementation.

8.4 Using SCAMPI[SM] to prepare for ISO 9001:2000 registration

We have previously seen how the CMMI® provides more detail and implementation guidance than ISO 9001:2000 does. Similarly, the SCAMPI[SM] method is detailed and procedure oriented, while ISO assessment provides only high-level guidance to assessors. Clearly, both assessment processes rely on the same types of evidence, although there is no formal equivalency established between these two assessment methods at this time.

An organization can use the SCAMPI[SM] method to prepare itself for an ISO certification assessment. In other words, if an organization has prepared objective evidence of its implementation of the CMMI®, it will be well on its way to preparing for an ISO registration audit. However, as pointed out

---

3. This particular TickIT certification was based on ISO 9001:1994.

in Chapter 7, achieving a certain CMMI® maturity level does not guarantee ISO certification.

The first step is to prepare for collection of objective evidence using the CMMI® PIIs. By using the CMMI®-to-ISO mapping, shown in Chapter 9, annotate each PII entry with the corresponding ISO statement. This will relate the CMMI®-required objective evidence to the ISO requirements and ensure that all ISO clauses corresponding to the CMMI® are addressed.

The organization can now collect the objective evidence needed to satisfy both appraisal methods using the same approach and the same data collection instruments. Then using a method similar to the one described in [12] this evidence can be correlated to a specific audit trail, thus facilitating the ISO audit.

Additional steps are required for organizations using the CMMI® to prepare for ISO certification. The ISO-to-CMMI® mapping shows that not all ISO 9001 clauses have corresponding CMMI® components. Following the structure established for the CMMI®, additional PIIs should be created for these ISO clauses. Remember that the mappings shown in Chapter 9 are many-to-many, meaning that one CMMI® statement may satisfy more than one ISO statement and vice versa. As with any other mapping and appraisal method, the whole model must be considered when attempting to show how objective evidence satisfies each individual practice.

8.5 Summary

In this brief overview, we have summarized highlights of the CMMI®, TickIT, and ISO assessment methods. The SCAMPI^{SM} method, being more comprehensive, consistent, and repeatable than the ISO assessment, can be used to gather objective evidence that may be used in the ISO certification process. TickIT is closely related to ISO and is a certification method in its own right. One significant advantage of the SCAMPI^{SM} method and the CMMI® is that they are in public domain, while both ISO 9001:2000 and TickIT are proprietary.

References

[1] CMMI® Product Team, *Standard CMMI® Appraisal Method for Process Improvement^{SM} (SCAMPI^{SM}), v1.1: Method Definition Document*, CMU/SEI-2001-HB-001, Pittsburgh, PA: Software Engineering Institute, December 2001.

[2] CMMI® Product Team, *Appraisal Requirements for CMMI®, v1.1*, CMU/SEI-2001-TR-034, Pittsburgh, PA: Software Engineering Institute, December 2001.

[3] Dunaway, D. K., and S. Masters, *CMM® Appraisal Framework, v1.0*, CMU/SEI-95-TR-001, Pittsburgh, PA: Software Engineering Institute, February 1995.

[4] *Systems Engineering Capability Model, Part 2: EIA/IS-731-2 Appraisal Method*, Washington, D.C.: Electronic Industry Association, 1998.

[5] *Information Technology—Software Process Assessment*, ISO/IEC TR 15504, Geneva, Switzerland: ISO, 1998.

[6] Dunaway, D. K., and S. Masters, *CMM®-Based Appraisal for Internal Process Improvement (CBA IPI), v1.2, Method Description*, CMU/SEI-01-TR-033, Pittsburgh, PA: Software Engineering Institute, November 2001.

[7] Byrnes, P., and M. Phillips, *Software Capability Evaluation, v3.0, Method Description*, CMU/SEI-96-TR-002, Pittsburgh, PA: Software Engineering Institute, 1996.

[8] *Guidelines for quality and/or environmental management systems auditing*, ISO 19011:2002, Geneva, Switzerland: ISO, 2002.

[9] Stimson, W. A., *Internal Quality Auditing: Meeting the Challenge of ISO 9000:2000*, Chico, CA: Paton Press, 2001.

[10] Wealleans, D., *The Quality Audit for ISO 9001:2000: A Practical Guide*, Oxon, England: Gower Publishing, 2000.

[11] O'Hanlon, T., *Quality Auditing for ISO 9001:2000: Making Compliance Value-Added*, Milwaukee, WI: American Society for Quality, 2001.

[12] Kymal, C., *How to Audit ISO 9001:2000, A Handbook for Auditors*, Chico, CA: Paton Press, 2002.

[13] *Guidelines for the Application of ISO/IEC 9001 to the Development, Supply, and Maintenance of Software*, ISO/IEC 9000-3, Geneva, Switzerland: ISO, 1997.

[14] DISC TickIT Office, *TickIT Guide*, Issue 5, British Standards Institution, 2001, http://www.tickit.org.

[15] Butler, K., and W. Lipke, *Software Process Achievement at Tinker Air Force Base, OK*, CMU/SEI-2000-TR-014, Pittsburgh, PA: Software Engineering Institute, September 2000.

CHAPTER 9

Contents

9.1 Mapping: ISO 9001:2000 to the CMMI®

9.2 Inverse mapping: CMMI® to ISO 9001:2000

References

Document Mapping

In this chapter, we provide mappings between ISO 9001:2000 and the CMMI®. Several attempts, both proprietary and public, have been to map standards and models to each other [1, 2]. One prominent mapping is that given in [3], which provides a mapping between several standards, models, and national awards documents. As with all mappings, it is subjective. A frequent complaint from users of that mapping is the granularity of the map. A high-level mapping may give a much better indication of correspondence than a more detailed, lower level map.

The mappings presented here address the middle ground. Each ISO *shall* statement has been mapped to a CMMI® practice, using only the most prominent correspondence. If an ISO *shall* statement strongly maps to a CMMI® specific practice, we do not indicate mappings to other specific practices that may show some weaker correspondence. The map thus serves as an indicator of correspondence rather than as an implementation guideline. The tables given in Section 9.1 represent roll-ups of the mappings from individual *shall* statements to CMMI® practices. One should keep in mind that this is still a many-to-many mapping, meaning that one ISO statement may correspond to more than one CMMI® specific or generic practice, and vice versa. Although maps are convenient, they cannot replace an understanding of the documents being mapped. Stretching the map correspondence could be counterproductive and misleading.

263

9.1 Mapping: ISO 9001:2000 to the CMMI®

Tables 9.1 through 9.5 show the mapping of each ISO 9001:2000 section to the CMMI®. "All" in the PA column means that generic practices in every PA correspond to that ISO statement. Similarly, "All" in the Practice column means that all specific practices in the indicated PA correspond to the specific ISO statement or a group of statements.

The tables do not indicate a mapping of CMMI® generic and specific goals and ISO requirements. Although the goals can be mapped to ISO statements, such a mapping has no meaning in CMMI® terms. In the CMMI®, specific or generic practices are associated with corresponding goals. In other words, goals aggregate those practices to indicate some unique characteristics of the PA or its institutionalization and do not stand by themselves.

Table 9.1 ISO 9001:2000 Section 4 to CMMI® Mapping

	ISO 9001:2000	PA	CMMI® Practices
4	Quality management system		
4.1	General requirements	All	GP 2.1, 2.2, 2.3, 2.6, 2.8, 2.9, GP 3.1, 3.2
		OPD	SP 1.1
		OPF	SP 1.1, 2.2
		SAM	GP 2.2, 2.7, 2.8, 2.9, SP 1.3, SP 2.2
4.2	Documentation requirements		
4.2.1	General	All	GP 2.1
		OPD	SP 1.1, 1.2, 1.3
4.2.2	Quality manual	All	GP 2.2
		OPD	SP 1.1
4.2.3	Control of documents	All	GP 2.6
		CM	All
		PP	SP 2.3
4.2.4	Control of records	All	GP 2.6
		CM	GP 2.2, All SP
		PPQA	SP 2.2

Table 9.2 ISO 9001:2000 Section 5 to CMMI® Mapping

	ISO 9001:2000	PA	CMMI® Practices
5	Management responsibility		
5.1	Management commitment	All	GP 2.1, 2.3, 2.10
5.2	Customer focus	All	GP 2.7

9.1 Mapping: ISO 9001:2000 to the CMMI®

Table 9.2 ISO 9001:2000 Section 5 to CMMI® Mapping *(continued)*

	ISO 9001:2000	PA	CMMI® Practices
		RD	SP 1.1-1, 1.1-2, 1.2, SP 2.1, SP 3.3, 3.4, 3.5
5.3	Quality policy	All	GP 2.1
		OPF	SP 1.1
5.4	Planning		
5.4.1	Quality objectives	All	GP 4.1
		OPF	SP 1.1
		QPM	SP 1.1, 1.2, 1.3
		OPP	SP 1.3
5.4.2	Quality management system planning	All	GP 2.2, 3.1
		OPD	All
5.5	Responsibility, authority, and communication		
5.5.1	Responsibility and authority	All	GP 2.4
5.5.2	Management representative	OPF	GP 2.4
5.5.3	Internal communication	OPD	GP 2.1
		OPF	GP 2.10, SP 1.1
5.6	Management review		
5.6.1	General	All	GP 2.6, GP 2.10
		OPF	SP 1.2, 1.3
5.6.2	Review input	All	GP 2.10
		PMC	SP 1.6, 1.7, SP 2.1, 2.2, 2.3
5.6.3	Review output	All	GP 2.10
		PMC	SP 1.6, 1.7, SP 2.1, 2.2, 2.3

Table 9.3 ISO 9001:2000 Section 6 to CMMI® Mapping

	ISO 9001:2000	PA	CMMI® Practices
6	Resource management		
6.1	Provision of resources	All	GP 2.3
		PP	SP 2.4
6.2	Human resources		
6.2.1	General	All	GP 2.5
6.2.2	Competence, awareness, and training	All	GP 2.5
		OT	SP 1.1, 1.2, 1.3, 1.4, SP 2.1, 2.2, 2.3
		PP	SP 2.5
		OEI	SP 1.3
6.3	Infrastructure	All	GP 2.3
		OEI	SP 1.2
6.4	Work environment	All	GP 2.3
		PP	SP 2.4
		OEI	SP 1.2

Table 9.4 ISO 9001:2000 Section 7 to CMMI® Mapping

	ISO 9001:2000	PA	CMMI® Practices
7	Product realization		
7.1	Planning product realization	All	GP 2.2, 3.1
		OPD	SP 1.1, 1.2, 1.3
		IPM	SP 1.1, 1.3, 1.4
		PP	SP 1.1, 1.2, 1.3, 1.4, SP 2.1, 2.2, 2.3, 2.4, 2.5, 2.6, 2.7
		QPM	GP 2.3, SP 1.1, 1.2
7.2	Customer-related processes		
7.2.1	Determination of requirements related to the product	RD	SP 1.1, 1.2, SP 2.1, 2.2, 2.3, SP 3.1, 3.2
		REQM	SP 1.1
		TS	SP 1.2
7.2.2	Review of requirements related to the product	RD	GP 2.7, 2.10, SP 1.1, SP 2.1, SP 3.5
		VER	GP 2.7, SP 2.2
		REQM	GP 2.6, GP 2.7, SP 1.1, 1.2, 1.3, 1.5
7.2.3	Customer communication	RD	GP 2.7
		REQM	SP 1.2
		MA	SP 2.4
		IPM	SP 2.1, 2.2, 2.3
7.3	Design and development		
7.3.1	Design and development planning	PP	All
		IPM	SP 1.1, 1.3, 1.4, SP 2.1, 2.2, 2.3, SP 3.1, 3.2, 4.1, 4.2, 4.3
		CM	All
		RD	GP 2.2, 2.8, 2.9
		REQM	GP 2.2, 2.8, 2.9
		TS	GP 2.2, 2.4, 2.7, 2.8, 2.9, SP 1.1, 1.2, 1.3, SP 2.1, 2.2, 2.3, 2.4, SP 3.1, 3.2
		PI	GP 2.2, 2.4, 2.7, SP 1.1, 1.2, 1.3, SP 2.1, 2.2
		VER	GP 2.2, 2.4, 2.7, SP 1.1
		VAL	GP 2.2, 2.4, 2.7, SP 1.1
		QPM	SP 1.1, 1.2, 1.3
7.3.2	Design and development inputs	RD	GP 2.7, 2.10, SP 1.1, 1.2, SP 2.1, SP 3.2, 3.3, 3.4, 3.5
7.3.3	Design and development outputs	TS	All
		IPM	SP 1.1
7.3.4	Design and development review	PMC	GP 2.7, SP 1.4, 1.6, 1.7
		TS	GP 2.8
7.3.5	Design and development verification	VER	GP 2.6, SP 1.1, 1.2, 1.3, SP 2.1, 2.2, 2.3, SP 3.1, 3.2

9.1 Mapping: ISO 9001:2000 to the CMMI®

Table 9.4 ISO 9001:2000 Section 7 to CMMI® Mapping *(continued)*

	ISO 9001:2000	PA	CMMI® Practices
7.3.6	Design and development validation	VAL	GP 2.6, SP 1.1, 1.2, 1.3, SP 2.1, 2.2
		PI	GP 2.6
7.3.7	Control of design and development changes	CM	All
		TS	GP 2.6
		PI	GP 2.6
7.4	Purchasing		
7.4.1	Purchasing process	SAM	GP 2.6, GP 2.9, SP 1.1, 1.2, SP 2.2, 2.3
		TS	SP 1.1, 1.2, 1.3, SP 2.4
		PI	SP 3.1
7.4.2	Purchasing information	SAM	SP 1.1, 1.3, SP 2.1
7.4.3	Verification of purchased product	SAM	SP 1.3, SP 2.1, 2.2, 2.3
		VER	SP 3.1
7.5	Production and service provision		
7.5.1	Control of production and service provision	TS	GP 2.2, 2.3, 2.6, 2.8, SP 3.1, 3.2
		PI	SP 3.1, 3.2, 3.3, 3.4
7.5.2	Validation of processes for production and service provision	VAL	All
		RD	SP 3.5
7.5.3	Identification and traceability	CM	SP 1.1, 1.3, SP 2.1, 2.2, 3.1
		REQM	SP 1.4
		PI	SP 3.1, 3.2, 3.3
7.5.4	Customer property		(Not covered by CMMI®)
7.5.5	Preservation of Product	PI	SP 3.4
7.6	Control of monitoring and measuring devices	VER	GP 2.8
		VAL	GP 2.8
		MA	GP 2.1, 2.2, 2.8, 2.9, 2.10

Table 9.5 ISO 9001:2000 Section 8 to CMMI® Mapping

	ISO 9001:2000	PA	CMMI® Practices
8	Measurement, analysis, and improvement		
8.1	General	All	GP 2.2, 2.8
		MA	GP 2.2, SP 1.1, 1.2, 1.3, 1.4
		QPM	SP 2.1, 2.2, 2.3, 2.4
8.2	Monitoring and measurement		
8.2.1	Customer satisfaction	MA	SP 1.1, 1.2, SP 2.2
		PMC	SP 1.5
8.2.2	Internal audit	OPF	GP 2.1, 2.2, 2.4, SP 1.1, 1.2, 1.3, SP 2.1, 2.2
		PPQA	GP 2.2, 2.4, 2.6, 2.9, All SP
		MA	SP 2.4

Table 9.5 ISO 9001:2000 Section 8 to CMMI® Mapping *(continued)*

	ISO 9001:2000	PA	CMMI® Practices
8.2.3	Monitoring and measurement of process	All	GP 2.8, GP 4.2
		MA	GP 2.2, SP 1.2, 1.3, 1.4
		QPM	SP 2.2, 2.3
		PMC	SP 2.1, 2.2, 2.3
8.2.4	Monitoring and measurement of product	MA	SP 2.1
		VAL	SP 1.3, SP 2.1, 2.2
		VER	SP 1.1, 1.3, SP 2.1, 2.2, 2.3, SP 3.1, 3.2
		REQM	SP 1.1
		SAM	SP 1.3
		PPQA	SP 1.2
		CM	SP 3.2
8.3	Control of nonconforming product	VER	GP 2.4, SP 1.3, SP 3.2
		VAL	GP 2.4, SP 1.3, SP 2.2
		PMC	SP 2.1, 2.2, 2.3
		CM	All
8.4	Analysis of data	All	GP 2.8, 3.2
		MA	SP 2.2, 2.3, 2.4
		OPF	SP 1.2, 1.3
		OPP	SP 1.1, 1.2, 1.3, 1.4, 1.5
		RD	SP 1.1, 1.2, SP 2.1, SP 3.1, 3.2, 3.3, 3.4
		QPM	SP 1.4
		CAR	SP 1.1, 1.2
		SAM	SP 2.2
8.5	Improvement		
8.5.1	Continual improvement	All	GP 5.1
		OPF	SP 1.1, 1.3
		OID	SP 1.1
		MA	SP 1.1, 1.2, 1.4, SP 2.1, 2.2
8.5.2	Corrective action	All	GP 5.2
		CAR	All
		OPF	SP 2.1, 2.2, 2.3
		PMC	SP 2.1, 2.2, 2.3
8.5.3	Preventive action	All	GP 5.2
		OPF	SP 2.4
		CAR	SP 1.1, 1.2, SP 2.1, 2.2, 2.3

9.2 Inverse mapping: CMMI® to ISO 9001:2000

The inverse mapping was obtained by mapping the CMMI® specific and generic practices to ISO 9001:2000. No attempt was made to indicate the strength of the correspondence. Table 9.6 shows the per-PA mapping from the CMMI® to individual ISO sections. Table 9.7 shows the mapping from CMMI® GPs to the corresponding ISO sections. A blank in the ISO column indicates that there is no correspondence between the documents.

9.2 Inverse mapping: CMMI® to ISO 9001:2000

Table 9.6 Mapping of CMMI® Process Areas to ISO 9001:2000

Goal	Specific Practice	Description	ISO 9001:2000
		Organizational Process Focus	
SG 1		Determine Process Improvement Opportunities	
	SP 1.1-1	Establish Organizational Process Needs	4.1, 5.3, 5.4.1, 5.5.3, 8.2.2, 8.5.1
	SP 1.2-1	Appraise the Organization's Processes	5.6.1, 8.2.2, 8.4
	SP 1.3-1	Identify the Organization's Process Improvements	5.6.1, 8.2.2, 8.4, 8.5.1
SG 2		Plan and Implement Process Improvement Activities	
	SP 2.1-1	Establish Process Action Plans	8.2.2, 8.5.1, 8.5.2
	SP 2.2-1	Implement Process Action Plans	4.1, 8.2.2, 8.5.1, 8.5.2
	SP 2.3-1	Deploy Organizational Process Assets	8.5.2
	SP 2.4-1	Incorporate Process-Related Experiences into the Organizational Process Assets	8.5.3
		Organizational Process Definition	
SG 1		Establish Organizational Process Assets	
	SP 1.1-1	Establish Standard Processes	4.1, 4.2.1, 4.2.2, 5.4.2, 7.1
	SP 1.2-1	Establish Life-Cycle Model Descriptions	4.2.1, 5.4.2, 7.1
	SP 1.3-1	Establish Tailoring Criteria and Guidelines	4.2.1, 5.4.2, 7.1
	SP 1.4-1	Establish the Organization's Measurement Repository	
	SP 1.5-1	Establish the Organization's Process Asset Library	
		Organizational Training	
SG 1		Establish an Organizational Training Capability	
	SP 1.1-1	Establish the Strategic Training Needs	6.2.2

Table 9.6 Mapping of CMMI® Process Areas to ISO 9001:2000 *(continued)*

Goal	Specific Practice	Description	ISO 9001:2000
	SP 1.2-1	Determine Which Training Needs Are the Responsibility of the Organization	6.2.2
	SP 1.3-1	Establish an Organizational Training Tactical Plan	6.2.2
	SP 1.4-1	Establish Training Capability	6.2.2
SG 2		Provide Necessary Training	
	SP 2.1-1	Deliver Training	6.2.2
	SP 2.2-1	Establish Training Records	6.2.2
	SP 2.3-1	Assess Training Effectiveness	6.2.2
		Organizational Process Performance	
SG 1		Establish Performance Baselines and Models	
	SP 1.1-1	Select Processes	8.4
	SP 1.2-1	Establish Process Performance Measures	8.4
	SP 1.3-1	Establish Quality and Process-Performance Objectives	8.4, 5.4.1
	SP 1.4-1	Establish Process Performance Baselines	8.4
	SP 1.5-1	Establish Process Performance Models	8.4
		Organizational Innovation and Deployment	
SG 1		Select Improvements	
	SP 1.1-1	Collect and Analyze Improvement Proposals	8.5.1
	SP 1.2-1	Identify and Analyze Innovations	
	SP 1.3-1	Pilot Improvements	
	SP 1.4-1	Select Improvements for Deployment	
SG 2		Deploy Improvements	
	SP 2.1-1	Plan the Deployment	
	SP 2.2-1	Manage the Deployment	
	SP 2.3-1	Measure Improvement Effects	

Table 9.6 Mapping of CMMI® Process Areas to ISO 9001:2000 *(continued)*

Goal	Specific Practice	Description	ISO 9001:2000
		Project Planning	
SG 1		Establish Estimates	
	SP 1.1-1	Estimate the Scope of the Project	7.1, 7.3.1
	SP 1.2-1	Establish Estimates of Work Product and Task Attributes	7.1, 7.3.1
	SP 1.3-1	Define Project Life Cycle	7.1, 7.3.1
	SP 1.4-1	Determine Estimates of Effort and Cost	7.1, 7.3.1
SG 2		Develop a Project Plan	
	SP 2.1-1	Establish the Budget and Schedule	7.1, 7.3.1
	SP 2.2-1	Identify Project Risks	7.1, 7.3.1
	SP 2.3-1	Plan for Data Management	4.2.3, 7.1, 7.3.1
	SP 2.4-1	Plan for Project Resources	6.1, 6.4, 7.1, 7.3.1
	SP 2.5-1	Plan for Needed Knowledge and Skills	6.2.2, 7.1, 7.3.1
	SP 2.6-1	Plan Stakeholder Involvement	7.1, 7.3.1
	SP 2.7-1	Establish the Project Plan	7.1, 7.3.1
SG 3		Obtain Commitment to the Plan	
	SP 3.1-1	Review Plans that Affect the Project	
	SP 3.2-1	Reconcile Work and Resource Levels	
	SP 3.3-1	Obtain Plan Commitment	
		Project Monitoring and Control	
SG 1		Monitor Project Against Plan	
	SP 1.1-1	Monitor Project Planning Parameters	
	SP 1.2-1	Monitor Commitments	7.3.4
	SP 1.3-1	Monitor Project Risks	
	SP 1.4-1	Monitor Data Management	
	SP 1.5-1	Monitor Stakeholder Involvement	8.2.1
	SP 1.6-1	Conduct Progress Reviews	5.6.2, 5.6.3, 7.3.4
	SP 1.7-1	Conduct Milestone Reviews	5.6.2, 5.6.3, 7.3.4
SG 2		Manage Corrective Action to Closure	
	SP 2.1-1	Analyze Issues	5.6.2, 5.6.3, 8.2.3, 8.3, 8.5.2

Table 9.6 Mapping of CMMI® Process Areas to ISO 9001:2000 *(continued)*

Goal	Specific Practice	Description	ISO 9001:2000
	SP 2.2-1	Take Corrective Action	5.6.2, 5.6.3, 8.2.3, 8.3, 8.5.2
	SP 2.3-1	Manage Corrective Action	5.6.2, 5.6.3, 8.2.3, 8.3, 8.5.2
		Supplier Agreement Management	
SG 1		Establish Supplier Agreements	
	SP 1.1-1	Determine Acquisition Type	7.4.1, 7.4.2
	SP 1.2-1	Select Suppliers	7.4.1
	SP 1.3-1	Establish Supplier Agreements	4.1, 7.4.2, 7.4.3, 8.2.4
SG 2		Satisfy Supplier Agreements	
	SP 2.1-1	Review COTS Products	7.4.2, 7.4.3
	SP 2.2-1	Execute the Supplier Agreement	4.1, 7.4.1, 7.4.3, 8.4
	SP 2.3-1	Accept the Acquired Product	7.4.1, 7.4.3
	SP 2.4-1	Transition Products	
		Integrated Project Management for IPPD	
SG 1		Use the Project's Defined Process	
	SP 1.1-1	Establish the Project's Defined Process	7.1, 7.3.1, 7.3.3
	SP 1.2-1	Use Organizational Process Assets for Planning Project Activities	
	SP 1.3-1	Integrate Plans	7.1, 7.3.1
	SP 1.4-1	Manage the Project Using the Integrated Plans	7.1, 7.3.1
	SP 1.5-1	Contribute to the Organizational Process Assets	
SG 2		Coordinate and Collaborate with Relevant Stakeholders	
	SP 2.1-1	Manage Stakeholder Involvement	7.2.3, 7.3.1
	SP 2.2-1	Manage Dependencies	7.2.3, 7.3.1
	SP 2.3-1	Resolve Coordination Issues	7.2.3, 7.3.1
SG 3		Use the Project's Shared Vision for IPPD	
	SP 3.1-1	Define Project's Shared-Vision Context	7.3.1

Table 9.6 Mapping of CMMI® Process Areas to ISO 9001:2000 *(continued)*

Goal	Specific Practice	Description	ISO 9001:2000
SG 4	SP 3.2-1	Establish the Project's Shared Vision	7.3.1
		Organize Integrated Teams for IPPD	
	SP 4.1-1	Determine Integrated Team Structure for the Project	7.3.1
	SP 4.2-1	Develop a Preliminary Distribution of Requirements to Integrated Teams	7.3.1
	SP 4.3-1	Establish Integrated Teams	7.3.1
Risk Management			
SG 1		Prepare for Risk Management	
	SP 1.1-1	Determine Risk Sources and Categories	
	SP 1.2-1	Define Risk Parameters	
	SP 1.3-1	Establish a Risk Management Strategy	
SG 2		Identify and Analyze Risks	
	SP 2.1-1	Identify Risks	
	SP 2.2-1	Evaluate, Categorize, and Prioritize Risks	
SG 3		Mitigate Risks	
	SP 3.1-1	Develop Risk Mitigation Plans	
	SP 3.2-1	Implement Risk Mitigation Plans	
Integrated Teaming			
SG 1		Establish Team Composition	
	SP 1.1-1	Identify Team Tasks	
	SP 1.2-1	Identify Needed Knowledge and Skills	
	SP 1.3-1	Assign Appropriate Team Members	
SG 2		Govern Team Operation	
	SP 2.1-1	Establish a Shared Vision	
	SP 2.2-1	Establish a Team Charter	
	SP 2.3-1	Define Roles and Responsibilities	
	SP 2.4-1	Establish Operating Procedures	
	SP 2.5-1	Collaborate among Interfacing Teams	

Table 9.6 Mapping of CMMI® Process Areas to ISO 9001:2000 *(continued)*

Goal	Specific Practice	Description	ISO 9001:2000
		Quantitative Project Management	
SG 1		Quantitatively Manage the Project	
	SP 1.1-1	Establish the Project's Objectives	5.4.1, 7.1, 7.3.1
	SP 1.2-1	Compose the Defined Process	5.4.1, 7.1, 7.3.1
	SP 1.3-1	Select the Subprocesses that Will Be Statistically Managed	5.4.1, 7.3.1
	SP 1.4-1	Manage Project Performance	8.2.3, 8.4
SG 2		Statistically Manage Subprocess Performance	
	SP 2.1-1	Select Measures and Analytic Techniques	8.1
	SP 2.2-1	Apply Statistical Methods to Understand Variation	8.1, 8.2.3
	SP 2.3-1	Monitor Performance of the Selected Subprocesses	8.1, 8.2.3
	SP 2.4-1	Record Statistical Management Data	8.1
		Requirements Management	
SG 1		Manage Requirements	
	SP 1.1-1	Obtain an Understanding of Requirements	7.2.1, 7.2.2, 8.2.4
	SP 1.2-2	Obtain Commitment to Requirements	7.2.2, 7.2.3
	SP 1.3-1	Manage Requirements Changes	7.2.2
	SP 1.4-2	Maintain Bidirectional Traceability of Requirements	7.5.3
	SP 1.5-1	Identify Inconsistencies between Project Work and Requirements	7.2.2
		Requirements Development	
SG 1		Develop Customer Requirements	
	SP 1.1-1	Collect Stakeholder Needs	5.2, 7.2.1, 7.3.2, 8.4
	SP 1.1-2	Elicit Needs	5.2, 7.2.1, 7.2.2, 7.3.2, 8.4
	SP 1.2-1	Develop the Customer Requirements	5.2, 7.2.1

Table 9.6 Mapping of CMMI® Process Areas to ISO 9001:2000 *(continued)*

Goal	Specific Practice	Description	ISO 9001:2000
SG 2		Develop Product Requirements	
	SP 2.1-1	Establish Product and Product-Component Requirements	5.2, 7.2.1, 7.2.2, 7.3.2, 8.4
	SP 2.2-1	Allocate Product-Component Requirements	7.2.1
	SP 2.3-1	Identify Interface Requirements	7.2.1
SG 3		Analyze and Validate Requirements	
	SP 3.1-1	Establish Operational Concepts and Scenarios	7.2.1, 8.4
	SP 3.2-1	Establish a Definition of Required Functionality	7.2.1, 7.3.2, 8.4
	SP 3.3-1	Analyze Requirements	5.2, 7.3.2, 8.4
	SP 3.4-3	Analyze Requirements to Achieve Balance	5.2, 7.3.2, 8.4
	SP 3.5-1	Validate Requirements	5.2, 7.2.2, 7.3.2
	SP 3.5-2	Validate Requirements with Comprehensive Methods	5.2, 7.2.2, 7.3.3
		Technical Solution	
SG 1		Select Product-Component Solutions	
	SP 1.1-1	Develop Alternative Solutions and Selection Criteria	7.3.1, 7.3.3, 7.4.1
	SP 1.1-2	Develop Detailed Alternative Solutions and Selection Criteria	7.3.1, 7.3.3, 7.4.1
	SP 1.2-2	Evolve Operational Concepts and Scenarios	7.2.1, 7.3.1, 7.3.3, 7.4.1
	SP 1.3-1	Select Product-Component Solutions	7.3.1, 7.3.3, 7.4.1
SG 2		Develop the Design	
	SP 2.1-1	Design the Product or Product Component	7.3.1, 7.3.3
	SP 2.2-3	Establish a Technical Data Package	7.3.1, 7.3.3
	SP 2.3-1	Establish Interface Descriptions	7.3.1, 7.3.3
	SP 2.3-3	Design Interfaces Using Criteria	7.3.1, 7.3.3
	SP 2.4-3	Perform Make, Buy, or Reuse Analyses	7.3.1, 7.3.3, 7.4.1
SG 3		Implement the Product Design	
	SP 3.1-1	Implement the Design	7.3.1, 7.3.3, 7.5.1

Table 9.6 Mapping of CMMI® Process Areas to ISO 9001:2000 *(continued)*

Goal	Specific Practice	Description	ISO 9001:2000
	SP 3.2-1	Develop Product Support Documentation	7.3.1, 7.3.3, 7.5.1
		Product Integration	
SG 1		Prepare for Product Integration	
	SP 1.1-1	Determine Integration Sequence	7.3.1
	SP 1.2-2	Establish the Product Integration Environment	7.3.1
	SP 1.3-3	Establish Product Integration Procedures and Criteria	7.3.1
SG 2		Ensure Interface Compatibility	
	SP 2.1-1	Review Interface Descriptions for Completeness	7.3.1
	SP 2.2-1	Manage Interfaces	7.3.1
SG 3		Assemble Product Components and Deliver the Product	
	SP 3.1-1	Confirm Readiness of Product Components for Integration	7.4.1, 7.5.1, 7.5.3
	SP 3.2-1	Assemble Product Components	7.5.1, 7.5.3
	SP 3.3-1	Evaluate Assembled Product Components	7.5.1, 7.5.3
	SP 3.4-1	Package and Deliver the Product or Product Component	7.5.1, 7.5.5
		Verification	
SG 1		Prepare for Verification	
	SP 1.1-1	Select Work Products for Verification	7.3.1, 7.3.5, 8.2.4
	SP 1.2-2	Establish the Verification Environment	7.3.5
	SP 1.3-3	Establish Verification Procedures and Criteria	7.3.5, 8.2.4, 8.3
SG 2		Perform Peer Reviews	
	SP 2.1-1	Prepare for Peer Reviews	7.3.5, 8.2.4
	SP 2.2-1	Conduct Peer Reviews	7.2.2, 7.3.5, 8.2.4
	SP 2.3-2	Analyze Peer Review Data	7.3.5, 8.2.4
SG 3		Verify Selected Work Products	
	SP 3.1-1	Perform Verification	7.3.5, 7.4.3, 8.2.4

Table 9.6 Mapping of CMMI® Process Areas to ISO 9001:2000 (continued)

Goal	Specific Practice	Description	ISO 9001:2000
	SP 3.2-2	Analyze Verification Results and Identify Corrective Action	7.3.5, 8.2.4, 8.3
		Validation	*7.5.2*
SG 1		Prepare for Validation	
	SP 1.1-1	Select Products for Validation	7.3.1, 7.3.6, 7.5.2
	SP 1.2-2	Establish the Validation Environment	7.3.6, 7.5.2
	SP 1.3-3	Establish Validation Procedures and Criteria	7.3.6, 7.5.2, 8.2.4, 8.3
SG 2		Validate Product or Product Components	
	SP 2.1-1	Perform Validation	7.3.6, 7.5.2, 8.2.4
	SP 2.2-1	Analyze Validation Results	7.3.6, 7.5.2, 8.2.4, 8.3
		Configuration Management	
SG 1		Establish Baselines	
	SP 1.1-1	Identify Configuration Items	4.2.3, 4.2.4, 7.3.1, 7.3.7, 7.5.3, 8.3
	SP 1.2-1	Establish a Configuration Management System	4.2.3, 4.2.4, 7.3.1, 7.3.7, 8.3
	SP 1.3-1	Create or Release Baselines	4.2.3, 4.2.4, 7.3.1, 7.3.7, 7.5.3, 8.3
SG 2		Track and Control Changes	
	SP 2.1-1	Track Change Requests	4.2.3, 4.2.4, 7.3.1, 7.3.7, 7.5.3, 8.3
	SP 2.2-1	Control Configuration Items	4.2.3, 4.2.4, 7.3.1, 7.3.7, 7.5.3, 8.3
SG 3		Establish Integrity	
	SP 3.1-1	Establish Configuration Management Records	4.2.3, 4.2.4, 7.3.1, 7.3.7, 7.5.3, 8.3
	SP 3.2-1	Perform Configuration Audits	4.2.3, 4.2.4, 7.3.1, 7.3.7, 7.5.3, 8.3
		Process and Product Quality Assurance	
SG 1		Objectively Evaluate Processes and Work Products	
	SP 1.1-1	Objectively Evaluate Processes	8.2.2
	SP 1.2-1	Objectively Evaluate Work Products and Services	8.2.2, 8.2.4
SG 2		Provide Objective Insight	

Table 9.6 Mapping of CMMI® Process Areas to ISO 9001:2000 *(continued)*

Goal	Specific Practice	Description	ISO 9001:2000
	SP 2.1-1	Communicate and Ensure Resolution of Noncompliance Issues	8.2.2
	SP 2.2-1	Establish Records	4.2.4, 8.2.2
		Measurement and Analysis	
SG 1		Align Measurement and Analysis Activities	
	SP 1.1-1	Establish Measurement Objectives	8.1, 8.2.1, 8.5.1
	SP 1.2-1	Specify Measures	8.1, 8.2.1, 8.2.3, 8.5.1
	SP 1.3-1	Specify Data Collection and Storage Procedures	8.1, 8.2.3
	SP 1.4-1	Specify Analysis Procedures	8.1, 8.5.1
SG 2		Provide Measurement Results	
	SP 2.1-1	Collect Measurement Data	8.2.4 8.5.1
	SP 2.2-1	Analyze Measurement Data	8.2.1, 8.4, 8.5.1
	SP 2.3-1	Store Data and Results	8.4
	SP 2.4-1	Communicate Results	7.2.3, 8.2.2, 8.4
		Decision Analysis and Resolution	
SG 1		Evaluate Alternatives	
	SP 1.1-1	Establish Guidelines for Decision Analysis	
	SP 1.2-1	Establish Evaluation Criteria	
	SP 1.3-1	Identify Alternative Solutions	
	SP 1.4-1	Select Evaluation Methods	
	SP 1.5-1	Evaluate Alternatives	
	SP 1.6-1	Select Solutions	
		Organizational Environment for Integration	
SG 1		Provide IPPD Infrastructure	
	SP 1.1-1	Establish the Organization's Shared Vision	
	SP 1.2-1	Establish an Integrated Work Environment	6.3, 6.4
	SP 1.3-1	Identify IPPD-Unique Skill Requirements	6.2.2
SG 2		Manage People for Integration	

Table 9.6 Mapping of CMMI® Process Areas to ISO 9001:2000 *(continued)*

Goal	Specific Practice	Description	ISO 9001:2000
	SP 2.1-1	Establish Leadership Mechanisms	
	SP 2.2-1	Establish Incentives for Integration	
	SP 2.3-1	Establish Mechanisms to Balance Team and Home Organization Responsibilities	
		Causal Analysis and Resolution	
SG 1		Determine Causes of Defects	
	SP 1.1-1	Select Defect Data for Analysis	8.4, 8.5.2, 8.5.3
	SP 1.2-1	Analyze Causes	8.4, 8.5.2, 8.5.3
SG 2		Address Causes of Defects	
	SP 2.1-1	Implement the Action Proposals	8.5.2, 8.5.3
	SP 2.2-1	Evaluate the Effect of Changes	8.5.2, 8.5.3
	SP 2.3-1	Record Data	8.5.2, 8.5.3

Table 9.7 Mapping of CMMI® Generic Goals and Practices to ISO 9001:2000

Generic Goal	Generic Practices	Description	Process Area	ISO 9001:2000
GG 1		Achieve Specific Goals		
	GP 1.1	Perform Base Practices		
GG 2		*Institutionalize a Managed Process*		
	GP 2.1	Establish an Organizational Policy	All	4.1, 4.2.1, 5.1, 5.3
			OPF	8.2.2
			OPD	5.5.3
			MA	7.6
	GP 2.2	Plan the Process	All	4.1, 4.2.2, 5.4.2, 7.1, 8.1
			CM	4.2.4
			PPQA	8.2.2
			OPF	8.2.2
			RD	7.3.1
			REQM	7.3.1
			PI	7.3.1
			TS	7.3.1, 7.5.1
			VER	7.3.1
			VAL	7.3.1
			MA	7.6, 8.2.3

Table 9.7 Mapping of CMMI® Generic Goals and Practices to ISO 9001:2000 *(continued)*

Generic Goal	Generic Practices	Description	Process Area	ISO 9001:2000
	GP 2.3	Provide Resources	All	4.1, 5.1, 6.1, 6.3, 6.4
			TS	7.5.1
			QPM	7.1
	GP 2.4	Assign Responsibility	All	5.5.1
			OPF	5.5.2, 8.2.2
			PPQA	8.2.2
			PI	7.3.1
			TS	7.3.1
			VER	7.3.1, 8.3
			VAL	7.3.1, 8.3
	GP 2.5	Train People	All	6.2.1, 6.2.2
	GP 2.6	Manage Configurations	All	4.1, 4.2.3, 4.2.4, 5.6.1
			PPQA	8.2.2
			SAM	7.4.1
			REQM	7.2.2
			VER	7.3.5, 7.3.6
			VAL	7.3.6
			PI	7.3.6, 7.3.7
			TS	7.3.7, 7.5.1
	GP 2.7	Identify and Involve Relevant Stakeholders	All	5.2
			RD	7.2.2, 7.2.3, 7.3.2
			REQM	7.2.2
			TS	7.3.1
			PI	7.3.1
			VER	7.3.1
			VAL	7.3.1
			PMC	7.3.4
			SAM	4.1
	GP 2.8	Monitor and Control the Process	All	4.1, 8.1, 8.2.3, 8.4
			RD	7.3.1
			REQM	7.3.1
			TS	7.3.1, 7.3.4, 7.5.1
			VER	7.6
			VAL	7.6
			MA	7.6
	GP 2.9	Objectively Evaluate Adherence	All	4.1
			MA	7.6
			PPQA	8.2.2
			SAM	7.4.1
			REQM	7.3.1
			RD	7.3.1
			TS	7.3.1
	GP 2.10	Review Status with Higher Level Management	All	5.6.1, 5.6.2, 5.6.3
			RD	7.2.2, 7.3.2
			MA	7.6
			OPF	5.5.3

Table 9.7 Mapping of CMMI® Generic Goals and Practices to ISO 9001:2000 (continued)

Generic Goal	Generic Practices	Description	Process Area	ISO 9001:2000
GG 3		Institutionalize a Defined Process		
	GP 3.1	Establish a Defined Process	All	4.1, 5.4.2, 7.1
	GP 3.2	Collect Improvement Information	All	4.1, 8.4
GG 4		Institutionalize a Quantitatively Managed Process		
	GP 4.1	Establish Quantitative Objectives for the Process	All	5.4.1
	GP 4.2	Stabilize Subprocess Performance	All	8.2.3
GG 5		Institutionalize an Optimizing Process		
	GP 5.1	Ensure Continuous Process Improvement	All	8.5.1
	GP 5.2	Correct Root Causes of Problems	All	8.5.2, 8.5.3

References

[1] Mutafelija, B., "Software Process Improvement: Synergy Between ISO 9001:2000 and CMMI®," *SERG Conference*, New Orleans, LA, 2001.

[2] Stromberg, H., and B. Mutafelija, "Using the CMMI® When Implementing ISO 9001:2000 for Software," *SERG Conference*, Phoenix, AZ, 2002.

[3] Ibrahim, L., et al., *The Federal Aviation Administration Integrated Capability Maturity Model® (FAA-iCMM®)*, Version 2.0, Washington, D.C.: FAA, September 2001.

Acronyms

AB	Ability to Perform (common feature)
ARC	Appraisal Requirements for CMMI®
BSI	British Standards Institution
CAF	CMM® Appraisal Framework
CAR	Causal Analysis and Resolution (CMMI® process area)
CBA IPI	CMM® Based Appraisal for Internal Process Improvement
CL	capability level
CM	Configuration Management (CMMI® process area)
CMM®	Capability Maturity Model®
CMMI®	Capability Maturity Model® Integrated
CMM®-SW	Capability Maturity Model® for Software
CO	Commitment to Perform (common feature)
DAR	Decision Analysis and Resolution (CMMI® process area)
DI	Directing Implementation (common feature)
DP	Defect Prevention (CMM® key process area)
EIA	Electronic Industries Alliance
EPG	engineering process group
EPIC	Enterprise Process Improvement Collaboration
FA	focus area (EIA/IS-731)
FAA	Federal Aviation Administration

FAM	FAA-iCMM® Appraisal Method
FI	fully implemented (SCAMPI[SM])
GA	generic attribute (EIA/IS-731)
GEIA	Government Electronic and Information Technology Association
GG	generic goal (CMMI®)
GP	generic practice (CMMI®)
IC	Intergroup Coordination (CMM® key process area)
iCMM®	Integrated Capability Maturity Model® (FAA iCMM®)
IDEAL[SM]	Initiating, Diagnosing, Establishing, Acting, and Learning
IEC	International Electrotechnical Commission
INCOSE	International Council on Systems Engineering
IPM	Integrated Project Management (CMMI® process area)
IPPD	Integrated Product and Process Development
IRCA	International Register of Certified Auditors
ISM	integrated software management (CMM® key process area)
ISO	International Organization for Standardization
IT	Integrated Teaming (CMMI® process area)
KPA	Key Process Area
LI	largely implemented (SCAMPI[SM])
MA	Measurement and Analysis (CMMI® process area)
ME	Measurement and Analysis (common feature)
ML	maturity level
MTTR	mean-time-to-repair
NI	not implemented (SCAMPI[SM])
OEI	Organizational Environment for Integration (CMMI® process area)
OID	Organizational Innovation and Deployment (CMMI® process area)
OPD	Organization Process Definition (CMM® key process area)

OPD	Organizational Process Definition (CMMI® process area)	
OPF	Organization Process Focus (CMM® key process area)	
OPF	Organizational Process Focus (CMMI® process area)	
OPP	Organizational Process Performance (CMMI® process area)	
OSSP	Organization's Set of Standard Processes	
OT	Organizational Training (CMMI® process area)	
PA	Process Area (CMMI®, FAA-iCMM®)	
PA	process attribute (ISO TR 15504)	
PAT	process action team	
PCM	Process Change Management (CMM® key process area)	
PDCA	Plan–Do–Check–Act (cycle)	
PEG	process engineering group	
PI	partially implemented (SCAMPI^{SM})	
PI	process improvement	
PI	Product Integration (CMMI® process area)	
PII	practice implementation indicator	
PMC	Project Monitoring and Control (CMMI® process area)	
PP	Project Planning (CMMI® process area)	
PPQA	Process and Product Quality Assurance (CMMI® process area)	
PR	Peer Review (CMM® key process area)	
QA	quality assurance	
QMS	quality management system	
QPM	Quantitative Process Management (CMM® key process area)	
QPM	Quantitative Project Management (CMMI® process area)	
RD	Requirements Development (CMMI® process area)	
REQM	Requirements Management (CMMI® process area)	
RM	Requirements Management (CMM® key process area)	
RSKM	Risk Management (CMMI® process area)	
SAM	Supplier Agreement Management (CMMI® process area)	

SCAMPI^{SM}	Standard CMMI® Appraisal Method for Process Improvement^{SM}	
SCE^{SM}	Software Capability Evaluation^{SM}	
SCM	Software Configuration Management (CMM® key process area)	
SE	software engineering	
SECM	Systems Engineering Capability Model	
SEI	Software Engineering Institute	
SEPG	software engineering process group	
SG	specific goal (CMMI®)	
SP	specific practice (CMMI®)	
SPA	software process assessment	
SPC	Software Productivity Consortium	
SPE	Software Product Engineering (CMM® key process area)	
SPICE	Software Process Improvement Capability Determination	
SPP	Software Project Planning (CMM® key process area)	
SPTO	Software Project Tracking and Oversight (CMM® key process area)	
SQA	Software Quality Assurance (CMM® key process area)	
SQM	Software Quality Management (CMM® key process area)	
SSM	Software Subcontract Management (CMM® key process area)	
TCM	Technology Change Management (CMM® key process area)	
TP	Training Program (CMM® key process area)	
TQM	total quality management	
TS	Technical Solution (CMMI® process area)	
VAL	Validation (CMMI® process area)	
VE	Verifying Implementation (common feature)	
VER	Verification (CMMI® process area)	
WBS	work breakdown structure	

About the Authors

Boris Mutafelija has more than 30 years of information technology experience as an engineer, software professional, and manager. He has coauthored more than 20 papers and is the coinventor of three U.S. patents. He is authorized by the Software Engineering Institute (SEI) as a lead assessor for performing the CMM® Based Appraisal for Internal Process Improvement and as the lead appraiser for performing SCAMPI[SM] appraisals. Mr. Mutafelija has led several organizations in reaching higher process maturity levels (as defined by the SEI). He has developed process architectures, worked on establishing process frameworks for efficient process improvement, and taught, tutored, and consulted many teams in process improvement. His process improvement interests include process frameworks, enterprise aspects of process engineering and improvement, measurements, statistical process control, and, of course, using standards in developing effective and efficient process improvement approaches.

Harvey Stromberg has more than 30 years of experience in software development, quality assurance, and process improvement. He has held a number of positions in the academic, defense, financial, and communications industries. Mr. Stromberg has been recognized by the American Society for Quality as a certified software quality engineer. He has managed software development projects, software quality assurance and software configuration management departments, and software engineering process groups. In those positions and as an independent consultant, he has helped bring several organizations to CMM® levels 2, 3, and 4. Mr. Stromberg's process improvement interests are in the use of quality assurance, measurements, and statistical techniques for process and project management.

Index

A
Ability to Perform (AB), 155, 157–59
Acting phase, 24
   defined, 24
   ISO–CMMI® synergy, 235–36
   sensitivity, 236
   See also IDEAL℠ model
advanced attributes (AAs), 49
advanced practices (APs), 49, 84
affirmations, 244
appraisal plan, 247–49
   purpose, 247
   sample contents for, 248
Appraisal Requirements for CMMI® (ARC), 240
appraisals, 208–9, 239–52
   class A, 241
   class B, 241
   class C, 208, 241
   conducting, 242, 249–51
   method selection, 239–40
   objectives, 239–40
   output, 209
   output example, 210
   planning/preparing for, 242, 247–49
   purpose, 239
   results, 208
   results, reporting, 242, 251–52
   scope, 241, 242
   verifying/validating, 251
   See also Standard CMMI® Appraisal Method for Process Improvement℠ (SCAMPI℠)

audience, this book, xv–xviii
audit trails, 255–56
   proposed, 256
   types of, 255

B
basic practices (BPs), 49
benchmarking, 207

C
capability levels
   cumulative, 174
   defined, 81
   EIA/IS-731, 48, 49–50
   FAA-iCMM®, 54
   ISO TR 15504, 44, 46
Capability Maturity Model®. *See* CMM®
Capability Maturity Model Integrated®. *See* CMMI®
Case 1, 212–24
   CMMI® implementation granularity, 213
   configuration management, 216, 220–21
   description, 212–13
   generic practices, 214
   illustrated, 212
   ISO–CMMI® synergy process improvement steps, 216–18
   management responsibility, authority, communication step, 216, 219
   measurement, tracking, review step, 217, 222–23
   measurement and analysis step, 217, 221–22

289

Case 1 (continued)
  other step, 218, 223–24
  PAs establishing/invoking practices, 215
  product realization step, 217, 222
  purchasing implementation step, 217, 222
  QMS definition/planning step, 216, 219–20
  quality assurance step, 216, 221
  quality policy step, 216, 219
  resource provision, 216, 220
  verification/validation step, 217, 222
  See also Transition cases
Case 2, 224–29
  approach for organizations at CMM® maturity level 2, 225
  approach for organizations at CMM® maturity level 3, 225–29
  configuration management step, 226
  defined, 224–25
  illustrated, 225, 229
  management responsibility, authority, communication step, 226
  measurement and analysis step, 227
  measurement tracking, reviewing, auditing step, 228
  other step, 228
  process improvement steps, 226–28
  product realization steps, 227
  purchase implementation step, 227
  QMS definition/plan step, 226
  quality assurance step, 227
  quality policy step, 226
  resource provision step, 226
  verification/validation step, 227
  See also Transition cases
Case 3, 229–32
  configuration management step, 231
  defined, 229
  illustrated, 233
  management responsibility, authority, communication step, 230
  measurement, tracking, reviewing, auditing step, 232
  measurement and analysis step, 231
  other step, 232
  process improvement steps, 230–32
  product realization steps, 231
  purchasing implementation step, 232
  QMS definition/plan step, 230

quality assurance step, 231
quality policy step, 230
resource provision step, 230
verification/validation step, 232
See also Transition cases
Case 4, 233–34
  challenge, 233
  ISO 9001:1994 organization operating at CMM® level 2, 234
  ISO 9001:1994 organization operating at CMM® level 3, 234
causal analysis and resolution (CAR), 117–18
  CMMI® to ISO 9001:2000 mapping, 279
  as maturity level 5 PA, 172–73
  purpose, 117
  See also Process areas (PAs)
CMM®
  appraisals, 121
  architecture, 41
  basis, 38
  CMMI® vs., 155–75
  common features, 39–40, 155
  defined, 35
  institutionalization, 155–61
  stable management processes, 123
  as staged model, 38
  sunset schedule, 79
  transitioning from, 177–201
CMM® Based Appraisal for Internal Process Improvement (CBA IPI), 22
CMMI®, 78–118
  Ability to Perform (AB), 157–59
  analysis of data, 148
  CMM® vs., 155–75
  Commitment to Perform (CO), 157
  commonalities, 129–31
  common features, 156
  continual improvement, 148
  continuous representation, 80, 83, 86–88, 173–74
  control of monitoring/measuring devices, 145–46
  control of nonconforming products, 148
  corrective action, 148
  creation, 3–4
  customer-related processes, 143–44
  customer satisfaction, 147
  defined, 4

Index

design and development, 144–45
as detailed document, 9
detail level, 134
differences, 131–32
Directing Implementation (DI), 159–60
FAA-iCMM® and, 56
features comparison, 122
goals, 79
institutionalization, 83–86, 155–61
internal audit, 147
ISO 9001:2000 relationship, 149–51
ISO 9001:2000 similarities, 8–9
ISO 9001:2000 synergy, 5, 7–10, 121–52
ISO requirements not covered by, 151–52
management responsibility and, 139–41
maturity levels, 10
maturity vs. capability levels, 81–82
measurement, analysis, improvement and, 146–49
model representations, 80, 81
monitoring/measurement of processes, 147
monitoring/measurement of product, 147–48
PAs, 98–118
planning, 142
premise, 123
preventative action, 149
process improvement illustration, 9
production and service provision, 145
product realization and, 142–46
product suite, 79
purchasing, 145
QMS and, 137–38
releases, 79
resource management and, 141–42
stable management processes, 123
staged representation, 80, 83, 86, 191–92
steward, 251
strengths, 132–33
stress management, 206
success, 78
systems approach, 80
terminology comparison, 126
Verifying Implementation (VE), 160–61
version 1.1, 80–81
weaknesses, 133–34
CMMI® to ISO 9001:2000 mapping, 268–81
causal analysis and resolution, 279
configuration management, 277
decision analysis and resolution, 278
defined, 268
of generic goals, 281
of generic practices, 280
integrated project management for IPPD, 272–73
integrated teaming, 273
measurement and analysis, 278
organizational environment and integration, 278–79
organizational innovation and deployment, 270
organizational process definition, 269–70
organizational process focus, 269
organizational process performance, 270
PAs, 269–79
process and product quality assurance, 277–78
product integration, 276
project monitoring and control, 271–72
project planning, 271
quantitative project management, 274
requirements development, 274–75
requirements management, 274
risk management, 273
supplier agreement and management, 272
technical solution, 275–76
validation, 277
verification, 276–77
See also Mappings
CMMI® transition, 177–201
alternative approaches, 182
basic approach, 180–92
CMM® maturity level 2 to CMMI® maturity level 3, 198–201
continuous approach, 200–201
continuous representation (implementing engineering PAs), 190–91
institutionalization approach, 182–83
institutionalization approach (continuous representation), 183–85
institutionalization approach (continuous representation variant), 185–89
with ISO 9001:1994/CMM® experience, 233–34
with ISO 9001:1994 experience/without CMM® experience, 229–32

CMMI® transition (continued)
  without ISO experience/with CMM®
      experience, 224–29
  maturity level 2, 192–95
  maturity level 3, 196–98
  potential transition cases, 211–34
  without previous process improvement
      experience, 212–24
  process improvement approaches, 181
  staged approach, 199–200
  staged representation, 191–92
  summary, 201
CMM® maturity levels, 21, 38
  achieving, 40
  defined level, 38, 42
  illustrated, 39
  initial level, 38
  KPAs, 38–43
  managed level, 38, 42
  optimizing level, 38, 42–43
  repeatable level, 38, 40–41
CMM®-SW, 3, 14, 35–43
  continuous process improvement basis, 33
  defined, 35–38
Commitment to Perform (CO), 155, 157
common features, 39–40
  CMM®, 155
  CMMI®, 156
configuration management (CM), 114–15
  CMMI® to ISO 9001:2000 mapping, 277
  as maturity level 2 PA, 165
  purpose, 114
  See also Process areas (PAs)
continual improvement, 63–64, 130
continuous representation, 80
  capability level 0, 86
  capability level 1, 86
  comparison, 83
  engineering PAs implementation, 190–91
  freedom, 133
  GGs/GPs, 87–88
  illustrated, 83
  institutionalization approach, 183–89
  PA implementation order, 174
  PAs, 81, 85
  See also CMMI®
customer focus, 61–62, 130, 140

D

decision analysis and resolution (DAR), 116–17
  CMMI® to ISO 9001:2000 mapping, 278
  purpose of, 116
  See also Process areas (PAs)
decision making, factual approach, 64, 131
defined maturity level
  defined, 38
  KPAs, 42
  See also CMM® maturity levels
defined process, 160
Diagnosing phase, 23
  defined, 23
  in ISO–CMMI® synergy, 207–9
  See also IDEAL℠ model
direct artifacts, 244
Directed Implementation (DI), 159–60
  CMM® key practices, 159
  new generic practices, 159
  See also CMMI®
document mapping, 263–81
  CMMI® to ISO 9001:2000, 268–81
  defined, 263
  ISO 9001:2000 to CMMI®, 264–68

E

EIA/IS-731, 47–53
  AAs, 49
  APs, 49
  architecture, 48
  BPs, 49
  capability levels, 48, 49–50
  defined, 47
  FAs, 51, 52
  focus areas, 51
  GAs, 51
  GCs, 51
  GPs, 51, 52
  parts, 47
Electronics Industry Alliance. See EIA/IS-731
engineering PAs, 99–104
  implementing, 190–91
  product integration (PI), 102–3, 170–71, 276
  requirements development (RD), 100–101, 274–75
  requirements management (REQM), 99–100, 162–63, 274

Index

technical solution (TS), 101–2, 169–70, 275–76
validation (VAL), 103–4, 148, 171, 277
verification (VER), 103, 148, 171, 276–77
See also Process areas (PAs)
engineering process group (EPG), 207
Enterprise Process Improvement Collaboration (EPIC), 47
equivalent staging, 80, 82
Establishing phase, 23–24
  defined, 23
  ISO–CMMI® synergy, 209–36
  potential transition cases, 211–34
  process improvement approaches, 209–11
  process improvement planning, 234–35
  See also IDEAL^{SM} model
evolutionary spiral process, 24–26
  defined, 25
  steps, 25–26

F

FAA-iCMM®, 6–7, 53–56
  Appraisal Method (FAM), 53
  architecture, 54
  capability levels, 54
  CMMI® and, 56
  defined, 53
  GPs, 54, 55–56
  PAs, 54, 56
  PAs by maturity level, 57
  process areas, 54
focus areas (FAs), 51
frameworks
  CMMI®, 78–118
  CMM®-SW, 35–43
  defined, 6, 31
  EIA/IS-731, 47–53
  FAA-iCMM®, 53–56
  as guidelines, 4
  introduction to, 31–57
  ISO 9001:1994, 34–35
  ISO 9001:2000, 59–78
  ISO TR 15504, 43–47
  process improvement approach relationship, 31–34
  quagmire, 2, 3
  revised, 59–118
  role in process improvement development, 4–5
  updated, 4

G

gap analysis, 202
  defined, 207
  implementation, 207–8
generic attributes (GAs), 51
generic characteristics (GCs), 51
generic goals (GGs), 83, 86–98
  achieve specific goals, 88–90
  CMMI® to ISO 9001:2000 mapping of, 281
  institutionalize a defined process, 95–96
  institutionalize a managed process, 90–95
  institutionalize a optimizing process, 98
  institutionalize a quantitatively managed process, 96–97
generic practices (GPs), 86–98
  assign responsibility, 92
  CMMI® to ISO 9001:2000 mapping of, 280
  collect improvement information, 96
  correct root causes of problems, 98
  defined, 51, 83
  EIA/IS-731, 52
  enabling PAs comparison, 188
  ensure continuous process improvement, 98
  establish a defined process, 95
  establish organizational policy, 90
  establish quantitative objects for process, 97
  FAA-iCMM®, 55–56
  identify/involve stakeholders, 93–94
  manage configurations, 93
  monitor/control the process, 94
  objectively evaluate adherence, 94
  perform basic practices, 88–90
  plan the process, 90–92
  provide resources, 92
  review status, 94–95
  stabilize subprocess performance, 97
  train people, 92–93

H

human resources, 72–73

I

iCMM®. *See* FAA-iCMM®
IDEAL^{SM} model, 6, 15, 21–26
  acting phase, 24, 235–36
  defined, 22

IDEAL^SM model (continued)
  Diagnosing phase, 23, 207–9
  Establishing phase, 23–24, 209–36
  illustrated, 23
  Initiating phase, 22, 206–7
  Learning phase, 24, 236–37
  managing improvement based on, 25
  process improvement guidance, 22
indirect artifacts, 244
infrastructure, 73
initial maturity level, 38
Initiating phase, 22
  defined, 206
  in ISO–CMMI® synergy, 206–7
  stress management, 206
  See also IDEAL^SM model
institutionalization, 83–86
  CMM® vs. CMMI®, 155–61
  GGs/GPs and, 85
  methods of address, 86
  staged representation and, 86
  synergy, 135–36
institutionalization approach, 182–83
  continuous representation, 183–85
  continuous representation variant, 185–89
  transition steps, 183
  See also CMMI® transition
integrated product and process development (IPPD), 80
integrated project management, 106–7, 142, 168–69
  CMMI® to ISO 9001:2000 mapping, 272–73
  maturity level 3 PA, 168–69
  purpose, 106
  See also Process areas (PAs)
integrated teaming, 108–9
  CMMI® to ISO 9001:2000 mapping, 273
  purpose, 108
  See also Process areas (PAs)
International Council on Systems Engineering (INCOSE), 47
inverse mapping, 268–81
ISO
  certification, 121
  family, 60
  Web site, 121
ISO 9000-3, 33
ISO 9000:1994, 34

ISO 9001:1987, 33
ISO 9001:1994, 3, 33, 34–35
  clauses, 35, 36–37
  defined, 34
  ISO 9001:2000 vs., 175–77
  nonconformity prevention, 176
  organization requirements, 35
  organization transition, 154
  transition to ISO 9001:2000, 201–4
ISO 9001:2000
  application, 122
  CMMI® relationship, 149–51
  CMMI® similarities, 8–9
  commonalities, 129–31
  differences, 131–32
  features comparison, 122
  ISO 9001:1994 vs., 175–77
  language, 176
  management responsibility, 69–72
  measurement, analysis, improvement, 76–78
  process improvement illustration, 9
  product realization, 73–75
  QMS, 67–69
  quality management principles, 61–65, 130–31, 175
  registration, SCAMPI^SM for, 260–61
  registration process, 252–57
  requirements, 66–78
  requirements not covered by CMMI®, 151–52
  resource management, 72–73
  Section 4 requirements, 177
  Section 5 requirements, 178
  Section 6 requirements, 178
  Section 7 requirements, 179
  Section 8 requirements, 179
  "shall" statements, 10
  as sparse document, 9
  strengths, 132–33
  stress management, 206
  terminology comparison, 126
  weaknesses, 133–34
ISO 9001:2000 to CMMI® mapping, 264–68
  Section 4, 264
  Section 5, 264–65
  Section 6, 265
  Section 7, 266–67
  Section 8, 267–68
  See also mappings

ISO 9001:2000 transition, 201–4
    difficulty, 201
    gap analysis and, 202
    with ISO 9001:1994/CMM® experience, 233–34
    with ISO 9001:1994 experience/without CMM® experience, 229–32
    without ISO experience/with CMM® experience, 224–29
    potential transition cases, 211–34
    without previous process improvement experience, 212–24
    steps, 202
ISO 9004:2000, 26–27
    defined, 26
    guidance, 26–27
ISO–CMMI® synergy, 5, 7–10, 134–52
    acting phase, 235–36
    advantages, 10
    approaches, 205–37
    diagnosing phase, 207–9
    establishing phase, 209–36
    illustrated, 9
    initiating phase, 206–7
    institutionalization, 135–36
    learning phase, 236–37
    management responsibility, 138–41
    measurement, analysis, improvement, 146–49
    PAs and SPs, 136–49
    process improvement, 205–6
    process improvement steps based on, 216–18
    product realization, 142–46
    QMS, 137–38
    relationships, 124, 149–51
    resource management, 141–42
ISO TR 15504, 3, 4, 17–21, 43–47
    assessment output analysis step, 20
    assessment scheme, 44
    attribute indicator sets, 46
    capability levels, 44
    capability levels and process attributes, 46
    communication/teamwork guidelines, 21
    compatibility, 43
    defined, 18, 43
    F attribute, 45
    gains sustain step, 21
    implementation step, 20
    improvement confirmation step, 21
    as international standard, 19
    L attribute, 45
    management practices, 47
    N attribute, 44
    needs/business goals step, 19
    Part 2, 43
    Part 5, 43
    Part 7, 18–19
    parts relationship, 18
    P attribute, 44
    performance monitoring step, 21
    process assessment step, 19–20
    process dimension, 45
    process improvement initiation step, 19
    process improvement steps, 19–21
    steps illustration, 20
    two-dimensional model, 44

K
key process areas (KPAs), 38–43
    common features, 39–40
    goals, satisfaction of, 39
    maturity level 2, 40–41
    maturity level 3, 42
    maturity level 4, 42
    maturity level 5, 42–43
    See also CMM® maturity levels

L
leadership, 62, 130
Learning phase, 24
    defined, 24, 236
    ISO–CMMI® synergy, 236–37
    See also IDEAL^SM model

M
managed maturity level
    defined, 38
    KPAs, 42
    See also CMM® maturity levels
managed process, 158
management
    configuration, 114–15, 165, 277
    integrated, 106–7
    process approach to, 65–66
    project, 104–9

management (continued)
  quality, 128
  quality project (QPM), 172
  quantitative project, 109, 274
  requirements, 99–100
  resource, 72–73, 141–42
  risk, 107–8, 273
  supplier agreement (SAM), 106, 164, 272
  system approach to, 63, 65–66
management responsibility, 69–72
  CMMI® and, 139–41
  commitment, 69–70
  customer focus, 70, 140
  planning, 71
  quality policy, 70–71
  responsibility, authority, communication, 71
  review, 72
  top management, 69
  See also ISO 9001:2000
mappings
  CMMI® to ISO 9001:2000, 268–81
  defined, 263
  ISO 9001:2000 to CMMI®, 264–68
maturity level 2 PAs, 161–66
  configuration management (CM), 165
  measurement and analysis (MA), 165–66
  process and product quality assurance (PPQA), 164–65
  project monitoring and control (PMC), 164
  project planning (PP), 163–64
  requirements management (REQM), 162–63
  supplier agreement management (SAM), 164
  See also Process areas (PAs)
maturity level 2 transition, 192–95
  defined, 192–93
  MA PA, 195
  PP PA, 194–95
  SAM PA, 195
  steps, 193
  systems engineering, 194
maturity level 3 PAs, 166–71
  integrated project management (IPM), 168–69, 189
  organizational process definition (OPD), 167–68
  organizational process focus (OPF), 166–67
  organizational training (OT), 168

product integration (PI), 170–71
requirements definition (RD), 169
technical solution (TS), 169–70
validation (VAL), 171
verification (VER), 171
See also Process areas (PAs)
maturity level 3 transition, 196–98
  MA PA, 198
  OPD PA, 196
  OT PA, 198
  steps, 197
maturity level 4 PAs, 171–72
  organizational process performance (OPP), 171
  quality project management (QPM), 172
  See also Process areas (PAs)
maturity level 5 PAs, 172–73
  causal analysis and resolution (CAR), 172–73
  organizational innovation and deployment (OID), 172
  See also Process areas (PAs)
Maturity Profile report, 251
mean-time-to-repair (MTTR), 147
measurement, analysis, improvement, 76–78
  CMMI® and, 146–49
  control of nonconforming product, 77
  data analysis, 77
  improvement, 77–78
  monitoring and measurement, 76–77
  See also ISO 9001:2000
measurement and analysis (MA), 116, 146, 165–66
  CMMI® to ISO 9001:2000 mapping, 278
  level 2 transition, 195
  level 3 transition, 198
  purpose, 116
  See also Process areas (PAs)
Measurement and Analysis (ME), 155

O

optimizing maturity level
  defined, 38
  KPAs, 42–43
  See also CMM® maturity levels
organizational environment for integration (OEI), 118, 141–42
  CMMI® to ISO 9001:2000 mapping, 278–79
  purpose, 118

organizational innovation and deployment
(OID), 113–14, 172
  CMMI® to ISO 9001:2000 mapping, 270
  purpose, 113
organizational process definition (OPD), 111,
137–38, 167–68, 185
  CMMI® to ISO 9001:2000 mapping, 269–70
  level 3 transition, 196
  purpose, 111
organizational process focus (OPF), 110–11,
139, 147, 166–67
  CMMI® to ISO 9001:2000 mapping, 269
  purpose, 110
organizational process performance (OPP),
112–13, 139, 171
  CMMI® to ISO 9001:2000 mapping, 270
  purpose, 112
organizational training (OT), 112, 168
organization set of standard processes (OSSPs),
135

P

people involvement, 62, 130
Plan–Do–Check–Act (PDCA) cycle, 6, 15, 16–17
  defined, 16
  as part of TQM, 16
  steps, 16–17
practice implementation indicators (PIIs), 244
preassessment, 252, 253–54
process action teams (PATs), 234–35
  determination, 235
  in pilot efforts, 236
  problems address by, 234
  typical contents, 235
process approach, 63, 65–66, 130
process areas (PAs), 98–118
  CMMI® to ISO 9001:2000 mapping of,
269–79
  for continuous representation, 81, 85
  enabling, GPs comparison, 188
  engineering, 99–104
  FAA-iCMM®, 54, 56
  by maturity level, 57
  maturity level 2, 161–66
  maturity level 3, 166–71
  maturity level 4, 171–72
  maturity level 5, 172–73
  process management, 110–14

project management, 104–9
specific goals (SGs), 84
specific practices (SPs), 84
for staged representation, 81, 84
support, 114–18
process improvement, 13–28
  continuous, 33
  cost, 1
  defined, 14
  difficulty, 14–15
  frameworks role in, 4–5
  goals, 14, 15
  identified in organization processes, 4
  implementation, 10, 13
  implied, 3
  ISO–CMMI® synergy and, 9
  issues, 15
  obstacles, 15
  problem-solving concepts, 13–14
  systematic concept, 7
  tasks, 5–6
process improvement approaches, 5–7, 13,
15–27
  alternative CMMI® transition, 182
  CMMI® transition, 181
  frameworks relationship to, 31–34
  plan development requirement, 31–32
process management PAs, 110–14
  organizational innovation and deployment
(OID), 113–14, 172, 270
  organizational process definition (OPD),
111, 137–38, 167–68, 185, 269–70
  organizational process focus (OPF), 110–11,
139, 147, 166–67, 269
  organizational process performance (OPP),
112–13, 139, 171, 270
  organizational training (OT), 112, 168
  See also Process areas (PAs)
process/product quality assurance (PPQA), 115,
147, 164–65
  CMMI® to ISO 9001:2000 mapping, 277–78
  purpose, 115
  See also Process areas (PAs)
product integration, 102–3, 170–71
  CMMI® to ISO 9001:2000 mapping, 276
  purpose, 102
  See also Process areas (PAs)

product realization, 73–75
  CMMI® and, 142–46
  customer-related processes, 74
  design and development, 74–75
  interactions, 143
  monitoring/measuring device control, 75
  planning, 73
  production and service provision, 75
  purchasing, 75
  See also ISO 9001:2000
project management, 104–9
  integrated, 106–7, 142, 168–69
  integrated teaming, 108–9, 273
  project monitoring/control, 105–6
  project planning (PP), 104–5, 163–64, 271
  quantitative, 109
  risk management, 107–8, 273
  supplier agreement management (SAM), 106, 164, 272
  See also Process areas (PAs)
project monitoring and control (PMC), 105–6, 164, 271–72
project planning (PP), 104–5, 163–64
  CMMI® to ISO 9001:2000 mapping, 271
  level 2 transition, 194–95
  purpose, 104
  See also Process areas (PAs)

Q

quality management, 128
quality management principles, 61–65, 130–31, 175
  continual improvement, 63–64, 130
  customer focus, 61–62, 130
  defined, 61
  factual approach to decision making, 64, 131
  involvement people, 62, 130
  leadership, 62, 130
  list of, 61
  mutually beneficial supplier relationships, 64–65, 130
  process approach, 63, 130
  system approach, 63, 130
  See also ISO 9001:2000
quality management system (QMS), 61, 67–69, 125–27
  answers, 68–69
  CMMI® and, 137–38
  defined, 67, 125
  documentation, 61, 67
  effectiveness measurement, 71
  quality manual, 125–27
  requirements, 67
  See also ISO 9001:2000
quality plan, 127–28
  integrated, 128
  requirement, 127
  topics, 127–28
quality project management (QPM), 172
quantitative project management, 109, 174

R

registration process, 252–57
  assessment, 254–57
  assessment plan, 253
  audit trails, 255–56
  documentation review, 254
  flow illustration, 253
  preassessment, 252, 253–54
  surveillance audits, 257
  See also ISO 9001:2000
repeatable maturity level
  defined, 38
  KPAs, 40–41
  See also CMM® maturity levels
requirements development (RD), 100–101, 169
  CMMI® to ISO 9001:2000 mapping, 274–75
  purpose, 100
  See also Process areas (PAs)
requirements management (REQM), 99–100, 162–63
  CMMI® to ISO 9001:2000 mapping, 274
  purpose, 99
  See also Process areas (PAs)
resource management, 72–73
  CMMI® and, 141–42
  human resources, 72–73
  infrastructure, 73
  provision of resources, 72
  work environment, 73
  See also ISO 9001:2000
risk management, 107–8
  CMMI® to ISO 9001:2000 mapping, 273
  purpose, 107–8
  See also Process areas (PAs)

Index

S

software process assessment (SPA), 240
Software Process Improvement Capability Determination (SPICE), 17
Software Productivity Consortium (SPC), 24
software quality assurance (SQA), 160
specific goals (SGs), 84
specific practices (SPs), 84
staged representation, 80
    activities vs. PAs, 173
    common features, 89
    comparison, 83
    illustrated, 82
    institutionalization and, 86
    PA implementation variations, 192
    PAs, 81, 84
    PA selection freedom, 191
    See also CMMI®
Standard CMMI® Appraisal Method for Process Improvement[SM] (SCAMPI[SM]), 147, 208, 240–52
    appraisal classes, 241
    appraisal method, 208–10, 240–52
    characterization concept, 245
    conduct appraisal phase, 242, 249–51
    development, 240–41
    goal setting process, 246
    history, 240–41
    interviews, 249
    for ISO 9001:2000 registration, 260
    organizational scope, 244
    output, 209
    overview, 242–52
    phases, 242
    PIIs, 244
    plan/prepare for appraisal phase, 242, 247–49
    report results phase, 242, 251–52
    type C appraisal, 208
    using, to prepare ISO 9001:2000 registration, 260–61
standards, 1–2
    advantages, 5
    changed, 2
    as guidelines, 4
    legacy, transitioning from, 153–204
    mapping, 129
    updated, 4

supplier agreement management (SAM), 106, 164
    CMMI® to ISO 9001:2000 mapping, 272
    level 2 transition, 195
    purpose, 106
    See also Process areas (PAs)
supplier relationships, 64–65, 131
support, 114–18
    causal analysis and resolution (CAR), 117–18, 172–73, 279
    configuration management (CM), 114–15, 165, 277
    decision analysis and resolution (DAR), 116–17, 278
    measurement and analysis (MA), 116, 146, 165–66, 278
    organizational environment for integration (OEI), 118, 141–42, 278–79
    process/product quality assurance (PPQA), 115, 147, 164–65, 277–78
    See also Process areas (PAs)
synergy. See ISO–CMMI® synergy
system approach, 63, 65–66, 130
systems engineering, 123–24
    defined, 123
    at maturity level 2, 194
Systems Engineering Capability Model (SECM), 47

T

tagging, 249
technical solution, 101–2, 169–70
    CMMI® to ISO 9001:2000 mapping, 275–76
    purpose, 101
    See also Process areas (PAs)
threads, 173–74
TickIT, 258–60
    defined, 258
    guide, 260
    parts, 259–60
    scope, 258
    structure, 259
    use example, 260
transition cases, 211–34
    with ISO 9001:1994 and CMM® experience, 233–34
    with ISO 9001:1994 experience/without CMM® experience, 229–32

transition cases (continued)
　without ISO experience/with CMM®
　　experience, 224–29
　list of, 211
　without previous process improvement
　　experience, 212–14
　See also CMMI® transition; ISO 9001:2000
　　transition

V

validation (VAL), 103–4, 148, 171
　CMMI® to ISO 9001:2000 mapping, 277
　purpose, 103
　See also Process areas (PAs)
verification (VER), 103, 148, 171
　CMMI® to ISO 9001:2000 mapping, 276–77
　purpose, 103
　See also Process areas (PAs)
Verifying Implementation (VE), 155, 160–61

W

work environment, 73

Recent Titles in the Artech House Computing Library

Advanced ANSI SQL Data Modeling and Structure Processing, Michael M. David

Advanced Database Technology and Design, Mario Piattini and Oscar Díaz, editors

Action Focused Assessment for Software Process Improvement, Tim Kasse

Building Reliable Component-Based Software Systems, Ivica Crnkovic and Magnus Larsson, editors

Business Process Implementation for IT Professionals and Managers, Robert B. Walford

Configuration Management: The Missing Link in Web Engineering, Susan Dart

Data Modeling and Design for Today's Architectures, Angelo Bobak

Developing Secure Distributed Systems with CORBA, Ulrich Lang and Rudolf Schreiner

Future Codes: Essays in Advanced Computer Technology and the Law, Curtis E. A. Karnow

Global Distributed Applications with Windows® DNA, Enrique Madrona

A Guide to Software Configuration Management, Alexis Leon

Guide to Standards and Specifications for Designing Web Software, Stan Magee and Leonard L. Tripp

Implementing Electronic Payment Systems, Cristian Radu

Internet Commerce Development, Craig Standing

Knowledge Management Strategy and Technology, Richard F. Bellaver and John M. Lusa, editors

Managing Computer Networks: A Case-Based Reasoning Approach, Lundy Lewis

Metadata Management for Information Control and Business Success, Guy Tozer

Multimedia Database Management Systems, Guojun Lu

Practical Guide to Software Quality Management, Second Edition, John W. Horch

Practical Process Simulation Using Object-Oriented Techniques and C++, José Garrido

Risk-Based E-Business Testing, Paul Gerrard and Neil Thompson

Secure Messaging with PGP and S/MIME, Rolf Oppliger

Software Fault Tolerance Techniques and Implementation, Laura L. Pullum

Software Verification and Validation for Practitioners and Managers, Second Edition, Steven R. Rakitin

Strategic Software Production with Domain-Oriented Reuse, Paolo Predonzani, Giancarlo Succi, and Tullio Vernazza

Successful Evolution of Software Systems, Hongji Yang and Martin Ward

Systematic Process Improvement Using ISO 9001:2000 and CMMI®, Boris Mutafelija and Harvey Stromberg

Systems Modeling for Business Process Improvement, David Bustard, Peter Kawalek, and Mark Norris, editors

User-Centered Information Design for Improved Software Usability, Pradeep Henry

Workflow Modeling: Tools for Process Improvement and Application Development, Alec Sharp and Patrick McDermott

For further information on these and other Artech House titles, including previously considered out-of-print books now available through our In-Print-Forever® (IPF®) program, contact:

Artech House
685 Canton Street
Norwood, MA 02062
Phone: 781-769-9750
Fax: 781-769-6334
e-mail: artech@artechhouse.com

Artech House
46 Gillingham Street
London SW1V 1AH UK
Phone: +44 (0)20 7596-8750
Fax: +44 (0)20 7630-0166
e-mail: artech-uk@artechhouse.com

Find us on the World Wide Web at:
www.artechhouse.com